Into Oblivion:

The Preventable Collapse of the University of the Arts

An Investigative Report on Belligerent Spending, Declining Enrollment, Academic Inbreeding, Missed Opportunities, and a Phantom Capital Campaign.

ISBN (Hardback): 978-1-955144-14-8
ISBN (Paperback): 978-1-955144-15-5
ISBN (EPUB): 978-1-955144-16-2

Library of Congress Control Number: 2025922281

Published by Andrew T. Hanna
Philadelphia, Pennsylvania

Printed in the United States of America
First Edition

Cover design and interior layout by Andrew T. Hanna

This book is a work of nonfiction based on publicly available documents, interviews, and firsthand research. While every effort has been made to ensure the accuracy of the information contained herein, the author assumes no responsibility for errors or omissions or for any consequences arising from the use of this information.

Preface

Who am I?

I am a sophisticated mind that relies on education, analysis, and technology to navigate the world. But beneath that lies raw aggression—an endless well of drive and resilience that refuses to surrender even when everything around me is collapsing. This duality—intellect sharpened by relentless energy—shapes how I confront challenges, blending strategic thought with unwavering persistence.

Raw aggression is no different than the fuel that lifts rockets into space. It burns hot, and when harnessed, it can carry a person far. Whether it's pursuing two engineering graduate degrees at once or investigating the collapse of a 150-year-old university, that drive has been the will that refuses to quit no matter how steep the climb.

There were times when I lacked knowledge, and passion drove me to overcome my limitations. There were other times when people placed deliberate obstacles in my path, and the same passion pushed me through— or around—them.

Yet like any rocket, fuel alone is not enough. Without a guidance system, it veers off course. My education, my command of technology, and my capacity for analysis are the systems that direct the raw power of aggression toward meaningful goals. Together, they define who I am.

What is my motivation?

I moved to Philadelphia in 1998 to attend the University of the Arts. It was a world I'd never experienced before—a dense metropolitan city, towering buildings, and a university teeming with more personality types than a candy store. I was out of my element and needed a plan, fast. So I began taking inventory of what I liked and disliked. I knew I liked challenges—and I liked working to overcome them. There's a certain thrill in facing something that seems insurmountable, only to look back on the path taken and feel that warmth of accomplishment replace the coldness of fear and uncertainty.

That fall, I set out to confront one of my deepest fears: dark alleyways. In the middle of the night, while the city slept, I sought out the darkest alleys I could find. Armed with only a pen and paper, I wrote down everything I feared might happen. Then I walked through. At the other side, I reviewed my notes to see what came true and what didn't. I repeated this ritual night after night, and eventually, fear gave way to familiarity. I did this for a year.

In the weeks following the sudden collapse of the University of the Arts, I saw several challenges emerge—none of them simple, all of them daunting. Could I shift my research skills from engineering to investigative reporting? Could I apply my background in engineering and mathematics to analyze the failure of a 150-year-old institution? And perhaps most personally: could I push my writing from academically functional to something more alive, more compelling—something readers might actually want to finish?

These questions became my new alleyways.

Table of Contents

Preface   5

Introduction   11

The Seeds of Collapse: UARTS' Path to Failure   13

UARTS: Granting Organization or University?   19

2009: The Year Enrollment Declined   29

Donating While in Debt: 41

UARTS' Morally Bankrupt Fundraising Strategy   41

2020: The Year UARTS Ignored the Alarm Bells   47

A Labor Contract That Set Faculty Back   59

A Mounting Legal Crisis: Lawsuits from Students and Faculty   65

Dangerously Low Student-to-Employee Ratios Undermined Financial Stability   79

Controversial Union Demands and Questionable Tactics During Negotiations   85

Missed Opportunities in Outreach, Branding, & Digital Strategy   89

Academic Inbreeding: How Insularity Stifled Innovation   99

A Phantom Capital Campaign Masked Financial Collapse   109

The Cohort Default Rate: An Overlooked Crisis at UARTS   129

2023: UARTS Slide into Oblivion   133

Conclusion   139

Epilogue   141

Afterword   145

Appendix A: Simplified Piecewise Arithmetic Formula for Faculty Step Increases   148

Appendix B: Simplified Piecewise Arithmetic Formula for Adjunct Step Increases   149

Appendix C: Table Listing UARTS Donations to External Organizations (2011-2022)   150

Appendix D: Legal Framework for Nonprofit Pass-Through Entities   157

Appendix E: Enrollment Trends for Sample Universities (2001–2023)   159

Appendix F: Foundation Grants to UARTS – (2016-2023)   191

Sources   193

Introduction

In June 2024, a crowd of students, alumni, and faculty gathered at Hamilton Hall to protest the sudden closure of their university. With each passing day, the crowd grew larger. What began as a small group of students occupying the steps swelled into a mass spilling into the street. Chants and shouts arose from the crowd asking, "Why did this happen?" Artists drew caricatures of current and past university presidents. Musicians performed impromptu jams. Others carried signs reading, "What happened to the money?"

The crowd smiled when someone spoke kind words, but beneath those smiles, anxiety and anger burned. Faculty and staff wondered how they would survive. Students asked how they would complete their education. As each day passed, edging closer to June 7, anger and anxiety grew. The final day came and went—faculty without jobs, students without a university. All begrudgingly accepted their new reality: their university was gone, and no amount of protest could resurrect their beloved institution.

Turmoil, upheaval, disruption—however one wishes to describe it—these were the scenes witnessed in the final days of the University of the Arts. The university had stood for 150 years, enduring countless artistic and social changes. From the cobblestone streets and horse-drawn buggies of its early days, through the Great Depression, and across all major artistic movements spanning the late 19th to early 21st centuries, it persevered. The day UARTS closed, Philadelphia didn't just lose an icon—America did. It was the only American university offering all the arts under one roof.

Protesters asked whether UARTS' closure was the fault of one person. Others wondered if real estate developers had conspired to shutter the school to make way for new condominiums. This investigation began soon after UARTS closed its doors. Fast forward one year, and it is undeniable that UARTS' collapse was not caused by one person. Instead, the collapse was caused by a series of events perpetuated by a series of people.

This report retraces that path. It examines what truly led to the collapse of the University of the Arts.

The Seeds of Collapse: UARTS' Path to Failure

UARTS: Granting Organization or University?

Between 2011 and 2022, UARTS donated over $86 million to external organizations — including the University of Pennsylvania, Drexel University, and Temple University, whose endowments dwarf UARTS's by a factor of 20. These donations continued during a period marked by declining enrollment, mounting legal settlements, and unsustainable corporate debt. Beneficiaries included the Mann Music Center, Pig Iron Theater, Opera Philadelphia, the Kimmel Center, Settlement Music School, the Philadelphia Museum of Art, and the Wilma Theater — among others. These gifts offered no measurable mutual benefit to UARTS. Rather than cultivating institutional pipelines or partnerships, UARTS behaved more like a grant-making foundation than a tuition-dependent university. This was not generosity — it was strategic dysfunction, emblematic of belligerent spending and an abdication of fiduciary responsibility.

2009: The Year Enrollment Declines

The seeds of UARTS' collapse were sown as early as 2009, the year stable enrollment gave way to decline. In a statistical review of 30 visual and performing arts colleges, 20 showed a striking pattern: overall enrollment increased, while 3 arts colleges enrollment stayed level. Yet while some art schools across the country saw enrollment grow, particularly in emerging creative sectors, Philadelphia-based institutions like UARTS faced the sharpest declines. Similar patterns appeared at nearby institutions like Moore College of Art & Design and the Pennsylvania Academy of the Fine Arts. Why did this region fare worse—and why didn't UARTS adapt?

Donating While in Debt: UARTS' Morally Bankrupt Fundraising Strategy

In a sign of deep institutional desperation, UARTS relied heavily on enrolled students, faculty, and staff to fund its operations. From 2020 to 2024, 29% of all donations came from current students and 13% from faculty. Accepting contributions from students already burdened by crushing debt wasn't just financially shortsighted—it was ethically indefensible. Instead of cultivating external donor networks, UARTS leaned on those least able to give. In some years, fundraising efforts actually resulted in net losses. Under the Buffington administration, modest fundraising brought in $250,000. Under President Yager, losses approached $400,000. These efforts, likely aimed at appeasing bondholders, rating agencies, and the public, only masked a deeper truth: UARTS could not fund raise competently or sustainably.

2020: The Year UARTS Ignored the Alarm Bells

By 2020, the financial warning signs were unmistakable. The university failed to secure a forgivable PPP loan during the COVID-19 pandemic—essentially free money and a lifeline used by many peer institutions. That same year, UARTS saw its bond rating downgraded and quietly paid legal settlements to two professors. Internally, the administration showed no sign of preparing for a crisis. Whether this was denial or incompetence is unclear—but either possibility is damning. 2020 was a pivotal moment: the last clear chance to act decisively before collapse.

A Labor Contract That Set Faculty Back

In February 2024, faculty and staff celebrated what they hoped was a turning point: UARTS' first-ever faculty labor contract. Optimism ran high, as union members believed their long wait for fair treatment was finally over. Yet, the contract's terms failed to keep pace with inflation, effectively causing union members to lose up to 3% in real income. Labor leaders neglected to factor in a healthy cost-of-living increase, leaving faculty financially behind despite their hard-fought agreement. What was meant as progress turned into a setback.

Controversial Union Demands & Questionable Tactics During Negotiations

Contract negotiations between the University of the Arts and United Academics of Philadelphia—the union representing UARTS faculty—began in 2021. While the administration has faced widespread scrutiny, union leadership also raised ethical and legal concerns. During early bargaining sessions, United Academics of Philadelphia proposed that future hiring decisions be codified by sex and race—both requests were denied by the university. In a later negotiation, UAP introduced a UARTS student into the bargaining room in what the administration described as an inappropriate attempt to sway discussions. The tactic was publicly condemned by UARTS as an act of student exploitation.

Dangerously Low Student-to-Employee Ratios Undermined Financial Stability

The last time UARTS maintained a student-to-employee ratio above 3:1 was in 2001 when it was 3.5:1. From 2009 until its closure, the ratio hovered between 2.9:1 and as low as 2:1—alarmingly low for a tuition-dependent institution. Such low ratios left UARTS highly vulnerable: even minor enrollment declines quickly translated into severe financial stress the university was ill-equipped to manage.

A Mounting Legal Crisis: Lawsuits from Students and Faculty

UARTS' legal troubles began in February 2019, when photography professor Harris Fogel successfully sued for wrongful termination. According to his complaint, Fogel's superior conspired with a student and an outside party to force his dismissal. In November 2020, musical theater vocal coach Benjamin Czarnota won a similar wrongful termination lawsuit after being fired due to an unfavorable end-of-semester student review that targeted him for being a white male. In both cases, the executive board swiftly approved the administration's recommendations.

Compounding these issues, legal settlements were improperly recorded on the university's IRS Form 990, hidden under categories like executive compensation and legal expenditures rather than disclosed transparently.

By November 2022, student civil rights litigation surfaced with John K.A. Doe alleging a musical theater professor infected him with syphilis. This case names eight defendants—the largest group of UARTS members ever accused in a single suit. As of September 2025, the case remains pending with ongoing motions from both sides.

Missed Opportunities in Outreach, Branding, & Digital Strategy

UARTS consistently failed to capitalize on low-cost, high-impact opportunities that could have sustained enrollment and enhanced visibility. Throughout the Philadelphia region, numerous school districts offer visual and performing arts programs. Yet UARTS never established strong partnerships with these districts to build a pipeline of aspiring students. In the digital realm, the university lacked a professional online presence. Its social media accounts saw minimal engagement, and many of its promotional videos fell short of industry standards in storytelling, design, and production. Perhaps most baffling, UARTS had access to world-renowned artists and creators—an untapped asset in its marketing efforts. Instead of investing in scalable, effective outreach, UARTS pursued high-cost strategies with little to no measurable return on investment.

Academic Inbreeding: How Insularity Stifled Innovation

From 2006 to 2024, UARTS consistently posted academic inbreeding rates—faculty hired from among their own graduates—well above accepted norms. In some schools within the university, the rate exceeded 50%, compared to the recommended ceiling of 10% that most institutions maintain to encourage fresh perspectives and innovation. At UARTS, the result was an insular culture resistant to change, with outdated programs that failed to keep pace with the evolving arts landscape. Over time, this inertia became a barrier to renewal and growth.

A Phantom Capital Campaign Masked Financial Collapse

In 2018, UARTS launched its first-ever capital campaign, setting a $50 million goal and later announcing with great fanfare that it had raised $67 million. On paper, it looked like a triumph—proof of a financially strong university weathering the pandemic. But a closer look at tax filings and foundation donations reveals a different story. Much of the campaign's success came from shifting money between accounts and repackaging existing funds. What David Yager celebrated as a fundraising victory was, in reality, a carefully crafted illusion. Behind the public relations gloss, UARTS was already circling the drain.

The Cohort Default Rate: An Overlooked Crisis at UARTS

UARTS' Cohort Default Rate (CDR)—the percentage of alumni in student loan default—climbed dangerously close to the federal sanction threshold of 30% by 2020. Crossing that line would have jeopardized access to federal student aid, the lifeblood of a tuition-dependent school. While records are incomplete, evidence suggests UARTS may already have crossed this threshold in recent years, exposing a hidden crisis that administrators failed to confront.

2023: UARTS' Slide Into Oblivion

By 2023, UARTS was running on financial fumes. Meeting payroll and basic obligations became a desperate month-to-month struggle. Successive bond downgrades and reliance on short-term credit signaled an institution circling the drain. Each domino — cash, debt, confidence — fell in quick succession, making survival less a plan than a fantasy.

UARTS: Granting Organization or University?

UARTS gave away millions it could not spare—leaving behind more questions than answers.

Beginning in 2011, the University of the Arts started making donations to external organizations in and around Philadelphia—something it had never done before. Between 2011 and 2022, these donations totaled $86 million. This was money that could have been used to improve academic programs, pay down debt, keep tuition stable, or prepare for unexpected financial crises. Instead, it went to other nonprofits.

Many recipients were local museums, theaters, and small arts organizations. More surprising, however, is that UARTS donated millions to major universities—Temple University, Drexel University, and the University of Pennsylvania—institutions whose financial endowments dwarfed UARTS' own at any point in its history.

Below is a selection of the largest known donations from 2011–2022. A complete breakdown is available in *Appendix C: Table Listing UARTS Donations to External Organizations (2011-2022)*.

- University of Pennsylvania – **$4.8 million**

- Temple University (including Tyler) – **$2.7 million**

- Philadelphia Museum of Art – **$2.6 million**

- Fabric Workshop & Museum – **$2 million**

- People's Light & Theater Company – **$2 million**

- Opera Company of Philadelphia – **$1.8 million**

- Mann Music Center for the Performing Arts – **$1.7 million**

- Pig Iron Theater – **$1.7 million**

- The Wilma Theater – **$1.6 million**

- Drexel University – **$1.4 million**

When viewed alongside the endowments of these larger universities, the contrast is stark:

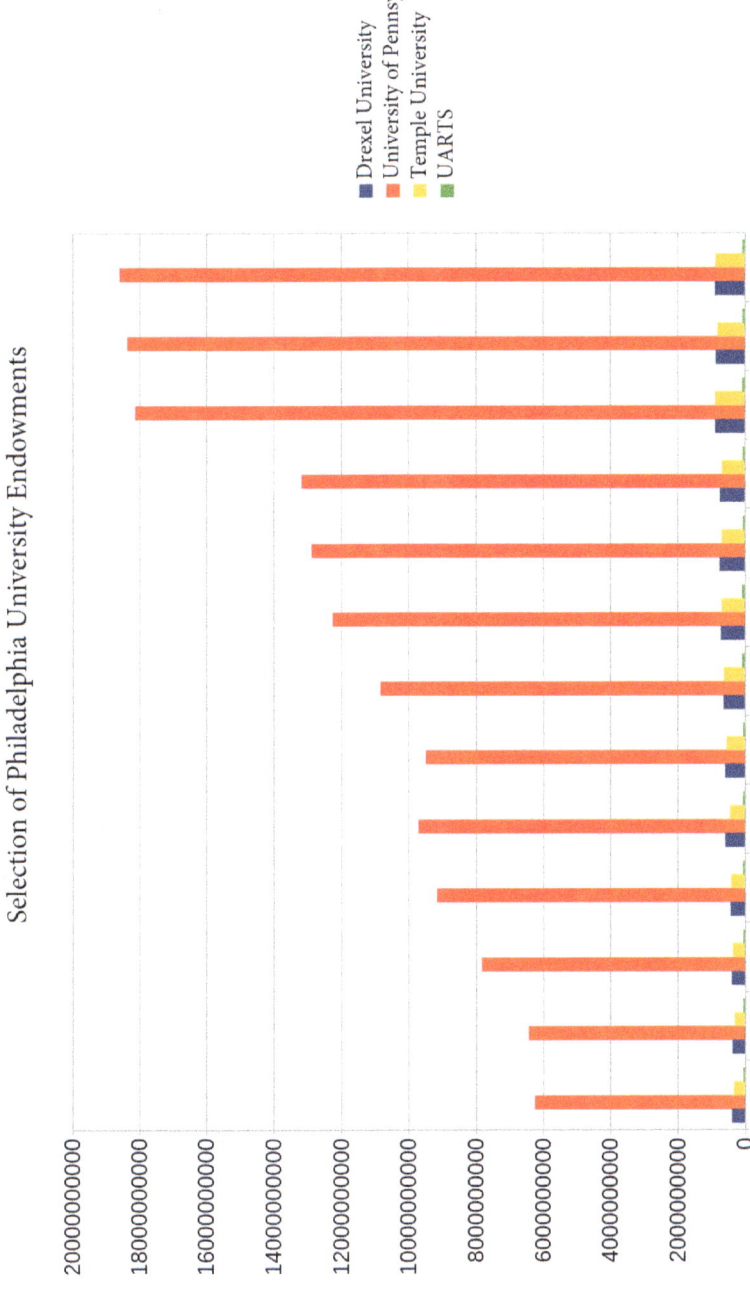

Figure 1: *Note Temple University's and Drexel University's endowments dwarfs UARTS endowment.*

This raises an unavoidable question:

*Why was a small, tuition-dependent university giving
away millions to institutions with far greater financial resources?*

Unanswered Questions

Just as striking is when UARTS began this practice—2011. There was no legal requirement for a nonprofit university to make such donations. The shift could only have been the result of an internal policy change approved by the administration and the Board of Trustees.

Equally puzzling is the absence of tangible return. During this 11-year period, there is no evidence that these donations produced mutually beneficial partnerships. Consider the Settlement Music School, which received $670,000 from UARTS. Despite being a city-wide music education institution, there's no indication it directed its students toward UARTS. If donations were meant to act as investments, the most basic business question should have been asked:

How does this expenditure improve our university?

From all available evidence, it appears that question was never seriously considered.

Possible Motives

Why persist in giving away millions—especially when financial strain became undeniable by 2020? Several possible motives emerge:

- **Financial Incompetence** - With tuition as the primary revenue source and enrollment steadily declining since 2009, UARTS should have scaled back donations to sustainable levels—or eliminated them entirely. Yet, even as student numbers fell and revenue shrank, the university continued giving away millions.

- **Projecting an Image of Legitimacy** - UARTS faced persistent negative publicity—from poor alumni reviews to ongoing civil rights lawsuits. High-profile philanthropy may have been used to project legitimacy and respectability among peers, masking internal instability.

- **Power Projection in the Arts** - As the only U.S. university to house all visual and performing arts disciplines under one roof, UARTS may have sought to position itself as a central player in the arts ecosystem. Large donations could be seen as a way to exert influence and enhance prestige within that community.

Figure 2: *UARTS donations to external organizations from 2011-2022. Note the sudden increase in donations during the pandemic years.*

The Curious Case of Paula Marincola & Her Relationship with UARTS

When analyzing University of the Arts officer compensation from 2000–2022, one finds the names and salaries of the highest paid officers. Many of these names belonged to people who were visible on campus and synonymous with UARTS leadership. But one name stands out: Paula Marincola.

Her name is absent from archived UARTS websites. She does not appear in the UARTS course catalog—the publication listing courses, officers, administrators, professors, deans, and department heads.

Yet Marincola regularly drew compensation from UARTS. Her job titles were inconsistent: sometimes listed as "director," other times "executive director," and in 2020 as "Executive Director – PCAH." However, no UARTS department of "PCAH" ever existed in university publications or organizational charts.

A closer review of UARTS records from 2000–2022 shows:

- Drew a UARTS salary in 2000–2003 and again from 2008–2024

- Never appeared in the UARTS organizational chart

- Never listed in course catalogs or administrative rosters

- Appeared only on UARTS tax returns under officer compensation

- Held vague, shifting job titles

These facts raise a simple but pressing question:

Who was she, and why was she paid by UARTS?

In 1997, the Philadelphia Exhibitions Initiative (PEI) was launched as a Pew Charitable Trusts program directed by Marincola, with UARTS serving as an administrative partner. In 2005, PEI and Marincola transitioned fully into Pew, where she became Executive Director of the newly formed Pew Center for Arts & Heritage (PCAH).

Despite holding this role at PCAH, Marincola began drawing a UARTS salary again in 2008. This overlapping relationship between PCAH and UARTS is striking, particularly given the similarities in their grantmaking patterns. While no evidence directly proves that Marincola directed UARTS's external giving, her dual affiliation and the alignment of grant priorities suggest that the two institutions operated in close tandem, with Marincola as a key connective figure.

Was UARTS a Pass-Through Entity?

One might argue that UARTS functioned as a pass-through entity for PCAH, receiving funds from Pew and redirecting them onward. Nonprofits can act as pass-through entities, but strict reporting requirements apply:

- All monies must be reported on the annual IRS Form 990

- Transfers must be designated as "restricted" or "unrestricted" on Schedule I

- Administrative fees may not exceed 10%

If UARTS had been operating in this manner, at least 90% of Pew funds would have been passed directly through. But the financial data show otherwise:

Year	Pew Charitable Trust Donations to UARTS ($)	UARTS Donations to External Organizations ($)	Money UARTS Donated (%)
2011	14,624,000	5,767,313	39
2012	9,746,000	5,147,724	53
2013	10,759,000	6,008,143	56
2014	12,250,000	7,361,466	56
2015	13,290,000	9,195,447	69
2016	12,137,000	6,005,204	49
2017	14,247,000	9,931,515	68
2018	11,765,000	6,918,776	59
2019	13,562,000	5,901,847	44
2020	13,663,685	4,118,274	30
2021	13,703,786	9,858,442	72
2022	12,738,261	9,454,090	74

Table 1: Comparison of PCAH and UARTS grantmaking, 2011–2022. While the two organizations often supported similar arts and cultural initiatives, the data reveal key differences. PCAH functioned as a direct grantmaker, while UARTS distributed only a portion of its Pew-derived funding to outside organizations—retaining significant amounts for internal use. The overlapping patterns suggest influence and alignment rather than a pass-through relationship.

Instead of meeting the 90% threshold, UARTS's percentages ranged from 30% to 74%. These figures clearly demonstrate that UARTS was **not** functioning as a pass-through entity for PCAH.

Further, UARTS tax returns contain no references to restricted funds earmarked for PCAH. The only explicit restriction appears in Pew's own 2004 tax return, which designated funds for PEI. But in UARTS's corresponding return, no such restriction was reported—likely due to looser pre-2009 reporting standards.

Conclusion

The evidence shows that UARTS was not a pass-through entity for PCAH. Its donations to external organizations were made at its own discretion, even if they often mirrored PCAH's priorities. This points not to a conduit relationship but to one of influence and alignment, with Paula Marincola serving as the central thread binding UARTS, Pew, and PCAH.

2009: The Year Enrollment Declined

2009 marks the first clear inflection point in the University of the Arts' trajectory toward collapse. That year, UARTS enrollment began a sustained decline. Prior to 2009, the university experienced steady growth followed by three years of stability. But after enrollment peaked in 2008, total numbers began to fall—and the trend never reversed.

As shown in Figure 3, UARTS' overall enrollment closely tracked its white student population. While other demographic groups remained comparatively stable, white student enrollment declined sharply after 2009, and the total student body followed the same trajectory. This was the first signal that UARTS' enrollment base was weakening.

University of the Arts - (Philadelphia, PA)

Enrollment by Race

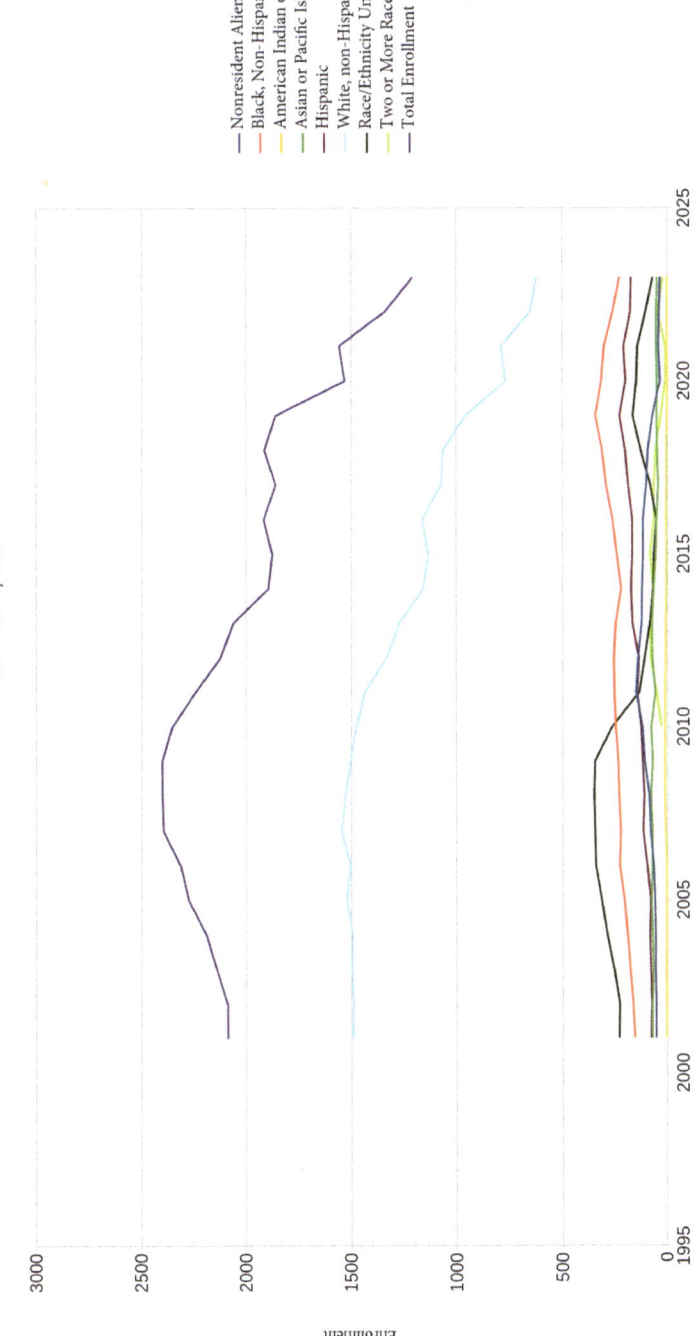

Figure 3: *Note the total enrollment tracks closely with white student enrollment.*

To determine whether this trend was unique to UARTS or part of a broader phenomenon, a comparative statistical analysis was conducted. A sample of 30 institutions was selected using the following criteria:

- Private nonprofit universities (501c3)

- Similar enrollment size to UARTS

- Exclusive programs in the arts

- Excluded schools offering non-arts degrees

- Included both visual and performing arts institutions

UARTS was already an outlier, offering both visual and performing arts degrees without the buffer of broader program diversification.

Results of Enrollment Based on Race & Nationality

The analysis revealed the following correlations between overall enrollment and demographic subgroups:

- **16 universities:** total enrollment correlated with white student enrollment

- **7 universities:** correlated with nonresident student enrollment

- **6 universities:** correlated with both white and nonresident student enrollment

- **1 university:** correlated with Hispanic and nonresident student enrollment

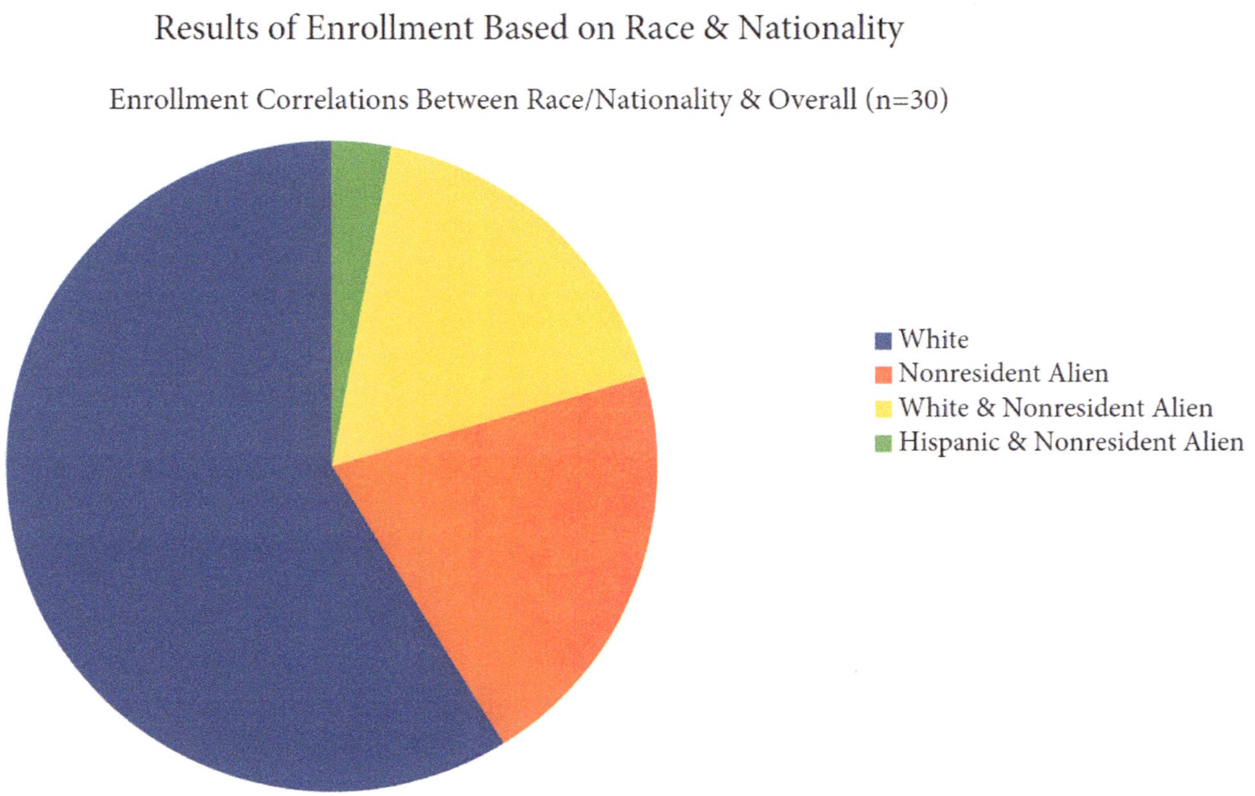

Results of Enrollment Based on Race & Nationality

Enrollment Correlations Between Race/Nationality & Overall (n=30)

- ■ White
- ■ Nonresident Alien
- ■ White & Nonresident Alien
- ■ Hispanic & Nonresident Alien

Figure 4 : *Statistical results showing a correlation between total enrollment and race/nationality.*

Trajectories of Enrollment, 2001–2023

The sample revealed three broad patterns of long-term enrollment:

- 20 universities experienced overall growth

- 7 universities experienced overall decline

- 3 universities remained relatively stable

Trajectories of Enrollment, 2001–2023

Private Nonprofit Visual & Performing Art Schools (n=30)

Increase
Decrease
Stable

Figure 5: *Of the 30 sampled conservatories, only 7 showed enrollment declines. Three of which were located in Philadelphia.*

Philadelphia's Arts Universities

An especially notable finding emerged when isolating Philadelphia's three major art schools: University of the Arts (UARTS), Pennsylvania Academy of the Fine Arts (PAFA), and Moore College of Art and Design (MCAD).

Each experienced enrollment decline, but at different points and rates:

- UARTS: decline began in 2009, slope of -85.43

- PAFA: decline began in 2010, slope of -7.69

- MCAD: decline began in 2003, slope of -16.1

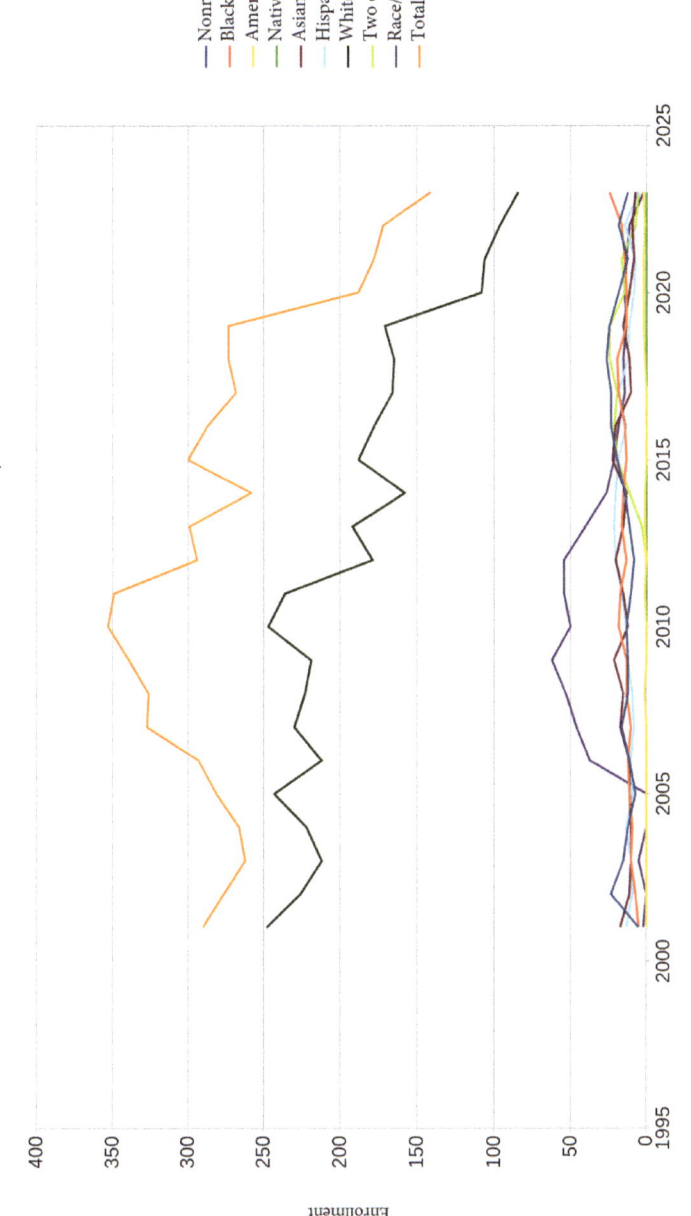

Figure 6: *PAFA experienced the same decline in student enrollment as UARTS.*

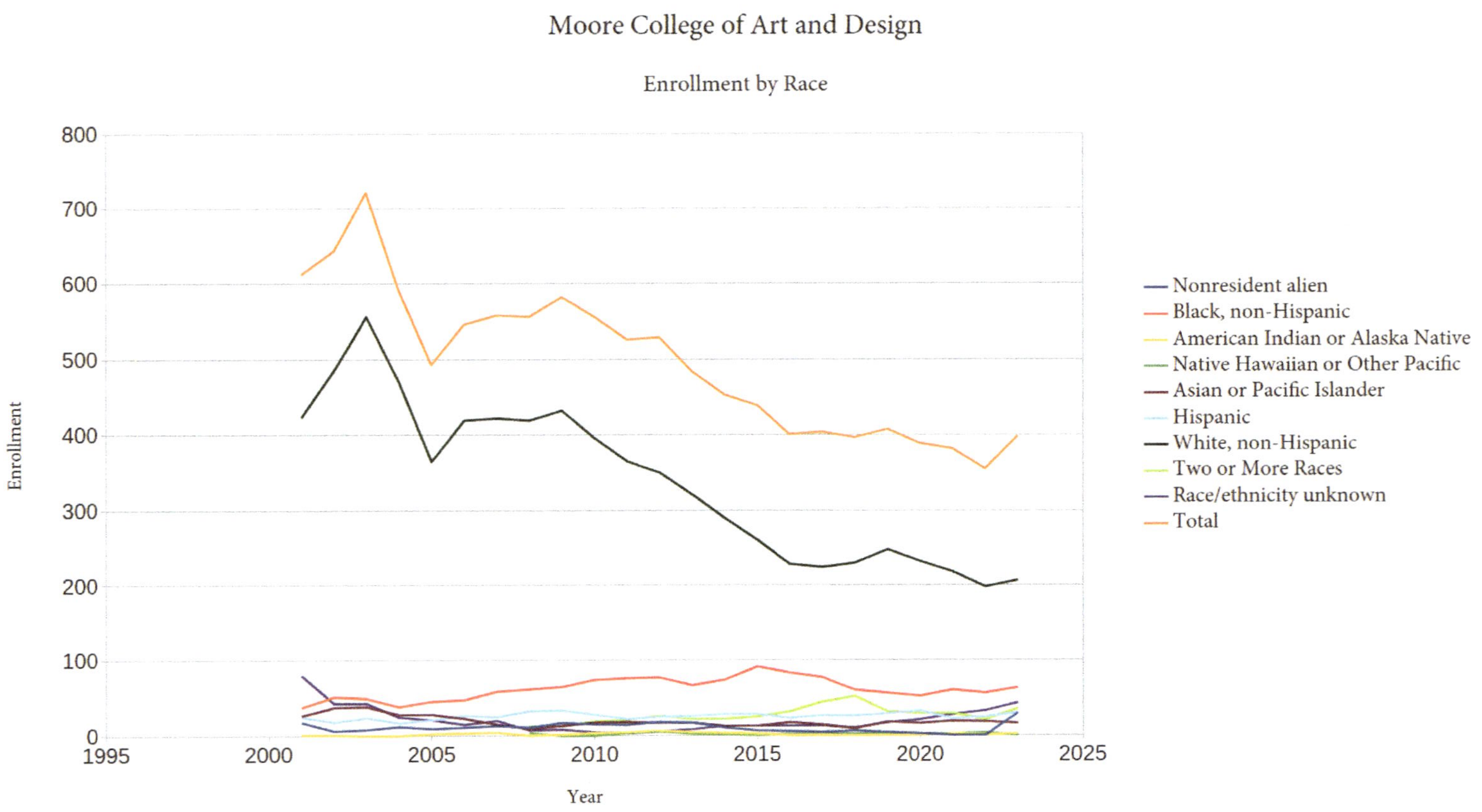
Moore College of Art and Design
Enrollment by Race
800
700
600
500
400
300
200
100
0
Enrollment
1995
2000
2005
2010
2015
2020
2025
Year
Nonresident alien
Black, non-Hispanic
American Indian or Alaska Native
Native Hawaiian or Other Pacific
Asian or Pacific Islander
Hispanic
White, non-Hispanic
Two or More Races
Race/ethnicity unknown
Total

Figure 7: *MCAD's student enrollment decline began 4 years earlier than UARTS. Note the steep decline in all three schools.*

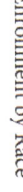

The Art Institute of Philadelphia, which closed in 2018, only reported enrollment data between 2012 and 2018, and only as percentages rather than aggregate counts.

Taken together, these data show that Philadelphia is over represented among art schools experiencing enrollment decline. Of the seven universities in the national sample with shrinking enrollment, three were located in Philadelphia.

This raises a larger question: **Why did so many Philadelphia-based arts institutions begin to lose students at roughly the same time, and why so sharply?** UARTS' enrollment decline in 2009 was not just a local downturn but part of a broader, citywide trend in arts education.

Donating While in Debt:
UARTS' Morally Bankrupt Fundraising Strategy

UARTS began conducting fundraising events in 2008. Between 2008 and 2015, these efforts generated modest gains, with a net profit of $250,000. In 2016, however, the university recorded its first loss from a fundraising event: $158,000. This decline coincides with the appointment of David Yager as UARTS' fourth president. From 2016 through 2022, fundraising events collectively lost $380,000. As shown in Figure 8, the downward trend highlights a persistent inability to generate reliable external revenue, indicating significant deficiencies in institutional leadership and strategic planning. For nonprofit universities, effective fundraising is essential to support academic programs, scholarships, and operational stability.

University of the Arts

Fundraising Events Net Profit - (2008-2022)

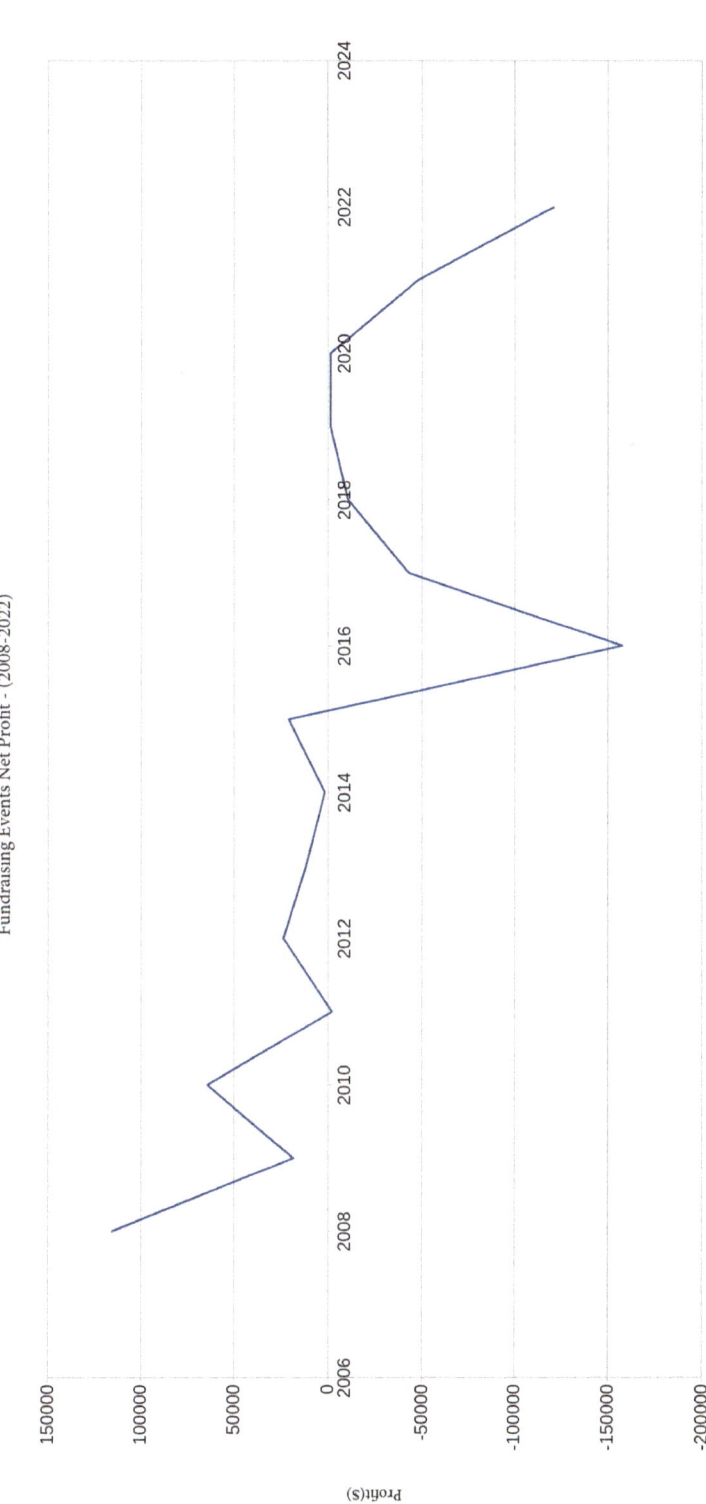

Figure 8: Net Gains/Losses from UARTS Fundraising Events, 2008–2022. (Note the loss in 2016 and UARTS inability to make a profit from 2016-2022.)

UARTS' fundraising strategies also raised ethical concerns. In 2020, the university launched its first Day of Giving, an annual online campaign soliciting donations from alumni, staff, parents, friends, and students. Across 2020, 2023, and 2024, students represented the largest number of donors, although there is no available data indicating which demographic contributed the most financially. In 2021 and 2022, a category labeled "Friends" accounted for a portion of donations, but the identity of these donors is unclear, making it difficult to assess engagement fully. Soliciting additional contributions from students—who are already financially burdened by tuition and student loans—reflects both an ethical concern and a symptom of institutional desperation.

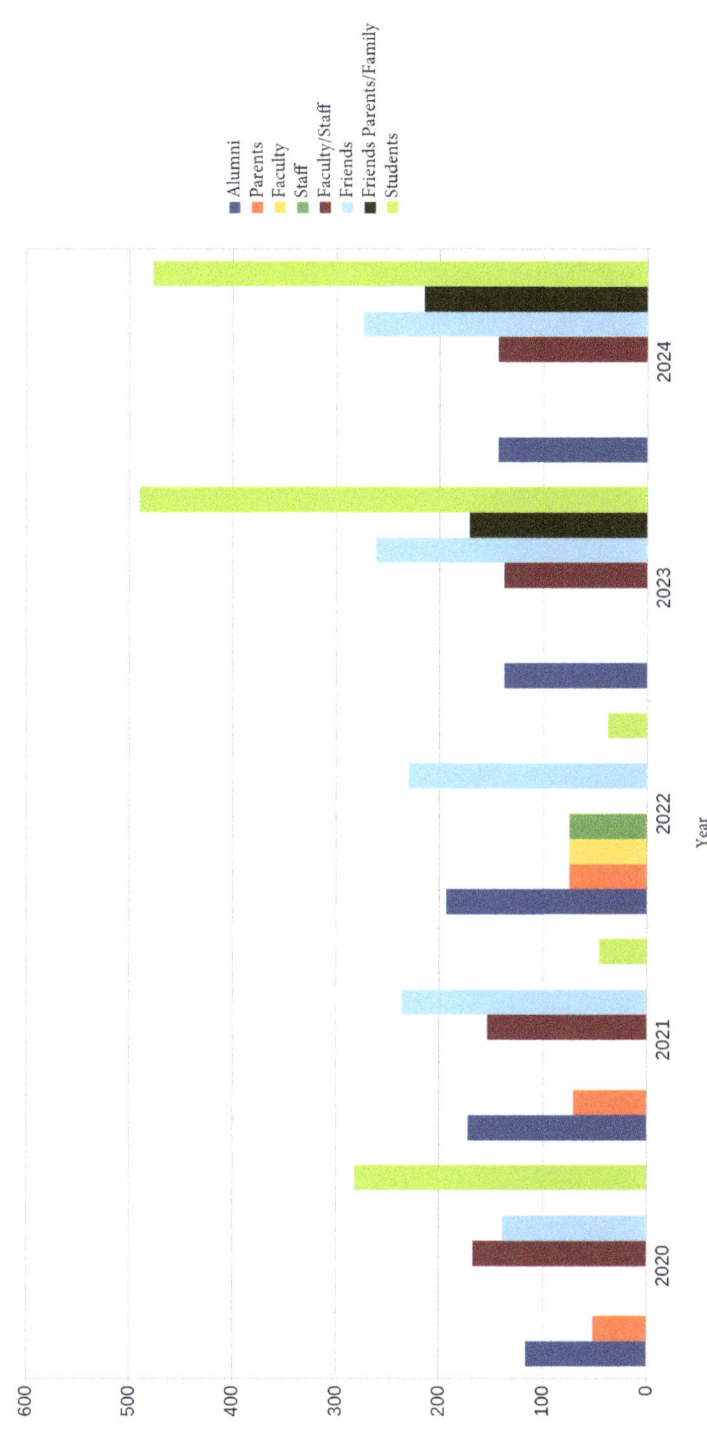

Figure 9: *Note the Number of Student Donors in UARTS Day of Giving, 2020–2024.*

As an outsider looking in, one must ask: was there a power imbalance between the university and the student body? Many students who participated in the Day of Giving are publicly identified, with only a small portion of donors are anonymous. Publicly available donor information creates the potential for favoritism from faculty and administration, raising ethical concerns about using students as a means to an end. This practice was not unique to fundraising at UARTS. As discussed in the section titled *Controversial Union Demands and Questionable Tactics During Negotiations*, the faculty union in one labor negotiation leveraged a student as a bargaining representative to negotiate a faculty contract.

Another ethical concern is whether UARTS informed donors of the university's financial difficulties. The donation website provided no information about how contributions would be used, leaving students and other donors without the ability to make fully informed decisions. Additionally, questions remain about the type of messaging students received: were implicit threats or benefits suggested based on whether they donated? Soliciting additional contributions from students—who are already financially burdened by tuition and student loans—reflects both an ethical concern and a symptom of institutional desperation.

Taken together, these examples indicate that UARTS was not only financially struggling but also morally compromised. The university's reliance on student donations, combined with questionable internal practices, illustrates a pattern of systemic mismanagement. The figures presented here show both the declining financial performance of fundraising efforts and the ethically problematic strategies employed, which disproportionately relied on students. The continued losses and aggressive solicitation practices underscore a lack of accountability and contributed directly to the broader financial and operational collapse of the university.

2020: The Year UARTS Ignored the Alarm Bells

Accountability and Transparency Concerns Surrounding UARTS' HEERF Grants

2020 was the second pivotal year in UARTS' decline, following 2009 when student enrollment began falling. Unlike 2009, 2020 exposed severe financial cracks that foreshadowed the institution's collapse.

During my research into UARTS' financial trajectory, I initially investigated their history with the Paycheck Protection Program (PPP) loans. Mapping PPP loan recipients along South Broad Street reveals that UARTS was the only major institution on that street not to secure a PPP loan—a concerning anomaly given the program's broad availability and minimal credit hurdles.

The PPP loan eligibility requirements were:

- 500 or fewer employees

- Eligible entity types including sole proprietors, independent contractors, non-profits, veterans organizations, business leagues, tribal businesses, news organizations, housing organizations

- In operation before February 15, 2020

- Minimal credit checks

UARTS met all but the employee count criterion. According to FY2019 data, UARTS employed 436 full-time and 336 part-time employees—a total of 772—well above the PPP's 500-employee cutoff.

Despite missing out on PPP funds, UARTS did qualify for and received federal pandemic relief from the Higher Education Emergency Relief Fund (HEERF), designed to support operations and student aid. HEERF funding required institutions to certify they would allocate at least 50% of the funds to direct student emergency aid and use the remainder for expenses such as remote learning, campus disruption, and technology investments.

HEERF eligibility requirements included:

- Eligibility as a Title IV institution (public, private, or for-profit college/university)

- Submission of a Certification & Agreement committing to fund usage requirements

- Maintenance of detailed documentation on HEERF fund expenditures

UARTS was awarded the following HEERF grants:

- HEERF I: $1,825,665 (FY2019)

- HEERF II: $2,708,958 (FY2020)

- HEERF III: $4,783,868 (FY2021)

However, what raises significant concern is that UARTS's tax returns from 2019 to 2022 show continued—and in fact increased—donations to external organizations during the same period they received these pandemic relief funds. The report section titled *UARTS: Granting Organization or University?* offers more detail, but in brief, UARTS donated roughly $20 million in these years amid profound economic and social insecurity.

Adding to the puzzling financial picture, UARTS reported a cumulative profit of $5.7 million between 2019 and 2021 but then suffered a $6 million loss in 2022.

This financial behavior prompts a critical question: **Were the HEERF grant monies truly used for their intended pandemic relief purposes, or were they diverted toward external donations?**

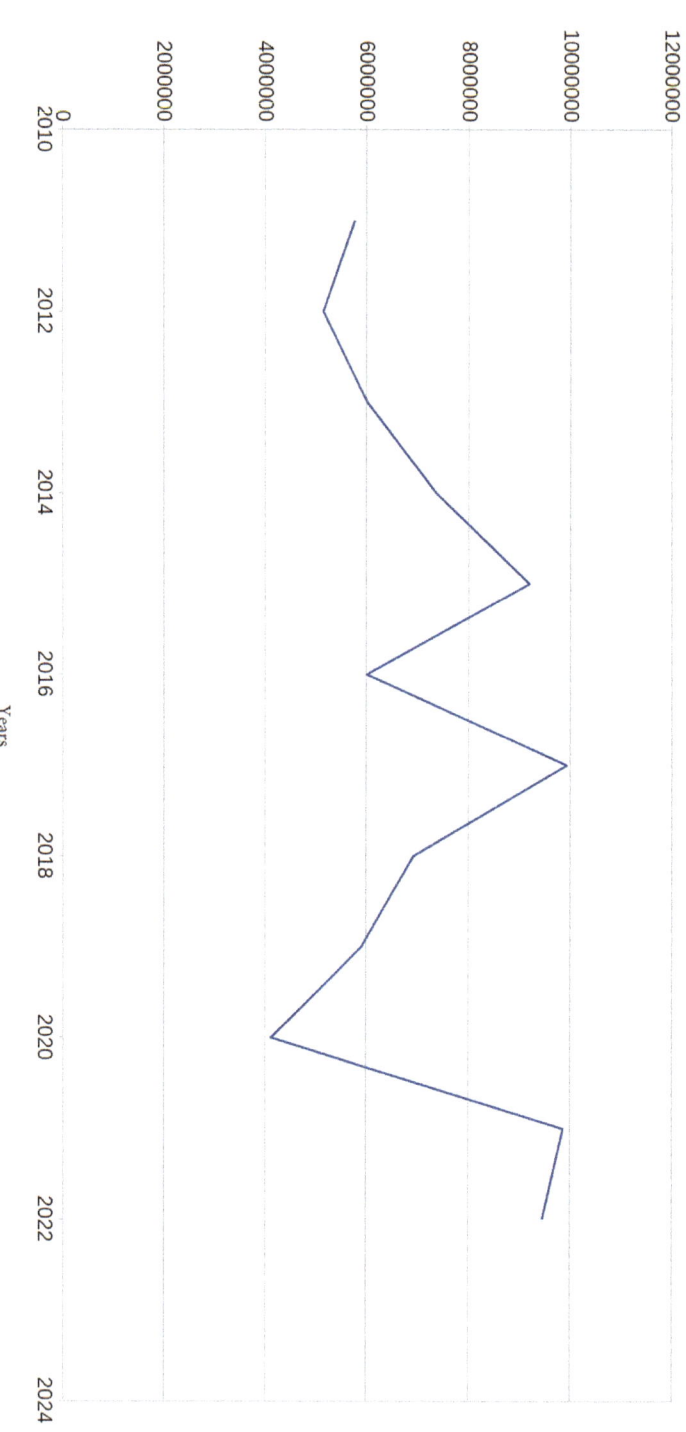

University of the Arts

Donations to External Organizations

Figure 10: *UARTS Donations to External Organizations, 2011–2022 (note significant increases during pandemic relief years)*

UARTS Bond: From Junk Bond to Default

In December 2017, the University of the Arts secured a conduit-issued municipal revenue bond through the Philadelphia Authority for Industrial Development (PAID). The bond had a face value of just over $50 million, with a total issuance cost approaching $53 million. While the exact allocation of the bond proceeds remains unclear, what is certain is that Fitch Ratings assigned it a BB+ grade at issuance—placing it squarely in non-investment-grade, or "junk bond," territory.

A BB+ rating signals elevated credit risk; in practical terms, it is a red flag that the borrower's financial position makes default a realistic, even probable, outcome without substantial improvement. In UArts' case, starting at BB+ left virtually no margin for deterioration. For senior leadership—particularly the Vice President of Finance—to overlook or underestimate this reality was, at best, a display of financial naïveté, and at worst, a severe lapse in fiduciary responsibility.

As the table below shows, Fitch downgraded the bond every single year following issuance, with each step down eroding confidence until 2024, when the university collapsed and the bond went into default.

Had UARTS not donated $20 million to external organizations during the pandemic years as explained in the subsection, *Accountability and Transparency Concerns Surrounding UARTS' HEERF Grants* and with the income earned from real estate sale of the Pine Street Dorms in 2023 for $10.7 million they could have weathered the COVID pandemic and remained in operation.

		Fitch's Bond Rating Schedule				
Rating	Category	Meaning	UARTS Bond Rating Date
AAA	Investment Grade	Best quality, minimal risk	
AA+		Very high quality; very strong capacity,	
AA		Very high quality; very strong capacity	
AA-		Same as AA, but closer to the next category down.	
A+		Strong capacity, but more vulnerable to changes in circumstances/economy.	
A		Strong capacity to meet obligations, though somewhat susceptible to adverse changes.	
A-		More susceptible to changes than A.	
BBB+		More likely to be affected by adverse changes.	
BBB		Lowest "safe" rating; medium credit risk.	
BBB-		Considered borderline speculative.	
Junk Bond Ratings			
BB+	Speculative	Faces major ongoing uncertainties; vulnerable to adverse conditions.	March 18, 2020
BB		Faces major uncertainties, but has some financial flexibility.	March 1, 2021
BB-		Elevated vulnerability to default risk	February 14, 2023
B+	Highly Speculative	Material default risk present.	January 23, 2024
B		Financial commitments being met but capacity very limited.	
B-		Material default risk; dependent upon favorable business/financial conditions.	
CCC	Distressed	Default appears a real possibility.	
CC		Default appears probable.	
C		Imminent default.	June 4, 2024
RD	Default	Restricted default—issuer has defaulted on one or more obligations but continues on others.	
D		Issuer has defaulted on all	August 28, 2024

Sudden Decline in Employee Head Count

In 2019, UARTS reported a workforce of 772 employees. By 2020, that figure had fallen to 544—representing a 25% reduction within a single year. The decline reflects a combination of layoffs, retirements, and non-renewed contracts. A workforce cut of this magnitude is extraordinary: in many industries, even a 1% reduction prompts widespread media scrutiny. Yet in this case, the sharp contraction at UARTS drew virtually no attention. Coverage was eclipsed by the overwhelming news cycle surrounding COVID-19, leaving this significant development largely unexamined by both local and niche media outlets.

Changes in Faculty Wages

When examining faculty wages from 2010–2023, two major inflection points stand out. The first occurred in 2013, when professor wages and benefits were reduced by 24% while other faculty positions continued on a steady upward trend. The second was in 2020, when all faculty positions experienced a reduction in wages and benefits.

Average Faculty Wage Declines in 2020

- Professor: 5%

- Associate Professor: 10%

- Assistant Professor: 5.5%

- No Academic Rank: 5.3%

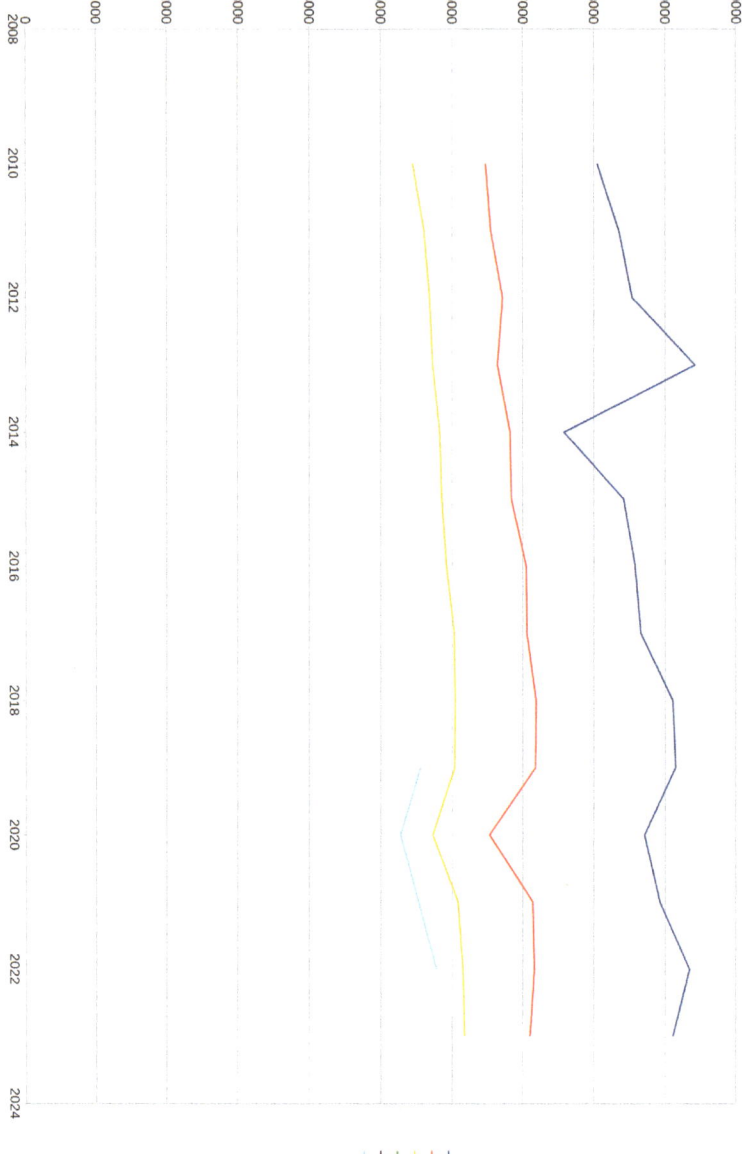

Figure 11: *Average faculty wages and benefits by position, 2010–2023 (showing 2013 and 2020 inflection points).*

These cuts allowed UARTS to save just over $1 million in 2020. However, they also had unintended consequences. Dissatisfaction over reduced pay contributed to faculty unionization efforts: faculty formed their union in 2020, and staff formed a separate union in 2022.

Unlike the faculty, there is no available data to confirm whether similar wage cuts were applied to non-teaching staff. Wages for most faculty positions returned to pre-2020 levels by 2021; professors were the exception, with full restoration delayed until 2022.

Post-2020, the number of faculty positions continued to decline in most categories. The only exception was the associate professor role, which dipped in 2020 but rebounded to baseline levels by 2022. Over the longer term, from 2010–2024, the data shows a steady overall decline in total faculty positions across the institution.

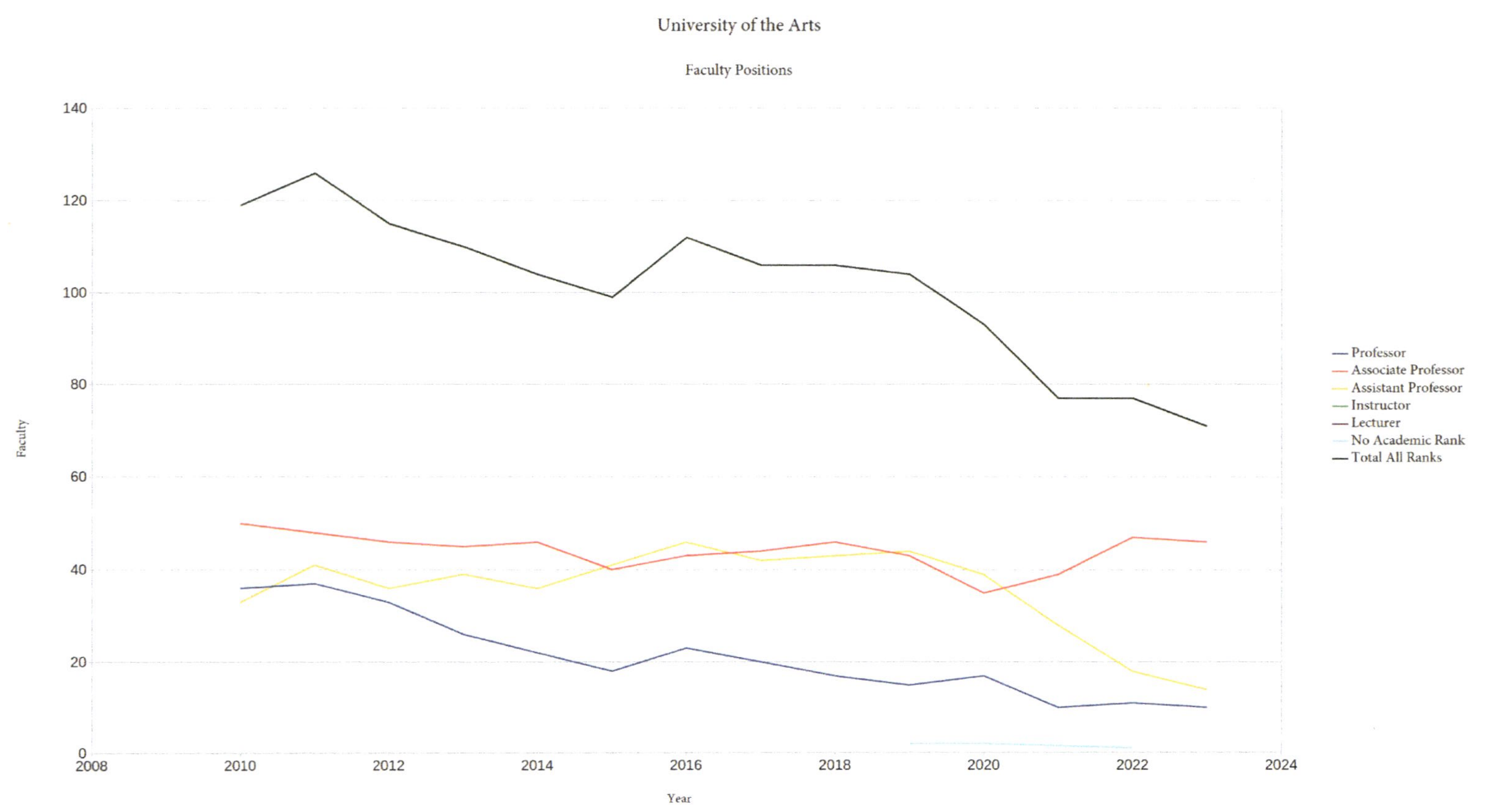
University of the Arts
Faculty Positions
140
120
100
80
60
40
20
0
Faculty
2008
2010
2012
2014
2016
2018
2020
2022
2024
Year
Professor
Associate Professor
Assistant Professor
Instructor
Lecturer
No Academic Rank
Total All Ranks

Figure 12: *Number of faculty by position, 2010–2023*

Legal Settlements: Another Crack in the Foundation

Amid the upheaval of 2020—donations to outside organizations, a newly formed faculty union negotiating its first contract, shrinking enrollment, and a declining faculty roster—UARTS also faced civil rights lawsuits that resulted in legal settlements with two former professors. While this report examines the broader legal landscape in *A Mounting Legal Crisis: Lawsuits from Students and Faculty*, it is important to note here that litigation was already adding to the institution's mounting pressures. These cases underscored that, even as financial and academic alarms were ringing, UARTS was also grappling with legal challenges that weakened its foundation further.

A Labor Contract That Set Faculty Back

2020 was the first time in UARTS 150 history to see a faculty union formed. Soon afterwards the UARTS staff formed their own union. Faculty and staff were represented by the fledgling United Academics of Philadelphia (UAP), a small labor union representing three locals – two at UARTS and one at Arcadia University. Faculty negotiations began in 2021. In February 2024, both sides reached an agreement.

When reading the labor agreement, contradictions and structural flaws appear.

- **First Contradiction.** Uneven pay steps for assistant professors – 8 steps, associate professors – 11 steps, and full professors – 5 steps.

- **Second Contradiction.** UARTS was only allowed to pay professors a maximum of two pay steps per year, yet other clauses state UARTS should treat each pay step as a minimum and could pay above and beyond the highest step.

- **First Structural Flaw.** Professors prior work history is not considered in determining the first pay step. Ultimately, a new hire with no prior work experience would be paid the same as a professor with 20 years of experience.

- **Second Structural Flaw.** Professors cannot advance past the highest step other than through a new contract. Such a structural flaw denies financial incentive for professors.

- **Third Structural Flaw.** The contract lasted three years, but with uneven steps and with a maximum of two steps being granted per year, the maximum steps should be six steps.

In addition to these structural flaws and contradictions, the contract contained the Financial Exigency Clause. It gave UARTS the ability to terminate all work agreements as soon as a financial emergency emerged. Was this foreshadowing of UARTS collapse three months later in May 2024?

In addition to the UARTS structural flaws and contradictions, the pay scale caused union members to lose gross income. Union leaders never incorporated a healthy 2% inflation rate in their negotiations. To better understand the wage losses, the following table first determines the wage increase as a percentage.

Adjunct Pay Scale – FY2024	Full Time Faculty Scale – FY2024
$$F = P*(1 + i)^n$$ $$F = Future\ Payment$$ $$P = Current\ Payment$$ $$n = number\ of\ steps$$ $$i = percent\ increase\ (decimal$$	
Steps 1-20	**Steps 1-8**
$1845 = 1275*(1 + i)^{20}$ $\left(\frac{1845}{1275}\right)^{\left(\frac{1}{20}\right)} - 1 = i$ $i = 1.86\%$	$64850 = 57850*(1 + i)^8$ $\left(\frac{64850}{57850}\right)^{\left(\frac{1}{8}\right)} - 1 = i$ $i = 1.44\%$
Steps 21-22	**Steps 9-20**
$1895 = 1870*(1 + i)^2$ $\left(\frac{1895}{1870}\right)^{\left(\frac{1}{2}\right)} - 1 = i$ $i = 0.66\%$	$80850 = 69850*(1 + i)^{11}$ $\left(\frac{80850}{69850}\right)^{\left(\frac{1}{11}\right)} - 1 = i$ $i = 1.34\%$
Steps 23-30	**Steps 21-25**
$2055 = 1950*(1 + i)^7$ $\left(\frac{2055}{1950}\right)^{\left(\frac{1}{7}\right)} - 1 = i$ $i = 0.752\%$	$85850 = 81850*(1 + i)^4$ $\left(\frac{85850}{81850}\right)^{\left(\frac{1}{4}\right)} - 1 = i$ $i = 1.20\%$

For this discussion, I will use the column analyzing Full Time Faculty Scale – FY2024.

- Full Time Faculty Steps 1-8, wage increases by 1.44%

- Full Time Faculty Steps 9-20 wage increases by 1.34%

- Full Time Faculty Steps 21-25 wage increases by 1.2%

Including the union dues of 1.75% and a 2% healthy inflation rate, the Full Time Faculty wage are:

- Full Time Faculty Steps 1-8, wage losses are:

    1.44%-1.75%-2% = -2.31%

- Full Time Faculty Steps 9-20 wage losses are:

    1.34% -1.75%-2% = -2.41%

- Full Time Faculty Steps 21-25 wage losses are:

    1.2% - 1.75% - 2% = -2.55%

This left faculty falling behind cost of living expenses and inflation rates. The winner in this agreement wasn't the faculty, but the union. The table below presents the information in a better format showing the mathematics behind these wage losses both for Adjunct and Full Time Faculty.

Adjunct Pay Scale – FY2024
$\Sigma T = i + f + u$ $T = total\ percentage\,(\%)$ $i = pay\ increase\,(\%)$ $f = inflation\ rate\,(\%) = -2.00\%$ $u = union\ dues\ (\%) = -1.75\%$
Steps 1-20
$i = 1.86\%$ $\Sigma T = i + f + u = 1.86 - 2.00 - 1.75 = -1.89\%$
Steps 21-22
$i = 1.44\%$ $\Sigma T = i + f + u = 1.44 - 2.00 - 1.75 = -2.31\%$
Steps 23-30
$i = 0.66\%$ $\Sigma T = i + f + u = 0.66 - 2.00 - 1.75 = -3.09\%$

Full Time Faculty Scale – FY2024
$\Sigma T = i + f + u$ $T = total\ percentage\,(\%)$ $i = pay\ increase\,(\%)$ $f = inflation\ rate\,(\%) = -2.00\%$ $u = union\ dues\ (\%) = -1.75\%$
Steps 1-8
$i = 1.44\%$ $\Sigma T = i + f + u = 1.44 - 2.00 - 1.75 = -2.31\%$
Steps 9-20
$i = 1.34\%$ $\Sigma T = i + f + u = 1.34 - 2.00 - 1.75 = -2.41\%$
Steps 21-25
$i = 1.20\%$ $\Sigma T = i + f + u = 1.20 - 2.00 - 1.75 = -2.55\%$

The UARTS faculty union contract, while historic in establishing formal representation, ultimately failed to deliver meaningful protections or financial security for its members. On paper, it offered a step system and the promise of raises, but in practice, it allowed for administrative discretion, limited advancement, and disregarded faculty experience. The financial framework of the agreement—marked by below-inflation raises and union dues—meant most faculty saw a net loss in real income over the course of the contract. Structurally, the agreement seemed more favorable to union leadership and university administrators than to the very educators it was meant to protect. That the agreement included a sweeping financial exigency clause—used just months later to shut down operations—raises troubling questions about the university's intent and the union's preparedness. Rather than serving as a stabilizing force, the contract may have inadvertently accelerated the institution's decline by masking deeper systemic and financial issues behind a veneer of collective bargaining.

A Mounting Legal Crisis:
Lawsuits from Students and Faculty

2018 marked the beginning of a series of high-profile lawsuits against UARTS, filed by both professors and students. In that year, Harris Fogel, a long-standing and popular photography professor, filed suit for wrongful termination based on sex discrimination. In 2020, shortly after the conclusion of Fogel's case, Benjamin Czarnota brought a lawsuit against UARTS for wrongful termination based on race. Following Czarnota's resolution, a student identified as John K.A. Doe filed a lawsuit alleging that Professor Daniel Dunn had infected him with a sexually transmitted disease. As of September 2025, motions continue to be filed by both plaintiffs and the university.

The following examines the claims brought by Fogel and Czarnota against the University of the Arts, as well as the impact of these lawsuits on UARTS' financial standing and institutional reputation.

Fogel v. University of the Arts

In Judge Kearney's memorandum, the court stated that Professor Fogel's allegations were to be "taken as true" for the purposes of evaluating the university's motion. This procedural standard does not establish the facts as proven but reflects the legal requirement to credit the plaintiff's allegations at this stage.

- **Differential treatment of complaints:** Fogel claimed that after receiving an unwanted kiss and hug from his supervisor, Anne Massoni, his complaint was dismissed without investigation by Lexi Morrison, UARTS' Title IX Coordinator. By contrast, when Jennifer Little, an Associate Professor of Art and Graphic Design at the University of the Pacific, reported that Fogel gave her an unwanted kiss and hug at a photography conference, Morrison conducted a full investigation.

- **March 2016 – Las Vegas conference:** At the Society for Photographic Education conference, Fogel hugged and kissed Little on the cheek. He also met Anne-Laurie Autin, to whom he accidentally handed his hotel key card instead of a business card. According to Fogel, both laughed at the mistake, and he corrected it by giving Autin his business card.

- **December 2017 – Complaints filed:** Twenty-one months later, Autin and Little submitted complaints to UARTS. Autin claimed the key card gesture was a hotel-room invitation, while Little escalated her original account of an unwanted kiss into a claim of forcible kissing, further alleging she tolerated his behavior in exchange for professional support.

- **Findings regarding Title IX process:** The court noted that Morrison applied the lower "preponderance of evidence" standard rather than the higher "clear and convincing" standard. Furthermore, Morrison refused to provide Fogel and his counsel with her investigative report, denied him the opportunity to respond in writing, and barred him from presenting witnesses in a live hearing. On January 23, 2018, Morrison concluded: "Professor Fogel had committed serious violations of the University's Sexual Misconduct, Sexual Harassment, and Other Forms of Harassment Policy.

- **Termination upheld:** In March 2018, Dean Mark Campbell terminated Fogel's employment. In August 2018, the university's executive board upheld the termination based on Morrison's recommendation.

Judge Kearney's memorandum allowed Fogel's claims to proceed into discovery, meaning the case had sufficient legal merit to survive dismissal. Faced with the prospect of extensive document production and potential exposure of administrative practices, the University of the Arts opted to settle before trial.

Reading Judge Kearney's memorandum, the sequence of events suggests that external complainants and internal administrators acted in concert to secure Fogel's dismissal. Rather than subject Morrison's conclusions to independent review, Dean Campbell and the executive board endorsed them without challenge. This lack of oversight highlights the absence of meaningful checks and balances within UARTS' governance — a failure that would contribute to the institution's mounting legal and financial troubles.

Fogel's case centered on allegations of sex-based discrimination. By contrast, the next lawsuit — *Czarnota v. University of the Arts* — focused on claims of racial discrimination.

Czarnota v. University of the Arts

In November 2020, vocal coach Benjamin Czarnota filed a lawsuit against the University of the Arts following his termination. In his initial complaint, Czarnota alleged that:

- UARTS Vice President of Academic Affairs Carole Graney terminated him because he is white.
- Graney's rationale for termination relied on a racially motivated end-of-semester course evaluation submitted by a student.
- The course evaluation stated:

> "I wonder if we would've made progress quicker if we hadn't had to navigate his social ignorance as a white man." The review further claimed that "learning is NEVER done for white people" [emphasis in original], and recommended that more voice teachers be hired — "just make sure they're not white."

Following Graney's decision, the UARTS executive board upheld her action. By May 2022, the case concluded with a settlement. As in *Fogel v. University of the Arts*, the court was preparing to move into discovery; however, both parties reached settlement beforehand.

Czarnota's case centered on alleged racial discrimination. The next section examines how these lawsuits — taken together — strained UARTS' finances and eroded its public reputation.

Costly Civil Rights Lawsuits

The civil rights cases settled with Harris Fogel and Benjamin Czarnota, along with the civil rights case still pending as of September 2025 brought by John K.A. Doe, imposed significant financial costs on UARTS. In Fogel's case, the number of administrators and faculty implicated suggests that his settlement was likely greater than a typical individual civil rights claim, while Czarnota's settlement may have been closer to the average. The exact settlement amounts remain unknown for several reasons. First, the agreements in both cases are sealed from the public. Second, UARTS did not disclose settlement amounts explicitly in either its IRS Form 990 filings or audited financial statements.

Nevertheless, the costs of litigation are visible in other ways. UARTS' 990 forms show escalating legal expenses that align with the lawsuits. The first indication of rising legal costs appears in UARTS' reported legal expenses

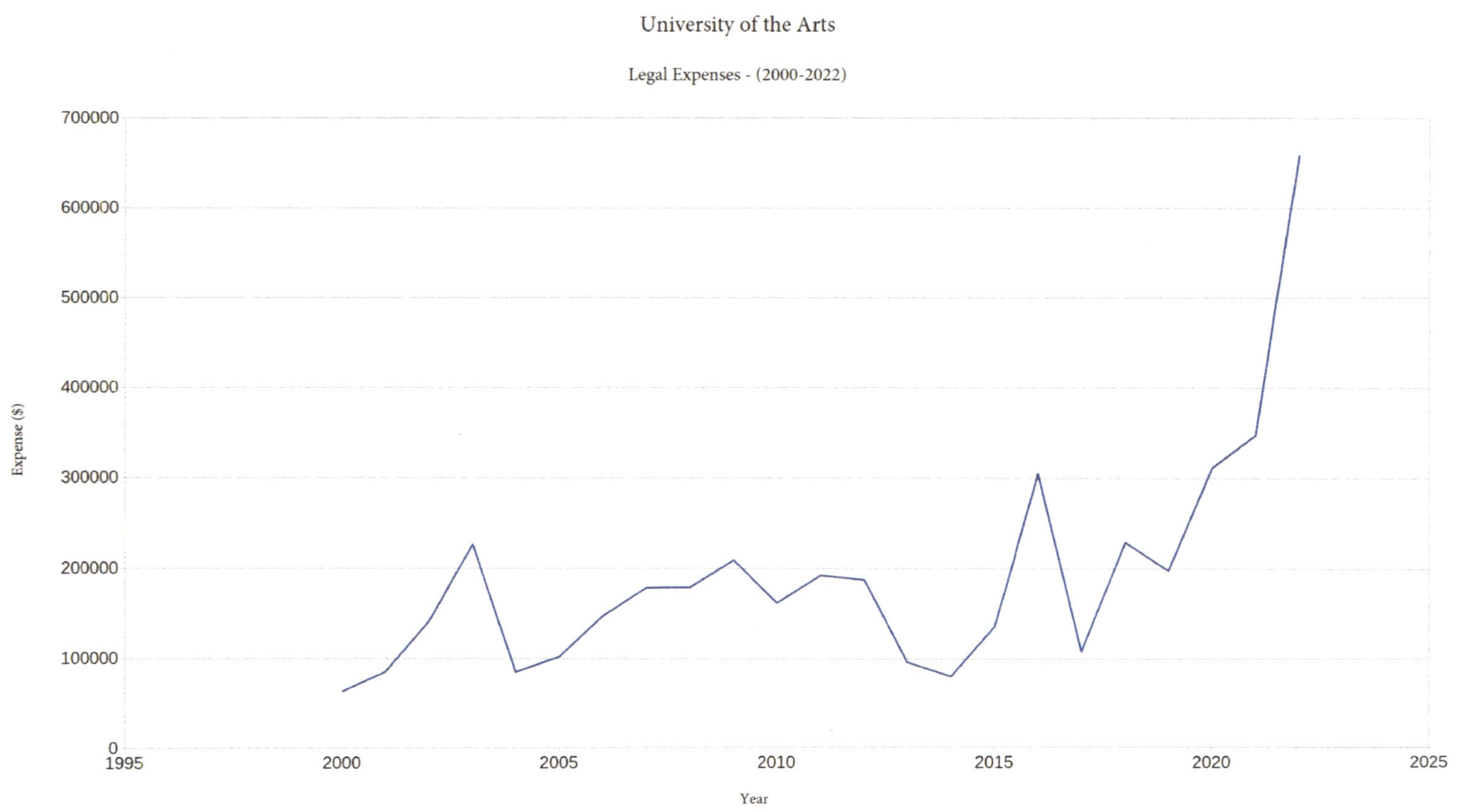

University of the Arts

Legal Expenses - (2000-2022)

Figure 13: *UARTS legal expenses nearly doubled in 2022 compared to the previous year, coinciding with multiple civil rights lawsuits. From 2018 to 2022, the university spent $1.7 million in this category, reflecting both legal fees and likely settlement costs.*

These escalating costs align closely with the timeline of successive lawsuits, suggesting that legal settlements are embedded within these figures. The most notable spike appears in 2022, when legal expenses nearly doubled from $347,000 in 2021 to $660,000. From 2018 to 2022 — the years when successive lawsuits were filed — UARTS spent $1.7 million on legal expenses. While the precise allocation between attorney fees and settlements is unclear, the trend underscores the financial toll of these civil rights cases.

Yet legal expenses are not the only area raising questions. A second area of the 990 filings that warrants scrutiny is total presidential compensation.

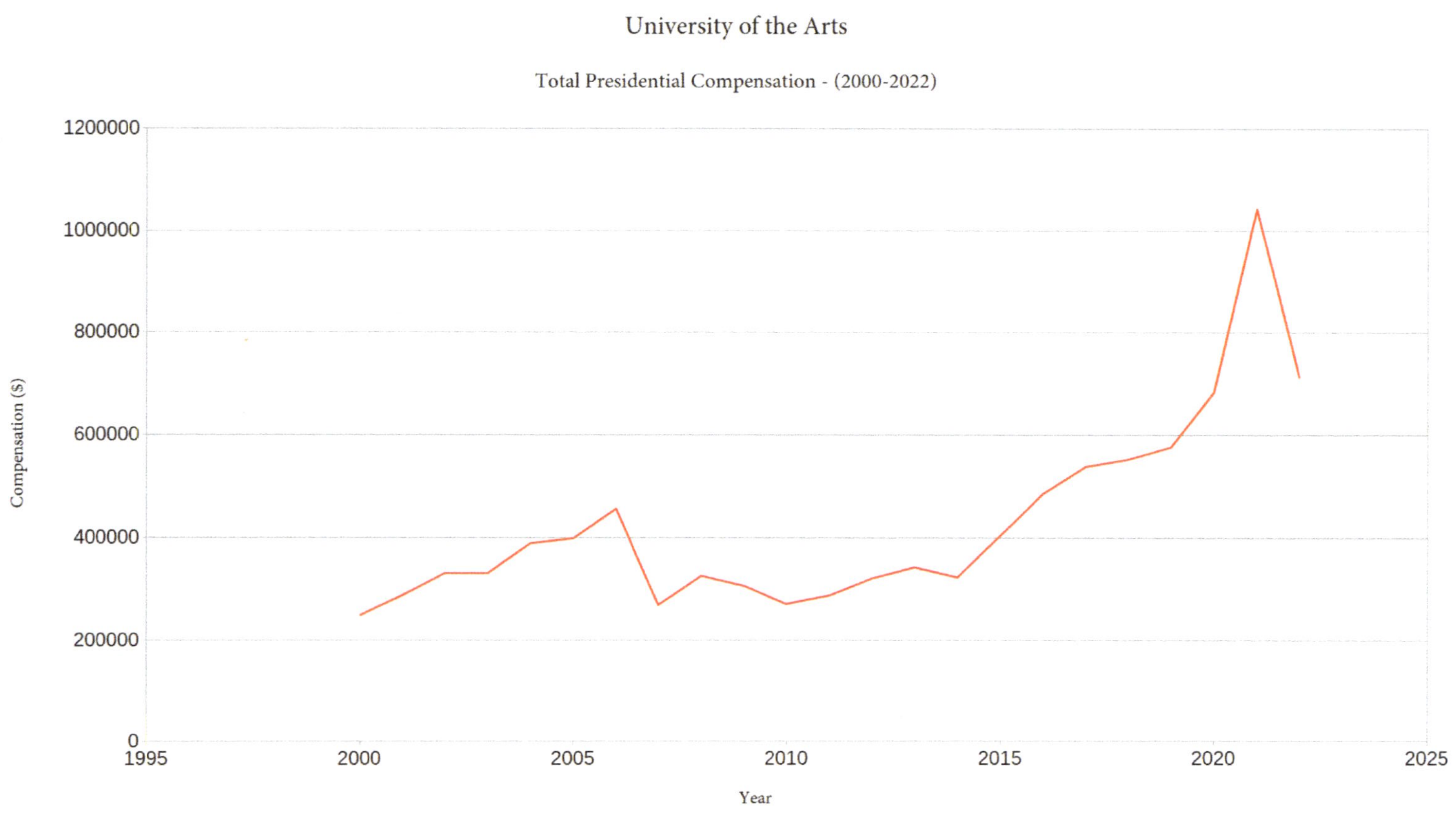

University of the Arts

Total Presidential Compensation - (2000-2022)

Compensation ($)

Year

Figure 14: *Total presidential compensation across four administrations. Compensation remained relatively steady under Corzo and Buffinton but rose sharply under Yager, peaking at more than $1 million in 2021.*

Yager's reported compensation levels not only surpassed his predecessor but also broke sharply from the long-term stability of prior administrations. From 2000 to 2006, total presidential compensation for Miguel Corzo (UARTS' second president) rose steadily. Between 2007 and 2014, Sean Buffington's pay remained relatively flat with minor fluctuations. In 2016, David Yager became the fourth president, and from that point forward, compensation levels diverged from historic norms. Two standouts are evident: Yager's pay far exceeded his predecessor's, and from 2020 to 2022, his reported compensation surged dramatically. In 2021, it exceeded $1 million; in 2022, it was reported at $712,000. To test whether these increases can be explained by normal growth, the following graph compares Yager's reported compensation to a projection based on historical trends.

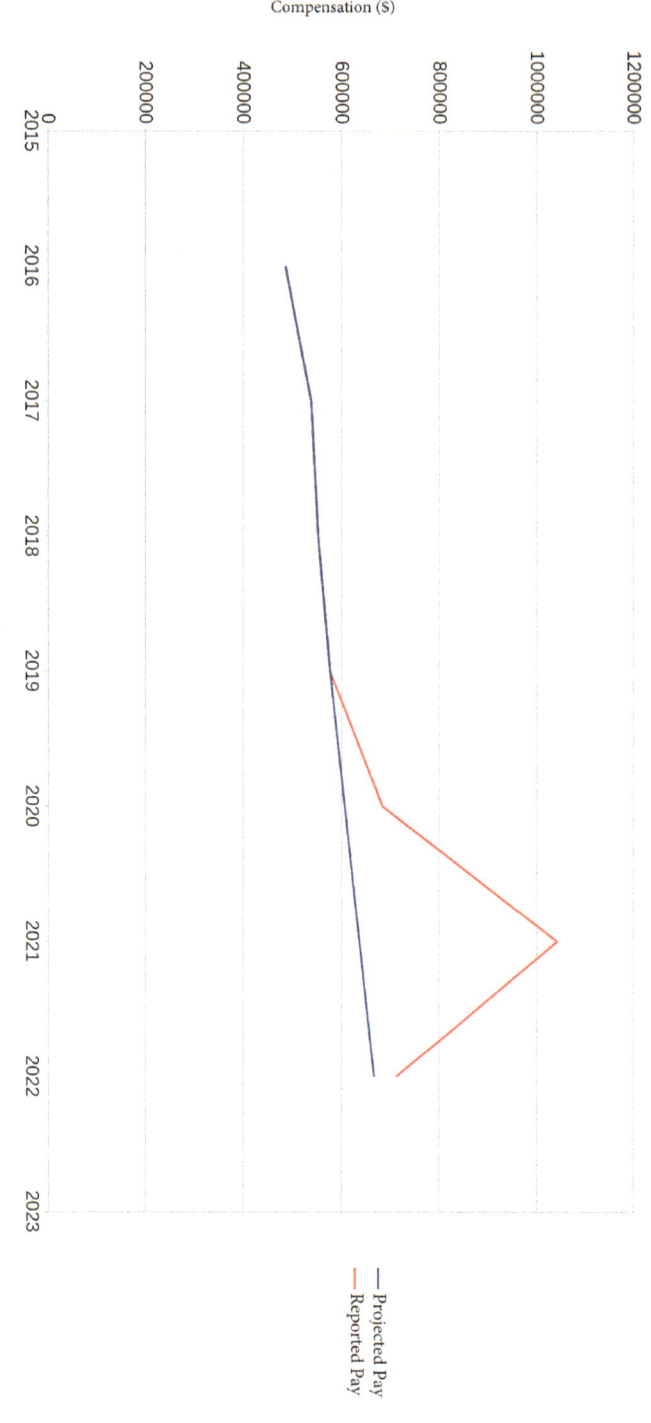

Figure 15: *Comparison of Yager's reported compensation and projected compensation based on prior growth trends. Between 2020 and 2022, his reported pay exceeded projections by $530,000, raising questions about whether some legal costs were masked as compensation.*

The $530,000 difference between reported and projected figures raises the possibility that reported compensation masked additional costs. Between 2020 and 2022, Yager's reported compensation totaled just over $2.4 million. Had his pay followed the historical growth trajectory, his projected compensation for those same years would have been $1.91 million — a difference of $530,000. Placing Yager's pay alongside his predecessors makes this divergence clearer.

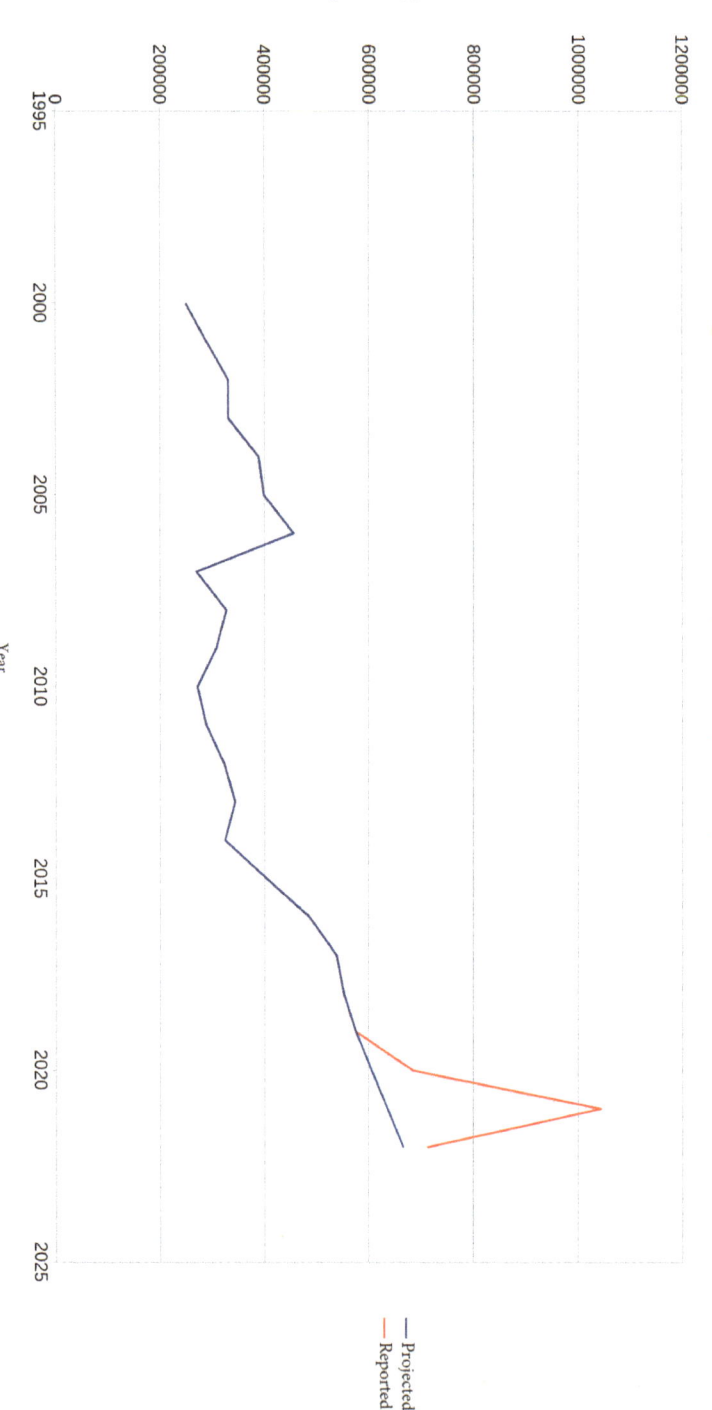

Figure 16: *When placed alongside his predecessors, Yager's projected compensation aligns with historical trends, while his reported compensation diverges dramatically — reinforcing the possibility of concealed legal expenditures.*

Seen in this broader context, Yager's pay trajectory was an outlier, reinforcing concerns that the 990s may have served as a vehicle to conceal settlements. Placed in historical context, Yager's projected salary growth aligns with the steady trajectory seen under Miguel Corzo. The sharp deviations in reported pay, however, are unique to Yager's tenure.

These anomalies occurred during the same years that UARTS was conducting its first-ever capital campaign and defending itself against costly civil rights lawsuits. The convergence of a campaign, sealed settlements, spiking legal expenses, and extraordinary reported compensation raises more than coincidence. It invites the question: did UARTS obscure some of its legal costs by embedding them in reported presidential compensation?

Between 2018 and 2022, UARTS faced a succession of civil rights lawsuits that not only damaged its public reputation but also placed a heavy financial burden on the institution. While the precise settlement amounts remain sealed, the university's rising legal expenses and the unusual surge in presidential compensation during David Yager's tenure suggest that the true costs were obscured from public view. Taken together, these trends raise the possibility that UARTS masked portions of its settlement payouts under the guise of executive pay — a practice that, if true, would explain both the financial strain and the irregularities in reported compensation.

Dangerously Low Student-to-Employee Ratios Undermined Financial Stability

Universities don't fail overnight. They erode year by year, until the numbers make collapse inevitable.

When UARTS collapsed in 2024, media outlets reported that roughly 700 employees were laid off and 1,200 students were displaced. This revealed an unusually low student-to-employee ratio—fewer than two students for every employee—a structural imbalance that had been building for decades.

The last time UARTS maintained a sustainable ratio was in 2001, when there were about 3.5 students per employee. From that point forward, the ratio steadily eroded, falling to 2.1:1 by 2022. Using media-reported figures from the 2024 closure, the final ratio was roughly 1.7:1—consistent with projections that the institution could not pull out of a financial nosedive.

The following graph illustrates the shrinking student-to-employee ratio between 2001 and 2022.

Figure 17: *UARTS student-to-employee ratio reached a high in 2001 and continued to shrink until 2024.*

For context, most small private universities maintain a student-to-employee ratio close to 10:1. That ratio provides a financial cushion and enables academic flexibility, including:

- Greater resilience during economic downturns
- The ability to build and protect cash reserves
- Protection against drastic tuition hikes
- Flexibility to sustain small classes that would otherwise be cut
- Space to experiment with new courses and programs

The next graph compares student enrollment and employee headcount. Between 2002 and 2019, employee numbers remained relatively stable while enrollment began to decline after 2009. A reduction in staffing finally occurred in 2020, but by then the structural imbalance was entrenched.

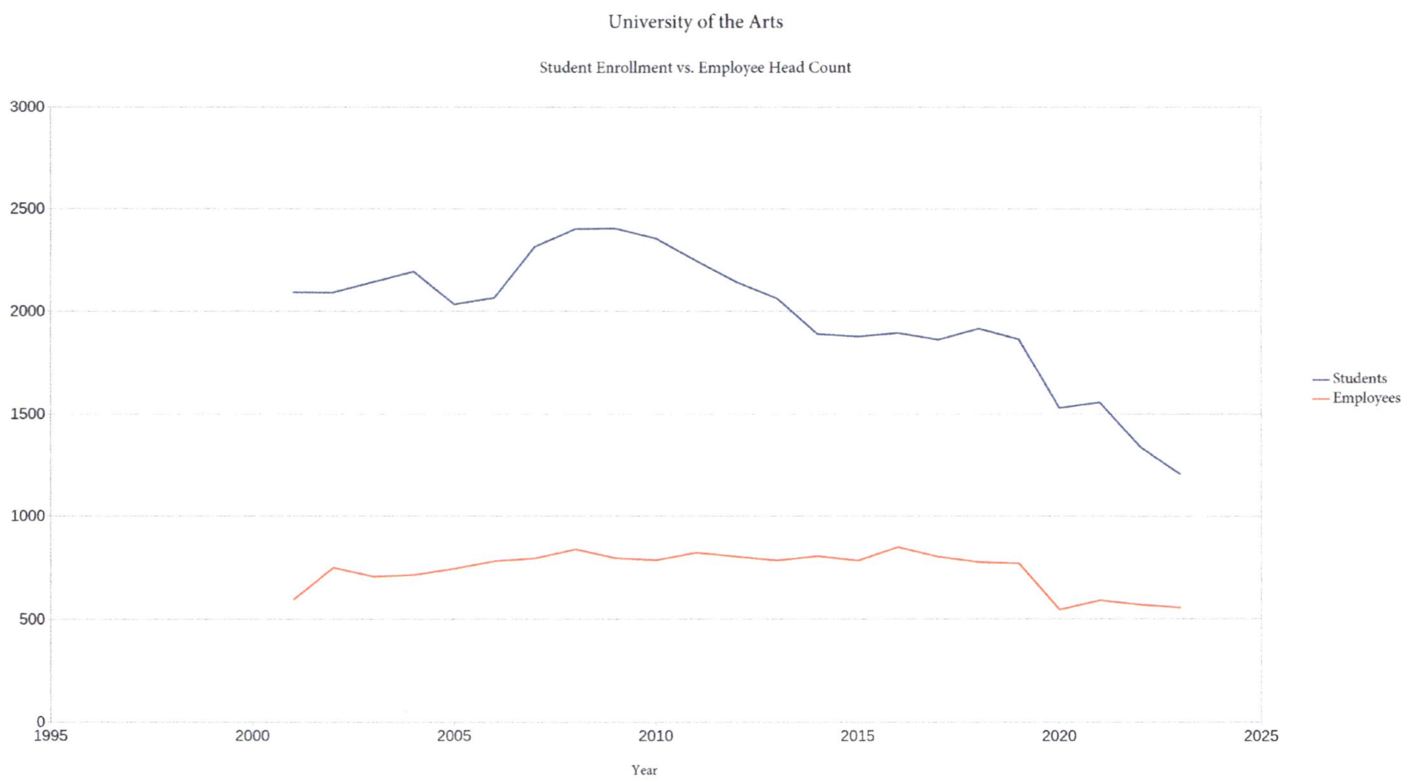

University of the Arts

Student Enrollment vs. Employee Head Count

Figure 18: Note the employee head count stayed level while student enrollment declined.

The risks of UARTS' low ratio far outweighed its limited advantages:

- Any decline in student enrollment amplified financial strain
- Cash reserves dwindled effectively to zero
- Tuition rose at a historical rate of 8% annually
- Small or experimental classes became financially unsustainable

UARTS had opportunities to change course if leadership had acted sooner. As outlined in the section on *Missed Opportunities in Outreach, Branding, and Digital Strategy*, alternative paths were available. Implementing even a few of these measures might have shifted the narrative from collapse to renewal—a story of resilience rather than closure.

Controversial Union Demands
and
Questionable Tactics During Negotiations

United Academics of Philadelphia (UAP), the labor union representing the UARTS faculty, began labor negotiations soon after forming in 2020. Their first contract was finalized in February 2024. Yet the road to this agreement was marred by questionable tactics and unusual demands.

From recognition to signing, negotiations stretched on for several years. According to UAP's own website, the union submitted numerous proposals, though which were accepted remains unclear. What is clear, however, is that in Session 8 (April 28, 2021) union leadership took the extraordinary step of bringing a student into the bargaining session to speak on behalf of faculty. This was not only unorthodox but raised serious ethical concerns.

Even if the student volunteered, the act placed her in a precarious position. Several questions naturally arise:

- Was there direct or indirect pressure from faculty or union leadership to participate?
- Did the student fully understand the risks of being inserted into a process that could affect her academic standing or relationship with the administration?

The administration's response was swift and pointed, accusing UAP of student exploitation. Under standard labor practice, when parties reach an impasse, arbitration or mediation is the path forward. Instead, UAP appeared to use the student as leverage in its dispute.

The union's own blog confirms the event:

> "UARTS administration left the bargaining table when Trina was introduced as a student invested in Shared Governance, accusing the Faculty Union of exploiting students. ... Trina made a statement that gracefully and powerfully encapsulates the feelings of this union on why Shared Governance matters, and why students should have a voice in these conversations: 'Our tuition dollars are what keep this school running. Between faculty salary, facility repairs and upkeep, food, housing, the administration's salary, I believe it's completely justified for students to be involved in these discussions with the representatives of the university.'"

A second area where UAP's demands raised concerns was in its push to codify hiring practices in accordance with Affirmative Action policies. UARTS refused this request. As noted in UAP's Session 9 (July 14, 2021) blog update, the union reported:

> *"Among their responses was a refusal to bargain over Affirmative Action. They refused to sign off on language directly from the faculty handbook … Throughout the session, the UARTS administration continued to express values they claim are important to the University, such as Shared Governance, Diversity, Equity, and Inclusion, while resisting implementation of policies that would meaningfully demonstrate those values."*

However, codifying race- or sex-based hiring in a collective bargaining agreement would have been illegal. Even if UARTS had agreed, such provisions would be unenforceable in court. More troubling, UAP's stance seemed blind to UARTS' own legal vulnerabilities: at least two lawsuits—*Fogel v. University of the Arts* (alleging termination on the basis of being male) and *Czarnota v. University of the Arts* (alleging termination on the basis of being white)—accused the university of race or sex discrimination. Both cases are addressed in detail in the section *A Mounting Legal Crisis: Lawsuits from Students and Faculty*.

These disputes at UARTS were not isolated. Across higher education, multiple high-profile cases highlight the risks universities face when race and sex enter hiring and tenure decisions:

- **University of Pennsylvania v. EEOC (1990)** – The U.S. Supreme Court ruled unanimously that universities must release peer-review materials to the EEOC in Title VII investigations, reinforcing accountability for discriminatory tenure and hiring decisions.

- **Jew v. University of Iowa (2019, appeal pending 2024)** – A female Asian-American professor sued under Title VII for harassment and race/sex discrimination in hiring and promotion. The Eighth Circuit revived her claims, emphasizing evidence of a hostile environment tied to bias.

- **Doe v. University of Washington (2023, settled)** – A faculty hiring search that explicitly considered race was terminated after internal and federal review confirmed Title VI violations. The case demonstrates that even informal DEI-based hiring practices can trigger federal enforcement.

- **America First Legal v. Northwestern University (2024, ongoing)** – A federal lawsuit alleges race-based hiring preferences discriminated against white male candidates, echoing the post-Students for Fair Admissions legal challenges to DEI-driven employment policies.

Taken together, these cases illustrate the precarious legal environment surrounding affirmative action in faculty hiring. By pressing UARTS to adopt such provisions, UAP not only pushed for a policy that would have been unenforceable, but also exposed its members—and the institution—to heightened legal risk.

This pattern of overreach tied directly to UAP's broader campaign for "Shared Governance." While shared governance is a recognized principle in higher education, UAP attempted to fold it into bargaining sessions, conflating the faculty's right to consultation with management's exclusive responsibility for institutional direction. From bringing a student to the bargaining table, to pressing for illegal hiring preferences, to demanding a voice in university governance structures, UAP repeatedly blurred the critical boundary between labor and management.

Such mission creep suggests that UAP leadership viewed the union not merely as a bargaining agent for compensation and working conditions, but as a parallel authority on the university's overall operations. The result was a union whose priorities strayed from core labor responsibilities into institutional policy making—an approach that was both legally dangerous and strategically self-defeating.

Missed Opportunities in Outreach, Branding, & Digital Strategy

Examining missed opportunities to use low cost high impact tactics to maintain enrollment, improve public connection, and maximize established online education platforms.

Missed Opportunity: Pipelines to the University

It became apparent in researching UARTS' collapse, one theme became abundantly clear: constant failure to take advantage of low cost, high impact strategies to stabilize or increase enrollment. As seen in figure , UARTS' enrollment decline began in 2009. By 2012, the downward trajectory was undeniable. There were many proactive strategies UARTS could have taken to engage prospective students, build community relationships, and showcase student talent. These tactics did not require large marketing budgets, they called for initiative, creativity, and communication.

A missed opportunity was connecting with high schools in surrounding counties to introduce students to the UARTS' artistic development process. These same missed opportunities extended to dance academies and charter schools such as Philadelphia High School for the Creative and Performing Arts (CAPA) and Girard Academic Music Program (GAMP).

All UARTS had to do was open its doors.

Opportunities Ignored:

- Conducting workshops and masterclasses at high schools
- Networking with high school music, art, and drama teachers to identify and nurture potential students
- Allowing high school student to attend theatrical, dance, and music rehearsals
- Offering students the chance to audit visual and performing arts classes
- Inviting students to attend senior jury exhibitions, critiques, and thesis performances

The above list could have been implemented with minimal cost. They required coordination and someone to see the big picture.

Who's at Fault:

- **Campus Administration** – for failing to coordinate and develop plans
- **Deans** – for failing to promote college programs to attract new students
- **Program Directors** – for failing to leverage student performances, teacher talents, and events for recruitment

By the Numbers:

To better understand the number of missed opportunities, the below lists the number of high school arts programs in surrounding counties.

County	High Schools Offering Visual & Performing Arts (Approx)
Philadelphia	51
Bucks	30-35
Montgomery	80
Chester	20-35
Delaware	20-35

Table 2: Approximate number of high schools in surrounding counties of Philadelphia.

Missed Opportunity: Paper Over Pixels

UARTS' communication strategy reveals a baffling inconsistency in the application of its creative resources. The university's relationship with media was deeply dichotomous. On one hand, its alumni publication The Edge and the annual admissions bulletin showcased exceptional graphic design. These print materials demonstrated a professional, thoughtful use of the graphic design department's capabilities. They left a lasting impression on prospective students — myself included. When I first saw the admissions bulletin in 1998, the design alone inspired me to take up graphic design, not as a profession but as a hobby. It impressed upon me the power of visual communication, and how design can shape perception and interest.

Graphic design was UARTS' flagship identity. Their official branding book covered every aspect of institutional visual identity — from letterhead, business cards, and signage to merchandise and web design. Yet, notably absent from this branding manual was any mention of video production or social media — channels that, by the 2010s, had become essential for public engagement.

This oversight is painfully clear when examining UARTS' online video presence. In sharp contrast to its polished print materials, much of the university's video content lacked basic storytelling, coherent branding, and adherence to even minimal industry standards. Many departmental YouTube channels went dark 10 to 15 years ago. In some cases, like the music department, videos resembled footage captured on early-generation mobile phones. The following table illustrates the last active date for various UARTS-affiliated YouTube channels:

Youtube Channel	Date of Last Upload	Subscriber Count
University of the Arts	Apr 10, 2024	1700
The University of the Arts Pre-College Programs	Mar 18, 2016	109
UArts School of Music	Jan 3, 2024	142
UArtsTheatre	Oct 7, 2009	112
Graduate Jazz Studies at UArts	Jan 18, 2019	71
UArts Admissions	Aug 6, 2013	37
University of the Arts Drum Department	Apr 27, 2021	180
UArts School of Dance	Feb 9, 2023	74
UartsMusicSchool	Jun 18, 2014	1110
UArts Career Services	Nov 2, 2022	2
UArts Animation	Dec 20, 2022	176

Table 3: *Youtube data collected July 2024*

It wasn't until the university's final three years that UARTS began producing videos of professional quality. These select examples displayed effective storytelling, polished visuals, and a competent use of creative resources. All were created in 2015 showing the ability to create compelling videos was available at UARTS:

- UArts Pre College Summer Institute Music Program

- UArts Pre College Summer Institute Creative Writing Program

- UArts School of Dance Program Portrait

These late efforts highlight what had been missing all along: a coordinated, strategic use of internal talent. UARTS had world-class departments in animation, film, design, and communications — yet failed to meaningfully involve them in its public-facing media. Producing high-quality video content did not require a massive marketing budget; it required leadership, collaboration, and vision.

What's even more perplexing is UARTS' use of Vimeo. Active since 2010, many of their Vimeo videos demonstrate higher production standards than those found on their YouTube channel — yet they have gone largely unnoticed. A manual review reveals that most videos have only 20 to 80 views, and the channel itself has around 500 subscribers.

Unlike YouTube, Vimeo is virtually unsearchable via Google — the dominant search engine on the Internet. To even find UARTS' Vimeo channel, a user must manually search Vimeo's internal site. Once found, however, the contrast is stark: the Vimeo videos contain strong university branding and all the hallmarks of professional production. This stands in sharp contrast to many of their departmental YouTube channels, where content is often amateurish and unpolished. In the university's final three years, the Vimeo channel posted mostly commencement videos — raising important questions. Why was Vimeo used for polished content while YouTube, the broader public platform, was populated with substandard material? Why were resources invested in a platform with limited reach?

More importantly, what types of videos could UARTS have produced that would have been both high-impact and low-cost?

- **Tips & Tricks** – Short, practical advice videos tailored to specific disciplines.
  Example 1: "I'm John Hamilton, coming to you from the University of the Arts in Philadelphia. Let's talk about the importance of long tones for wind musicians…"
  Example 2: "I'm Mary Anderson, and in my After Effects course at UARTS, students learn JavaScript integration. Today I'll show you a simple snippet that will make your scene transitions come alive."

- **Historical Videos** – UARTS had a 150-year legacy. With the right approach, they could have produced powerful short- and long-form historical content. One example: a spotlight on composer and professor Vincent Persichetti, whose book *Twentieth Century Harmony* made advanced concepts accessible to generations of composers.

- **Collage Videos** – A hybrid documentary montage. Picture a cold open: black screen, no music, just ambient sound — footsteps, rustling paper. Then a voice: "This is the script. We have two months. Let's make it happen." The video follows students from script distribution through rehearsals, dress runs, and backstage moments, culminating in a packed audience rising to a standing ovation.

These are just a few possibilities. Here's a broader list of video types UARTS could have embraced:

- Tips and Tricks

- Historical Features

- Tutorials / How-To Guides

- Explainer Videos

- Lectures / Seminars

- Animated Whiteboard Segments

- Demonstrations

- Mini-Documentaries

- Faculty/Student Profiles

- Behind-the-Scenes (BTS) Content

- Branded Video Series

With the talent and resources at its disposal, UARTS had everything it needed to build a dynamic online presence. Its creative departments were so skilled that they could have taken a monotone-speaking professor and, with proper coaching and editing, made them engaging and accessible to a broad audience.

Instead, UARTS chose to invest in high-cost, low-impact gestures — such as draping Anderson Hall with a building-sized promotional banner. The cost of producing, installing, and removing such a display likely ran into the thousands. And yet, unlike digital video content, there was no scalable audience and no measurable return on investment.

This contradictory communication strategy raises important questions: Why was UARTS hyperfocused on legacy media, while treating video and social media as afterthoughts? Why invest in exceptional graphic design for print, but ignore the platforms where modern audiences live — YouTube, Instagram, etc.? UARTS' fixation on paper over digital reflects a broader institutional failure: the inability to adapt to the demands of a digital-first world.

Missed Opportunity: Maximizing Online Course Delivery

Over the past two decades, universities have increasingly embraced online education as a way to expand enrollment, build brand recognition, and remain competitive in a changing higher education landscape. According to the National Center for Education Statistics, by 2018 nearly 50% of students had taken at least one course online. It is therefore baffling that UARTS appeared oblivious to this trend and the robust platforms available for distributing their curriculum. The following are some of the most widely used platforms for universities to share courses globally:

- **Coursera** – A leading U.S.-based platform offering Massive Open Online Courses (MOOCs).
- **edX** – A MOOC platform founded by Harvard and MIT, offering university-level courses from top institutions.
- **FutureLearn** – A UK-based MOOC provider with international reach.
- **Kadenze** – A MOOC platform specializing in visual and performing arts.
- **OpenLearning** – An Australian-based provider supporting creative and academic course content.

UARTS had a range of courses that could have seamlessly transitioned to an online format—particularly first-year seminars, creative writing, art history, literature critique, and music theory. Students could have completed these requirements remotely, on their own schedule. This kind of flexibility is now a standard expectation, not a bonus.

Beyond convenience, online courses would have served as a powerful tool for brand building. With its access to top-tier visual and performing arts talent, UARTS had the potential to produce highly engaging, professionally polished online lectures. Yet, a search for any UARTS presence on major MOOC platforms yields nothing. Was the university even aware of this ecosystem—and the opportunities it presented?

Academic Inbreeding:
How Insularity Stifled Innovation

Looking into University of the Arts academic inbreeding rate and its impact on program innovation.

A striking pattern emerges when reviewing the educational backgrounds of UARTS faculty and administrators: a significant number earned their degrees from the very same institution. Between the school years 2006–2009 and 2011–2023, the university's overall academic inbreeding rate rose from 27% to 35%. By comparison, many universities aim to keep such rates below 10% in order to foster new ideas, innovation, and creativity. UARTS, however, moved in the opposite direction, reinforcing insularity and institutional inertia.

Efforts to normalize the data across 2006–2023 proved difficult due to frequent restructuring and renaming of colleges. For instance, liberal arts faculty were alternately categorized as "liberal arts," "critical studies," or "university professors," with the last designation pooling professors from multiple colleges. Attempts were made to sort faculty back into their proper colleges, but the lack of consistent records made the task nearly impossible.

To illustrate these trends more concretely, the following graph presents the overall academic inbreeding rates for the university between 2006 and 2009:

University of the Arts

Academic Inbreeding Rates - (2006-2009)

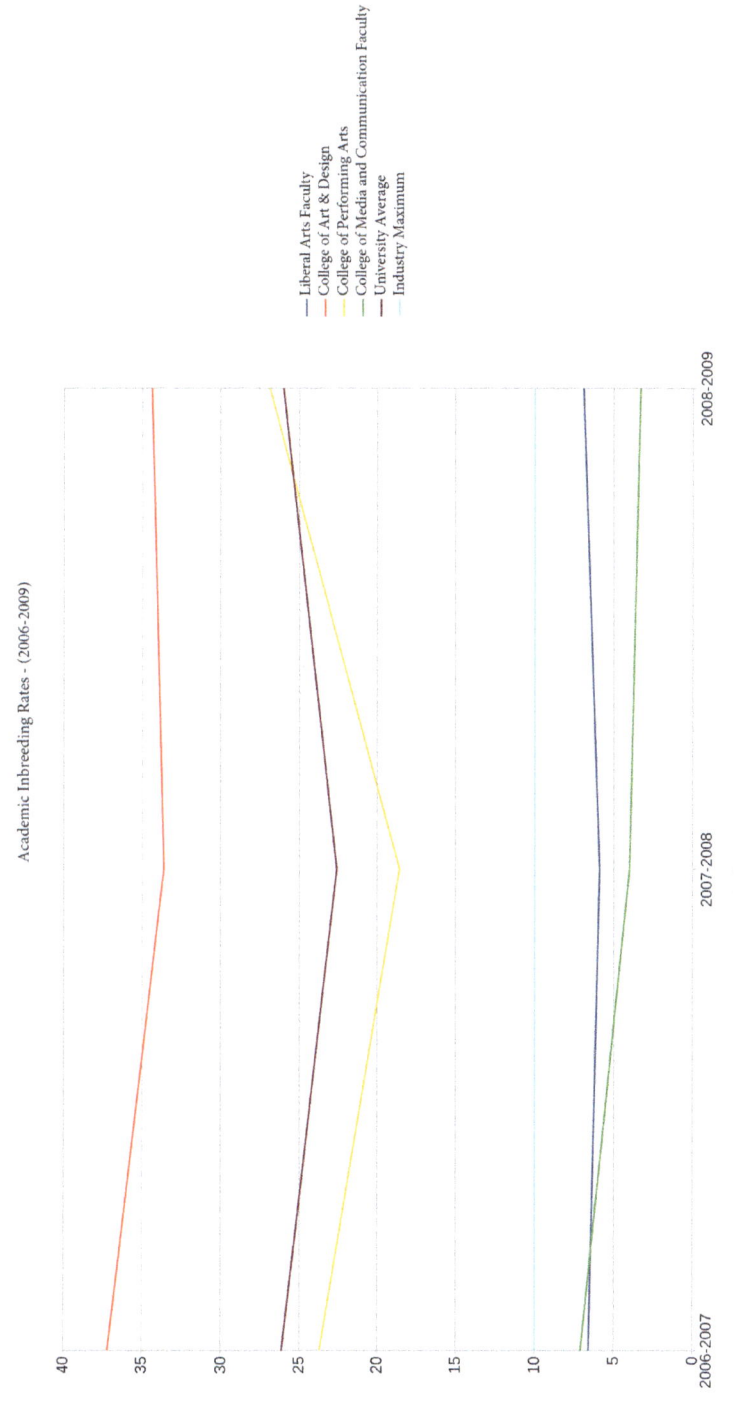

Figure 20: *Note the Liberal Arts and College of Media & Communication faculties are below industry standard of 10% while the other colleges are well above industry standard.*

The clearest data comes from the school years 2006–2009, which in some cases break faculty down by degree program. The College of Art and Design is one such example. Its overall inbreeding rate ranged from 34% to 37%— well above industry standards. Within its visual arts faculties in 2006, 10 out of 11 reported rates between 29% and 52%, with graphic design the highest. The only exception was art therapy, a statistical outlier with just three faculty members and an inbreeding rate of 0%, slightly lowering the college's overall average.

The following breakdown highlights inbreeding rates by individual program during this same period:

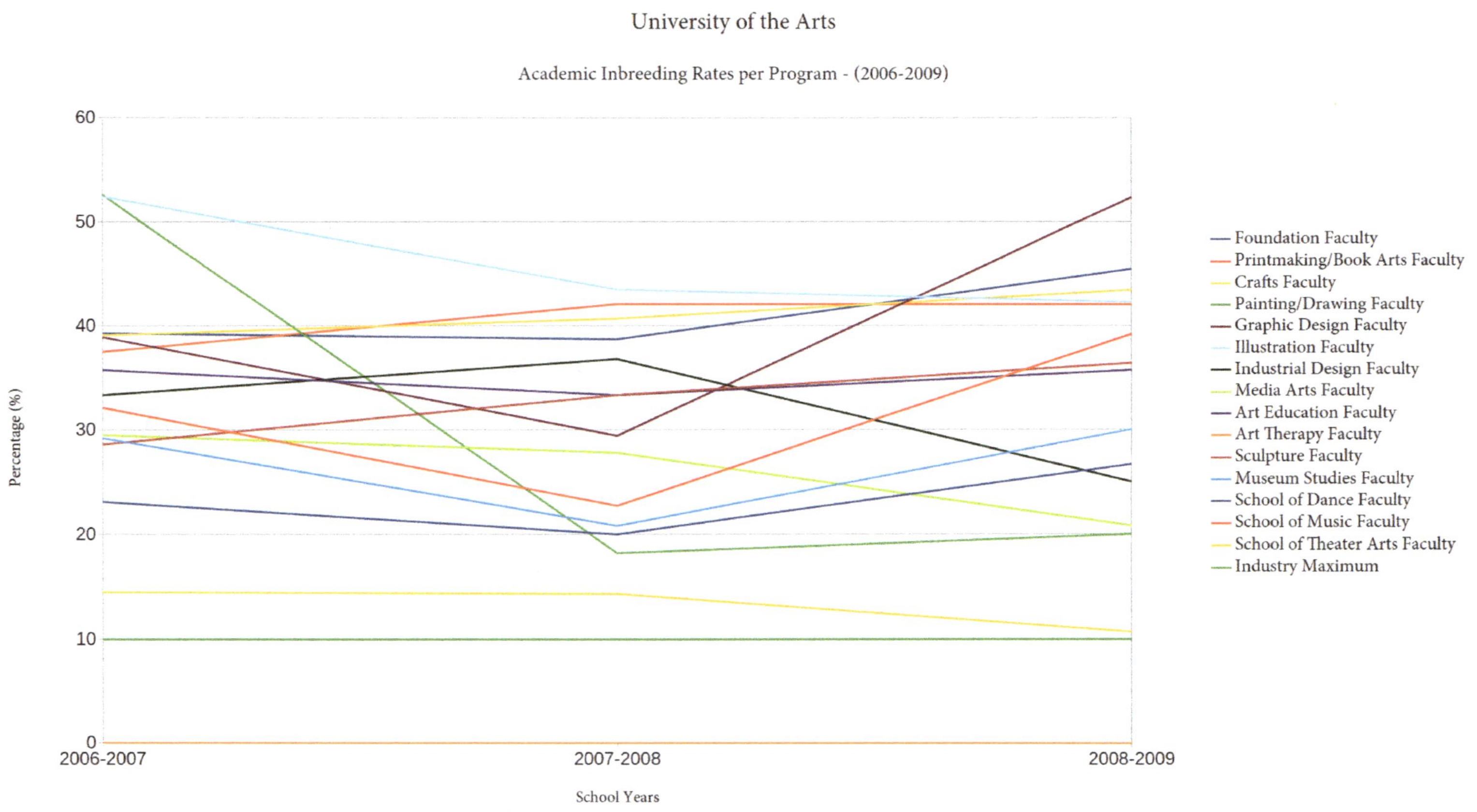
University of the Arts
Academic Inbreeding Rates per Program - (2006-2009)
60
50
40
30
20
10
0
Percentage (%)
2006-2007
2007-2008
2008-2009
School Years
Foundation Faculty
Printmaking/Book Arts Faculty
Crafts Faculty
Painting/Drawing Faculty
Graphic Design Faculty
Illustration Faculty
Industrial Design Faculty
Media Arts Faculty
Art Education Faculty
Art Therapy Faculty
Sculpture Faculty
Museum Studies Faculty
School of Dance Faculty
School of Music Faculty
School of Theater Arts Faculty
Industry Maximum

Figure 21: *Academic Inbreeding Rates per Program (2006-2009). Individual programs in CMAC had extreme academic inbreeding rates. The statistical outlier being Arts Therapy Faculty at 0%.*

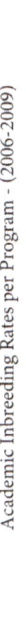

Other notable patterns appear in the College of Performing Arts. From 2006–2009, the School of Music had inbreeding rates between 22% and 39%, levels that persisted into UARTS' final years when the colleges were restructured under the "School of…" model. By contrast, the School of Dance saw rates of 20%–29% in 2006–2009 but later dropped to 12%–14%—an improvement, though still above the 10% ceiling.

The graph below provides a snapshot of academic inbreeding rates from the final years of UARTS, covering 2022–2024:

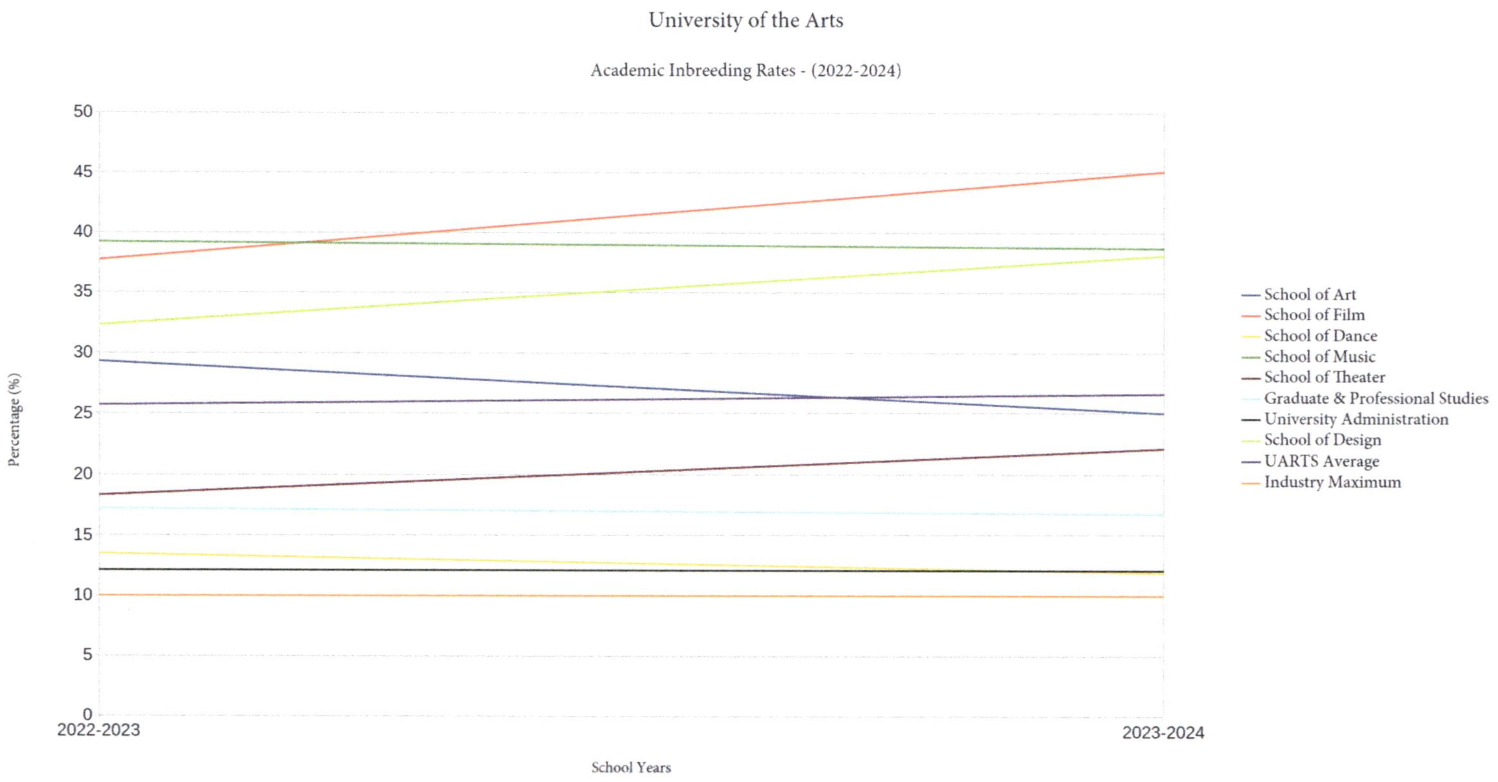
University of the Arts
Academic Inbreeding Rates - (2022-2024)
50
45
40
35
30
25
20
15
10
5
0
Percentage (%)
2022-2023
2023-2024
School Years
School of Art
School of Film
School of Dance
School of Music
School of Theater
Graduate & Professional Studies
University Administration
School of Design
UARTS Average
Industry Maximum

Figure 22: *UARTS academic inbreeding rate continued to remain high until 2024.*

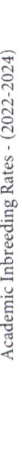

During these years, a clearer picture also emerged for administration. Administrative inbreeding ranged from 9%–11%. While this figure hovers around the industry maximum, it remained lower than rates observed in most of the academic schools.

Additional historical data, spanning 2011–2018, further illustrates the persistence of elevated inbreeding across multiple colleges:

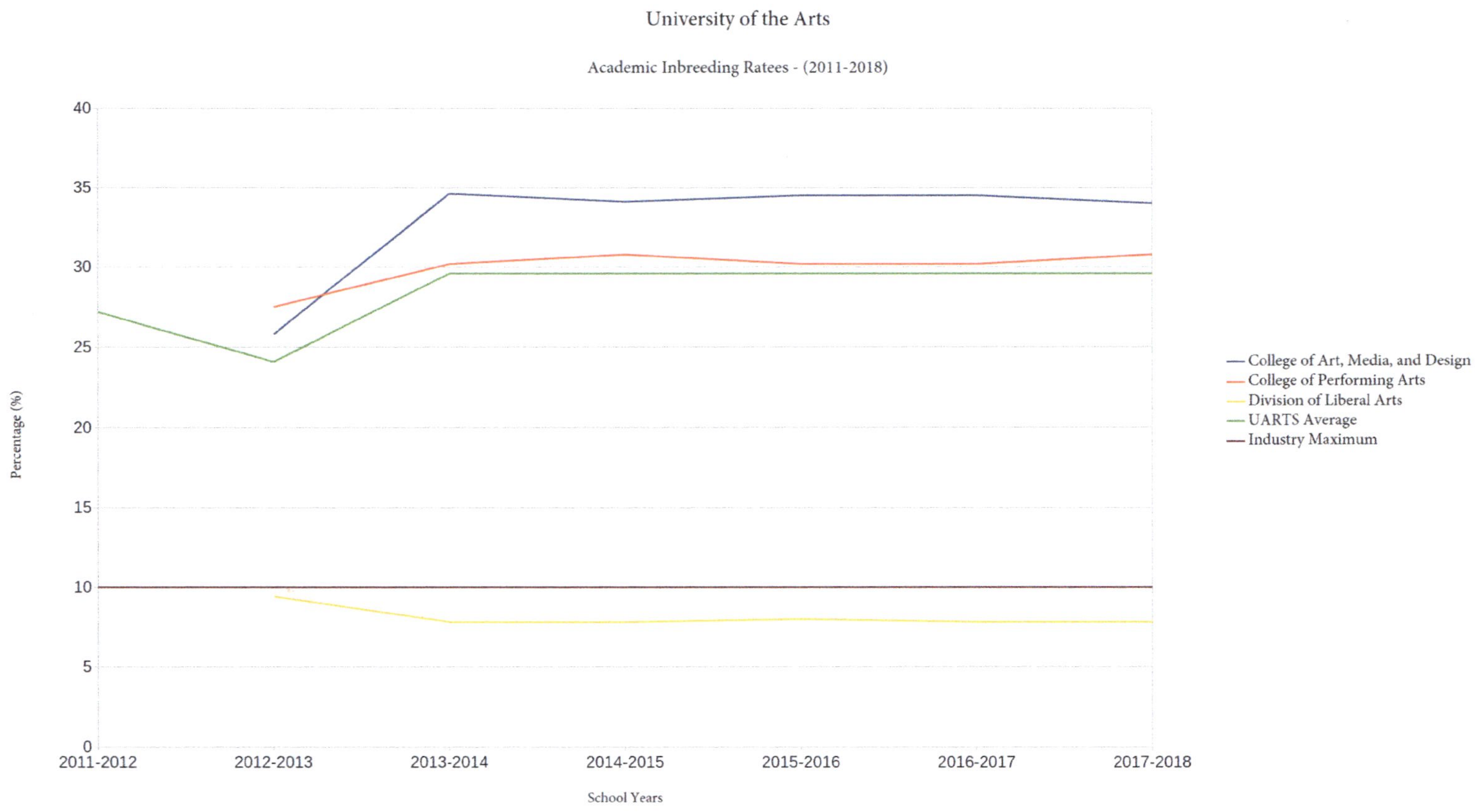

University of the Arts

Academic Inbreeding Ratees - (2011-2018)

Figure 23: *Restructuring the colleges negatively impacted the academic inbreeding rate by increasing the per college/school rate.*

The cumulative effect of UARTS' high inbreeding rates was predictable: insularity and inertia. These conditions stifled the development of new ideas and discouraged risk-taking. As discussed in the section *Missed Opportunities in Outreach, Branding, and Digital Strategy*, UARTS had numerous paths available to revitalize enrollment and strengthen its online presence. Yet with faculty and administrators so deeply rooted in the same institutional culture, the likelihood of pursuing—let alone enacting—innovative solutions was minimal.

A Phantom Capital Campaign
Masked Financial Collapse

In 2018, UARTS launched its first-ever capital campaign, announced by President David Yager with a goal of $50 million. Four years later, Yager declared the campaign a success, boasting that it had raised $67 million. Yet, a review of UARTS' tax returns and financial statements tells a very different story. Rather than reflecting new external funding, the campaign appears to have relied on shifting internal monies, creative accounting, and a carefully orchestrated public relations strategy that masked the university's deepening financial collapse.

To better understand what a capital campaign should look like — both from the perspective of the public and on a university's IRS filings — it is useful to break down the contrast.

What a Capital Campaign Looks Like to the Average Person

- **Visible on-campus advertising:** posters, banners, and the classic fundraising thermometer tracking progress.
- **Donor recognition:** buildings, scholarships, or programs named in honor of contributors.
- **Public announcements:** foundations and major donors publicly declaring their support.

What a Capital Campaign Looks Like on a University's 990 Tax Return

- **Direct Public Support (Line 1e):** primary line for donations; should spike during active campaign years.
- **Schedule B (Contributors):** identifies major individual or foundation donors (though details may be redacted).
- **Part VIII (Statement of Revenue):** distinguishes contributions from tuition and program service revenue.
- **Part X (Balance Sheet):** "Net assets with donor restrictions" should rise if pledges are booked.
- **Schedule D (Endowment Funds):** indicates whether new endowment contributions were actually received.
- **Multi-Year Pledges:** may be reported upfront, inflating totals without corresponding cash flow.

- **Foundation Grant Cross-Check:** foundation 990-PF filings should corroborate claimed donations.
- **No Gala Glow:** unlike the glossy PR campaign, the 990 provides only raw numbers — often revealing smaller inflows than advertised.

These contrasting views establish the framework for the analysis that follows. By comparing UARTS' public narrative with its financial filings, we can test President David Yager's capital campaign claims against the reality of the university's finances.

In 2022, the *Philadelphia Inquirer* reported on the campaign's outcome. The article, *University of the Arts raises $67 million in its first capital campaign. Here's how it'll be used*, detailed how the supposed $67 million would be allocated:

- **$24 million** to be kept in perpetuity in the endowment.
- **$17 million** for capital projects, such as a new student center in the Gershman Y building, the Laurie Wagman Recording Studios, and "Living Steps," a gathering space for students.
- **$14 million** in restricted funds for programs and academic disciplines.
- **$5.5 million** for scholarships.
- **$5 million** in discretionary funds for tuition relief, housing costs, food expenses, and art supplies.

Each of these claims can be examined against UARTS' tax returns and financial statements to test whether the promises align with reality.

"The biggest chunk, about $24 million, will be kept in perpetuity in endowment."

During the campaign years (2018–2022), UARTS' endowment did not experience the kind of growth that would indicate a $24 million infusion. In fact, the only significant spike occurred two years earlier, in FY2016, when the endowment jumped from $49 million to $72 million. This increase was followed by a sharp withdrawal of $17 million in FY2019. The timing matters: the sudden increase in 2016 occurred before Yager's campaign was even announced.

Equally troubling is the use of the phrase "in perpetuity." This wording implies that the campaign successfully added $24 million in new donations to the endowment. Yet, the filings show no such sustained growth. An endowment is meant to be a university's nest egg, generating investment income from which roughly 5% can be drawn annually for scholarships, salaries, and maintenance. If Yager's claim were accurate, the endowment totals should have reflected a permanent $24 million rise — but they do not.

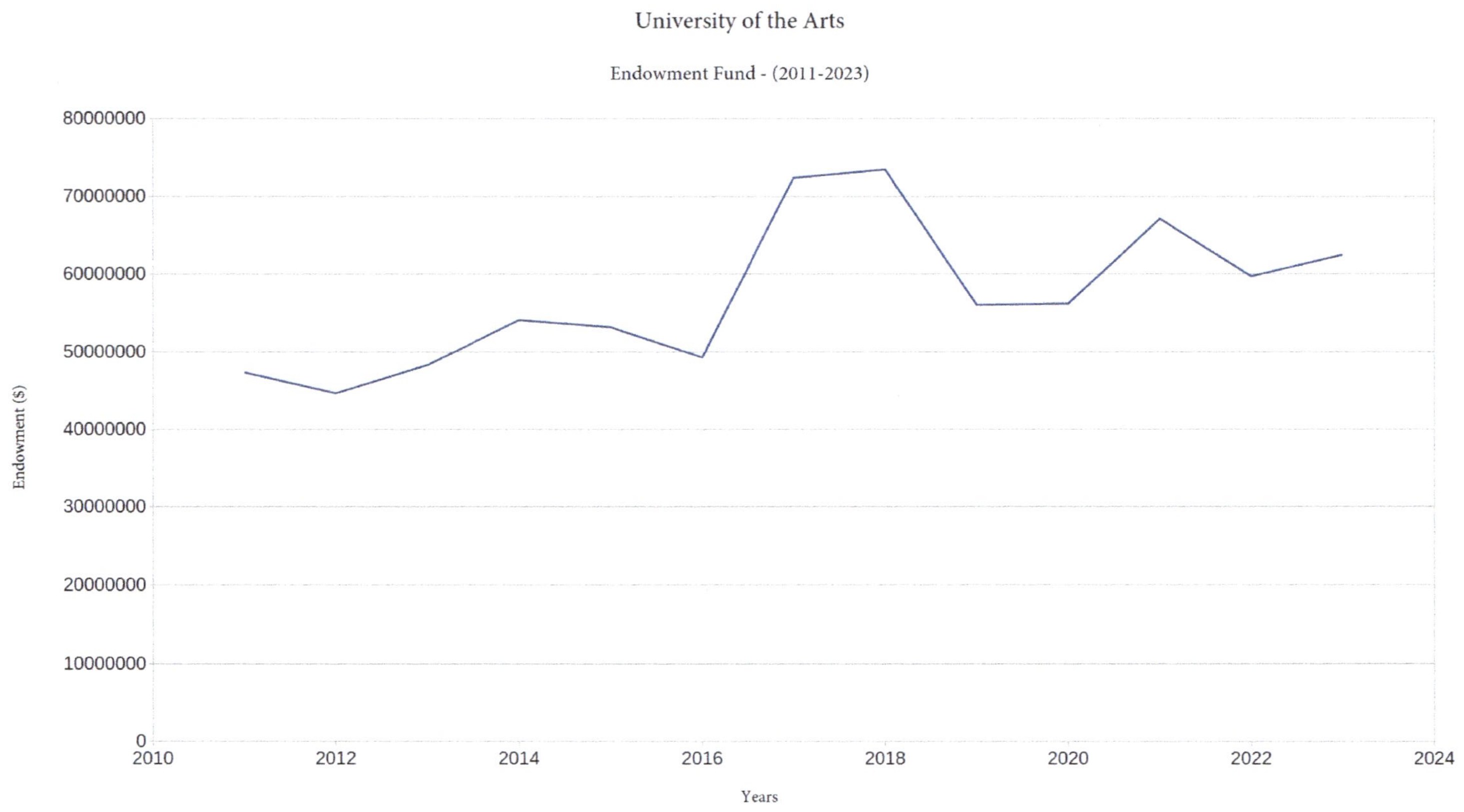

University of the Arts

Endowment Fund - (2011-2023)

Figure 24: Note the endowment increase & decrease by $17 million in 2017 & 2019.

The likeliest explanation for the 2016 spike is not donor generosity but financial maneuvering. UARTS appears to have bolstered its endowment with internal transfers in preparation for its December 2017 bond issuance, creating the appearance of stability to reassure lenders. This raises a critical question: where did that $23 million actually come from?

The Inquirer offered one possible explanation, citing Yager's claim that the campaign's single-largest gift was $25 million from the estate of philanthropist Dorrance "Dodo" Hill Hamilton. But this claim does not withstand scrutiny. In FY2018, the Hamilton Family Foundation (HFF) reported net assets of just $18.9 million, which declined to $11.6 million by 2022. According to its tax returns, HFF's total contributions to UARTS in 2018 amounted to only $13,000. For HFF to donate $25 million outright — or even over several years — would have been financially impossible without dismantling its long-standing support for dozens of other arts, cultural, and community organizations across Philadelphia.

To test whether Yager's $24 million claim could have originated elsewhere, I reviewed UARTS' tax returns and audited statements for alternative inflows. With the exception of a spike in direct public support in FY2016 ($33.4M, up from $15.6M in FY2015) and a one-time bump in cash from the Merriam Theater sale in FY2017, no other revenue lines show unusual increases. Government grants, investment income, and restricted gifts all follow ordinary patterns inconsistent with an endowment gift of that magnitude. The audited financials confirm this: no cash flow anomalies or donor-restricted assets suggest an inflow anywhere close to $24 million.

The only anomaly that stands out is a sudden surge in pledges. In FY2017, pledges jumped from just $295,000 in 2016 to $19.5 million. Yet pledges are not liquid assets; they represent promises to give, often contingent or spread across years. They can bolster a campaign's appearance of success on paper but do not solve the immediate financial strain of a university struggling to pay its bills.

The following line graph illustrates UARTS' reported pledges from 2009 to 2022, highlighting the extraordinary 2017 spike that coincided with Yager's capital campaign narrative.

University of the Arts

Pledges - (2009-2023)

Pledges ($)

Year

Figure 25

"$17 Million for Capital Projects . . ."

Yager claimed that $17 million was allocated to capital projects, including a new student center in the Gershman Y building, the Laurie Wagman Recording Studios, and Living Steps, a gathering space for students. However, the reality tells a different story. His statement appears to be a slight-of-hand technique, as the $17 million figure corresponds to the portion of the endowment withdrawn in FY2019, which left the university with $56 million in total endowment funds.

As with many of Yager's claims, UARTS' 990 tax returns and audited financial statements reveal a more nuanced picture. Between 2016 and 2022, a total of $32.2 million was actually spent on capital projects. The work was primarily carried out by JacobsWyper Architects, responsible for designing all of UARTS' capital improvements, and C. Erickson and Sons, Inc., the contractor executing the construction.

The bar graph below details payments to JacobsWyper Architects and C. Erickson and Sons, Inc., showing how the $32.2 million in capital project spending was actually allocated over the 2016–2022 period.

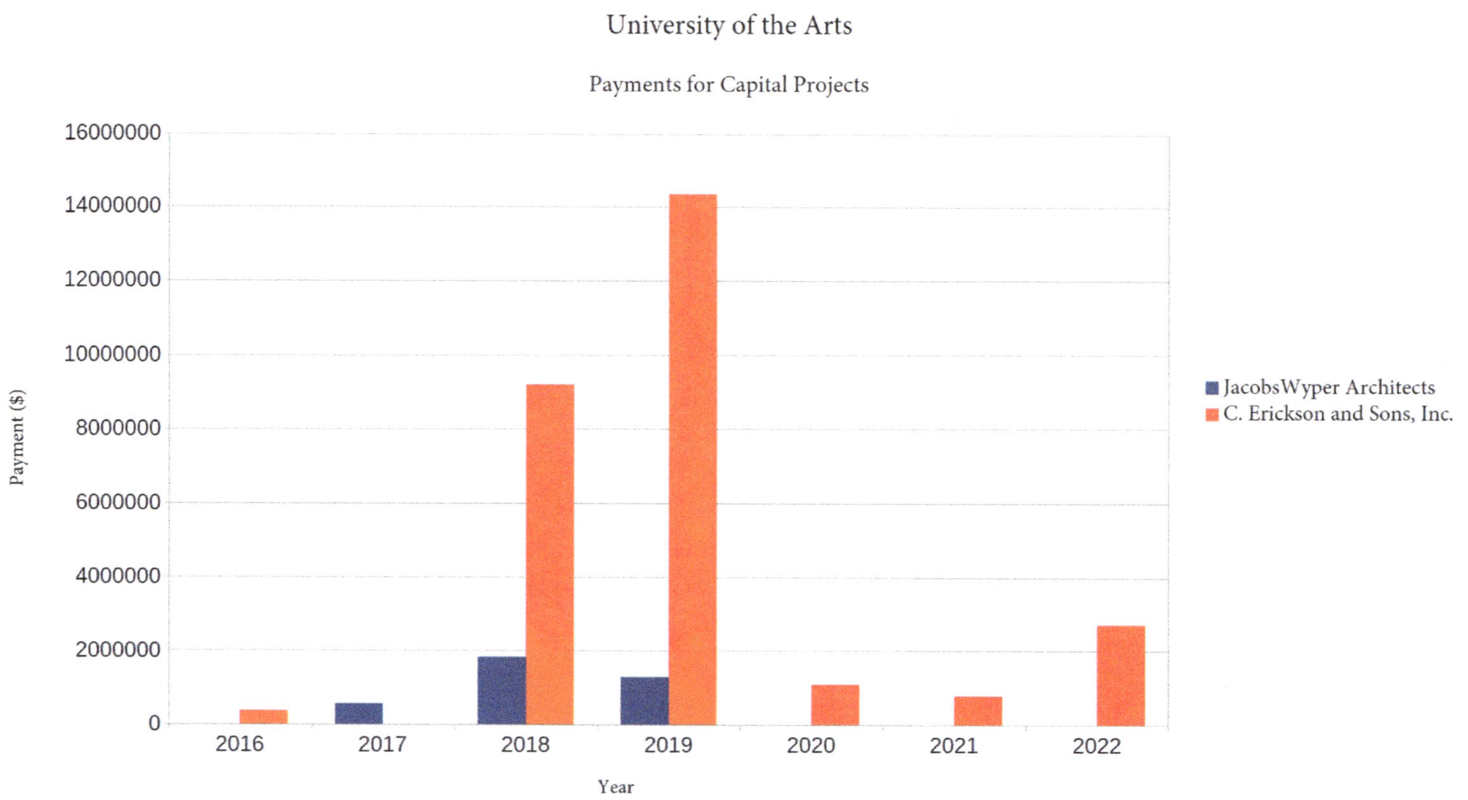

University of the Arts
Payments for Capital Projects
16000000
14000000
12000000
10000000
8000000
6000000
4000000
2000000
0
Payment ($)
2016
2017
2018
2019
2020
2021
2022
Year
JacobsWyper Architects
C. Erickson and Sons, Inc.

Figure 26: *The total expenditures on the capital projects was $32.2 million – far above the claimed $17 million.*

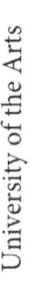

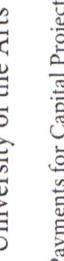

"$14 Million in Restricted Funds for Programs and Academic Disciplines"

Yager claimed that $14 million from the capital campaign would be used for programs and academic disciplines. While UARTS' audited financial statements for the four-year campaign period do show restricted and temporarily restricted funds, the sources of those funds complicate verification. Analysis of foundation donations shows that most contributions were labeled vaguely as "program support," "school support," or left blank entirely, with no clear indication of specific restrictions in the donors' 990-PF tax returns.

In other words, while restricted contributions existed, their intended purpose and allocation are unclear, making it impossible to confirm that $14 million was specifically designated for programs and disciplines, or that it was spent accordingly. A comparison of restricted funds balances versus actual program expenses over the campaign years can provide context, but even this only suggests plausibility, not certainty.

"$5.5 Million for Scholarships & $5 Million in Discretionary Funds"

Yager's claims of $5.5 million for scholarships and $5 million in discretionary funds can be analyzed together because both relied primarily on monies from the Higher Education Emergency Relief Fund (HEERF). HEERF was a federal COVID-era grant program designed to provide financial lifelines to universities that did not qualify for Paycheck Protection Program (PPP) loans. For additional context on HEERF and its impact on UARTS, see the section *2020: The Year UARTS Ignored the Alarm Bells*. Here, the focus is solely on HEERF funding.

Before receiving HEERF, UARTS' government grants typically ranged from $600,000 to $700,000 per year. With pandemic-related restrictions and financial pressures, UARTS received $10.9 million from HEERF and annual government grants during the emergency period. HEERF funds came with specific restrictions: a portion had to be spent on student aid, while the remainder could be allocated at the university's discretion.

The following graph illustrates how HEERF monies were allocated for student aid versus discretionary spending for 2019–2021.

University of the Arts

Government Grants & Higher Education Emergency Relief Fund (HEERF)

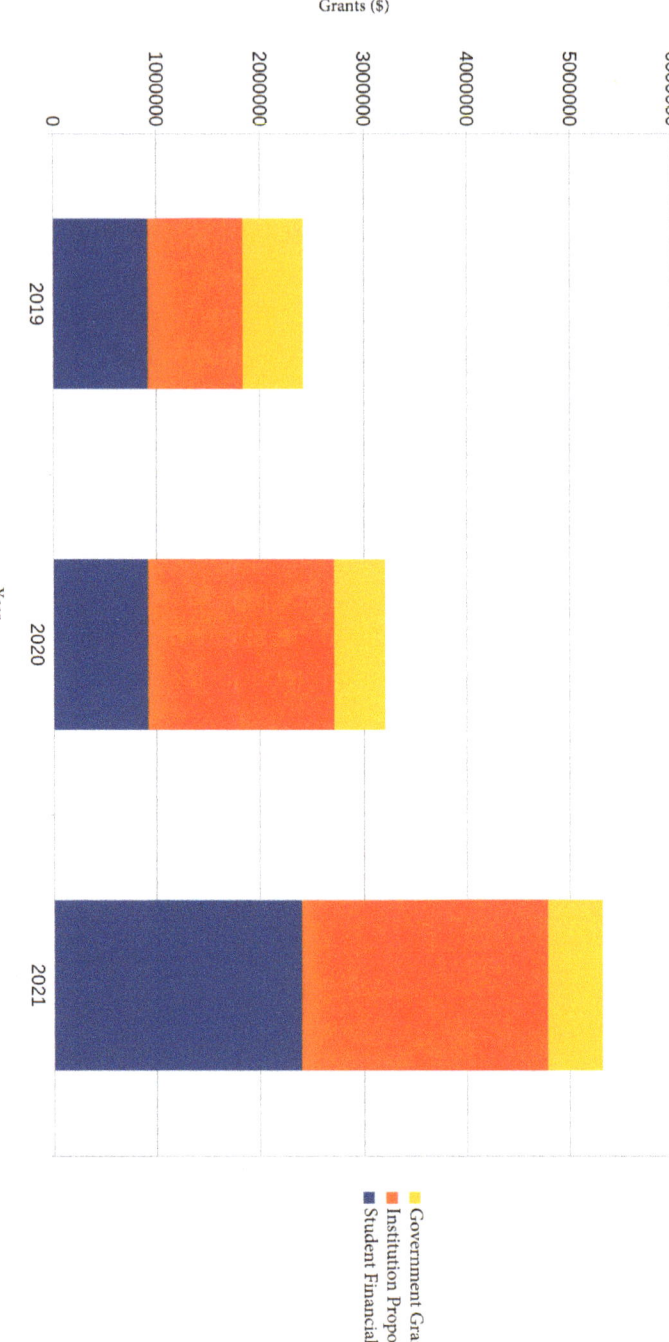

Figure 27: *UARTS received $9.3 million in HEERF funding during the pandemic years.*

Of the $10.9 million, $9.3 million came from HEERF, with the remaining $1.6 million from annual government grants. These are the funds underlying Yager's claims about scholarships and discretionary spending. His statement is an example of a slight-of-hand tactic: while technically the funds came from external sources, they were federal and state government grants — not donations from foundations, alumni, or wealthy private donors, which is what most people would assume when hearing "raised for scholarships."

To further illustrate the role of government grants in UARTS' finances, the following graph shows government grant revenue from 2009 to 2022.

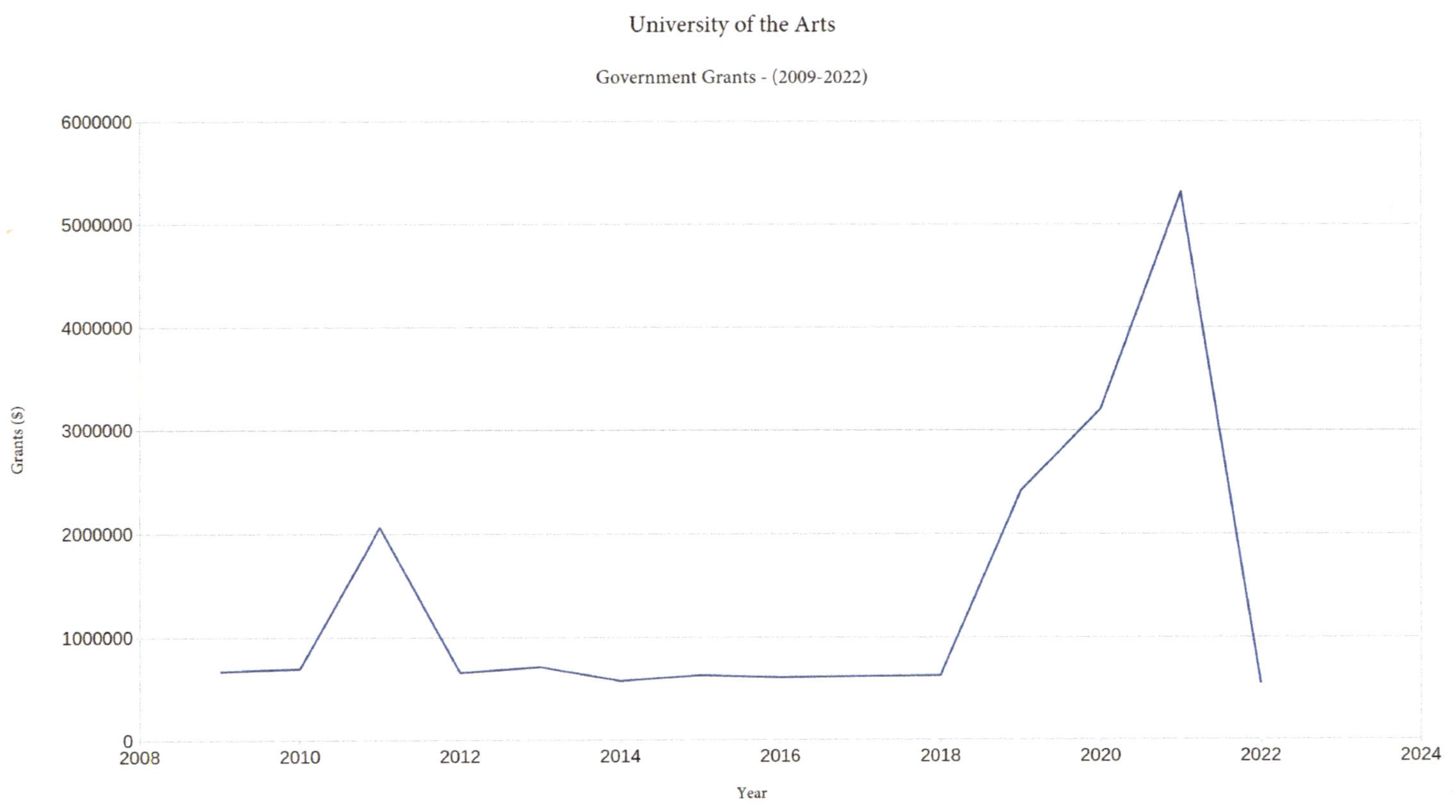

University of the Arts

Government Grants - (2009-2022)

Grants ($)

6000000

5000000

4000000

3000000

2000000

1000000

0
2008   2010   2012   2014   2016   2018   2020   2022   2024

Year

Figure 28: Note the sudden spike in government grants between 2019-2021.

No Grand Foundational Grants

A hallmark of university capital campaigns is large foundation donations. Such gifts are typically accompanied by a media campaign, on-campus announcements, and the naming of buildings or halls. This pattern is absent in UARTS' capital campaign.

Examining 990-PF tax returns from Philadelphia's largest arts foundations shows that from 2017–2023, the total contributed to UARTS was only $2.9 million. The largest foundation, The William Penn Foundation, with net assets of $3.2 billion in 2023, donated just $152,000 during this period. Similarly, the Greenfield Foundation, after whom UARTS' library is named, gave only $400,000, and the Hamilton Family Foundation (HFF), namesake of Hamilton Hall, donated just $73,500 from 2016 to 2020. Requests to HFF for grant breakdowns from 2019–2022 were not answered.

The list below summarizes total donations from regional foundations to UARTS, 2017–2023. Further details on foundation grants can be found in *Appendix F: Foundation Grants to UARTS – (2016-2023)*.

Foundation Grants to UARTS (2017–2023)

- Neubauer Family Foundation – $66,000

- William Penn Foundation – $152,000

- Wyncote Foundation – $200,000

- William B. Dietrich Foundation – $625,000

- Presser Foundation – $524,000

- Greenfield Foundation – $400,000

- W W Smith Charitable Trust – $350,000

- Zeldin Family Foundation – $23,000

- T/W Mary F. Lindback Residuary Tr Nect – $20,000

- Charlotte Cushman Foundation – $17,500

- Howard A. & Martha R. Wolf Fund – $74,000

- Richard & Jean Coyne Family Foundation – $143,000

- Jeff & Jenifer Westphal Foundation – $60,000

- Henry Nias Foundation – $15,000

What is not present are large, multi-million-dollar gifts — the hallmark of a true capital campaign. Among named buildings and departments, only the Greenfield Library carries a donor designation. It is likely that foundations perceived UARTS as financially unstable, a situation exacerbated by the university's $50 million bond issuance, which may have discouraged larger contributions.

The Illusion of Growth Through Pledges

A closer look at UARTS' reported contributions shows that much of Yager's claimed capital campaign success relied on pledges rather than actual cash. Pledges are promises to donate, often paid over several years, and sometimes never fulfilled. Despite this uncertainty, institutions can book pledged amounts as revenue in the year they are pledged, allowing them to present an inflated picture of financial health.

Between 2015 and 2016, UARTS' pledges surged from $294,777 to $19.5 million — an increase of nearly $19 million in a single year. This spike coincided with the 2017 bond issuance and the public launch of Yager's capital campaign. From 2016 through 2022, pledge values remained consistently high, fluctuating between $17 million and $22 million annually.

While these figures suggest apparent momentum, there is no corresponding increase in cash or unrestricted funds. Instead, operating liquidity continued to decline, leaving the university with fewer usable resources to meet obligations or service debt.

Yager's claim of raising $67 million through the campaign relied heavily on these pledges, creating a public impression of success while providing minimal practical relief for UARTS' deteriorating financial position. The campaign, in effect, was robust on paper, but weak in tangible, available funds.

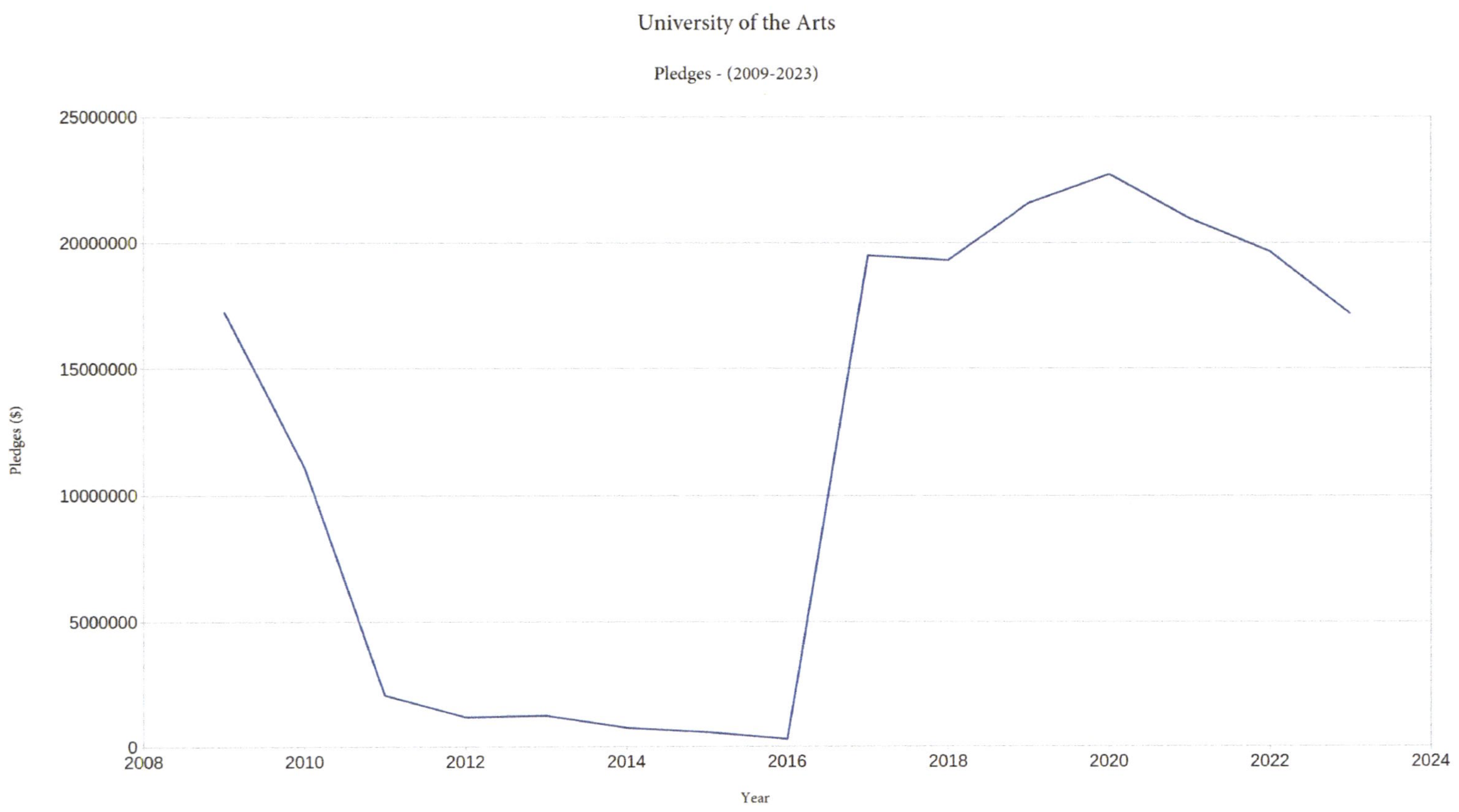

University of the Arts

Pledges - (2009-2023)

Pledges ($)

25000000

20000000

15000000

10000000

5000000

0

2008   2010   2012   2014   2016   2018   2020   2022   2024

Year

Figure 29: *2017 saw an extraordinary spike in pledges by $19 million.*

Concluding Thoughts

Taken together, Yager's capital campaign was one of illusion rather than substance, built on slight-of-hand public relations messaging. Students, faculty, alumni, and the public were led to believe that UARTS was pulling out of a financial nosedive, but the financial reality was the opposite.

The absence of large, multi-million-dollar foundation gifts — the hallmark of successful campaigns at other universities — underscored the lack of confidence in UARTS' financial management. Instead, the campaign relied on shifting monies from one account to another, a practice that allowed UARTS to appear financially healthy to the public and, crucially, to bond rating agencies.

The reliance on pandemic-era grants and the strategy of booking pledges as revenue further reinforced this illusion. These choices projected momentum but offered little in the way of usable resources. In the end, the campaign revealed vulnerabilities rather than strengths, eroding trust among donors, accreditors, and the very community it claimed to serve.

The Cohort Default Rate:

An Overlooked Crisis at UARTS

The Cohort Default Rate (CDR) is a federal metric used by the U.S. Department of Education (DOE) to measure how many students default on their federal student loans. Beyond being a compliance measure, CDR carries broader implications: it reflects borrower financial responsibility, the health of the job market, and, to some extent, how well a university prepares its students for gainful employment.

For students, a loan is counted as "in default" only after 540 days without payment following graduation. This includes the standard 180-day grace period and an additional 360 days. Once that threshold is crossed, the student is officially in default and contributes to the school's CDR.

For universities, crossing certain CDR thresholds triggers serious consequences:

- **30% or higher for three consecutive years (but below 40%)** – The school loses the ability to originate federal student loans. Students may still attend, but they must secure loans independently.

- **40% or higher in any single year** – The school is permanently barred from originating federal student loans.

Evidence suggests UARTS crossed the 30% threshold. According to DOE records, the university received virtually no federal loan disbursements between FY2017 and FY2019 (with the lone exception of about $10,000 in FY2017, negligible compared to the millions received before and after this period). This gap strongly implies that UARTS was prohibited from originating student loans during those years, likely because its CDR exceeded 30% for FY2014–FY2016.

The more recent CDR data strengthens this inference. UARTS reported a CDR of 23.4% in FY2019 and 26% in FY2020—figures alarmingly close to the 30% threshold. From FY2021–FY2024, CDR figures were unavailable due to COVID-era federal policies that suspended reporting.

Taken together, the data points to a pattern: UARTS likely triggered sanctions in the mid-2010s, temporarily losing access to federal loans, only to return with dangerously high default rates in the years leading to its closure.

This raises a critical question: when then-president Kerry Walk described the school's collapse as an "unforeseen financial crisis," was the real crisis already baked into UARTS' long-term struggle with student loan defaults and federal sanctions?

2023: UARTS Slide into Oblivion

On May 31, 2024, the University of the Arts announced its sudden closure. That same day, UARTS president Kerry Walk and Judson Aaron, Chair of the Board of Trustees, published an open letter claiming that the university had ". . . a cash position that has steadily weakened, [and] we could not cover significant, unanticipated expenses. The situation came to light very suddenly." Contrary to those claims, an examination of UARTS' audited financial reports from 2015 through 2023 reveals a financial trajectory far less sudden than Walk and Aaron suggested.

To understand the university's financial condition, one must distinguish between short-term and long-term debt. Long-term obligations include corporate bonds, mortgages, and retirement funds. Short-term obligations, by contrast, include salaries, operating expenses, and leases. Meeting these short-term debts requires liquidity—that is, readily available cash and cash equivalents. The following line graph illustrates UARTS' liquidity (cash and cash equivalents) from 2015 through 2023:

Figure 30: *UARTS cash & cash equivalents on a downward trajectory starting in 2017.*

Two points in the graph stand out. First, in 2016, UARTS' cash reserves increased by approximately $13 million, largely driven by the $11 million sale of the Merriam Theater. Second, beginning in 2017, the university's liquidity shows a steady downward trend. By 2023, UARTS' cash and cash equivalents stood at just $3.9 million at the close of the fiscal year. Without the infusion from the Merriam Theater sale, UARTS would likely have faced a liquidity crisis years earlier than 2024.

When looking at the graph above, there was nothing "sudden" about UARTS' liquidity decline. It is evident that liquidity had been decreasing over the years. If the trend were projected into 2024, UARTS could very well have had cash and cash equivalents of around $1 million. One could spend time making detailed financial projections for fiscal year 2024, but given UARTS' reliance on a line of credit to cover short-term debts, it is unlikely their liquidity spontaneously rose above $4 million. Regardless of precise projections, having liquidity this low placed UARTS in dangerous financial territory—as we saw in 2024, such low liquidity can precipitate institutional collapse.

Additional financial stressors compounded the problem in 2023:

- UARTS' $7 million line of credit with TD Bank was reduced to $6 million—likely in response to Fitch's downgrade of its bonds.
- The university drew $2 million from this line to cover short-term obligations, signaling severe liquidity strain.
- On February 14, 2023, Fitch Ratings downgraded UARTS' corporate bonds to B+, a deep speculative grade that increased borrowing costs and reduced investor confidence.
- UARTS sold the Pine Street Dorm for $10.7 million; however, $3.5 million of the proceeds was placed into a defeasance escrow account, locking those funds for future bond payments and making them unavailable for operations.
- UARTS' bond covenants included a 30-day clean-up provision on its credit line. In practice, the university had to fully repay its borrowings and maintain sufficient liquidity within 30 days. Failure to do so risked penalty interest rates and further loss of credit access.

Time Line of Events

All figures and events are drawn from primary sources, detailed in the appendix.

- 2016 – David Yager becomes UARTS' fourth president.
- 2016 – UARTS endowment stands at $49 million (IRS Form 990).
- 2016 – UARTS sells the Merriam Theater for $11 million.
- 2017 – UARTS operational revenue (tuition) reaches $75 million.
- 2017 – UARTS issues Series 2017 PAID Revenue Bonds (corporate bond).
- 2017 – UARTS endowment rises to $72 million (IRS Form 990).
- 2018 – UARTS operational revenue (tuition) declines to $43 million.
- 2018 – UARTS announces its first capital campaign with a goal of $50 million (alleged progress; HEERF grants were inappropriately counted, foundation contributions were minimal, and no sudden increase in donations occurred).
- 2019 – Laurie Wagman Recording Studios completed in December.
- 2019 – UARTS endowment decreases by $17 million, ending the year at $56 million (IRS Form 990).
- 2021 – Living Steps (Dorrance Hamilton Hall) project begins and is completed.
- 2022 – UARTS announces the end of their capital campaign.
- 2023 – UARTS sells Pine Street Dorm for $10.7 million.
- 2023 – New Student Center project announced.
- 2023 – David Yager retires in June.
- 2023 – Kerry Walk becomes UARTS' fifth president in August.
- 2023 – UARTS' cash and cash equivalents decrease to $3.9 million (end of fiscal year).
- 2023 – Fitch Ratings lowers UARTS bond rating to B+ in February.
- 2023 – TD Bank reduces UARTS' line of credit due to bond rating decrease.
- 2023 – UARTS draws $2 million to cover short-term debts.
- 2024 – UARTS collapses in May.

Conclusion

When looking at UARTS cash flows, it is evident that their cash position wasn't "sudden," it was predictable. The capital projects that began during the Yager administration would have enhanced the university. After reviewing JacobsWyper Architect's floor plans and artist renderings for the Gershwin building, I, as an alumnus, would have loved to see these plans come to fruition. Students would have benefited from the proposed renovations. But the reality is these campus changes came at the wrong time.

There is one question that remains unanswered: Why did Kerry Walk and her administration not take action sooner? UARTS was already in financial decline the moment she became the university's fifth president. Understandably, no leader wants their legacy defined as the president who oversaw a university closure. Yet given the options—a graceful and respectful wind-down, or the sudden and disruptive collapse witnessed in 2024—the former would have been far less damaging to students, faculty, and alumni.

Conclusion

The evidence presented throughout this report confirms a clear conclusion: UARTS' collapse was not the product of a single decision or individual. Instead, it was the cumulative effect of financial, administrative, and operational missteps, each compounding the next over more than a decade.

Financially, decisions such as donating over $86 million to external institutions between 2011 and 2022, reliance on a high-cost municipal bond exceeding $50 million, poorly timed capital projects totaling over $32 million, and escalating line-of-credit usage steadily eroded the university's capacity to sustain operations. Administratively, leadership failures—including mismanaged campaigns, opaque oversight, and a lack of accountability—magnified the impact of these financial choices. Operationally, declining tuition revenue (from $74M in 2017 to $34M in 2023), missed opportunities to strengthen relationships with local schools, and strategic misalignment further weakened the institution.

This analysis reveals a systemic pattern: UARTS' collapse was theoretically preventable, but in practice it was the result of repeated errors and oversights by multiple actors over time. No single decision caused the downfall; it was the interplay of policies, leadership choices, and operational missteps that ultimately brought the university to insolvency.

Ultimately, UARTS' experience offers a cautionary tale for higher education institutions. Even culturally significant universities are vulnerable when financial, operational, and governance decisions fail to align consistently. As noted in the Introduction, no one person caused this collapse—it was a series of events perpetuated by a series of people. Understanding this complex interplay is essential for preventing similar failures in the future.

Epilogue

After the collapse of UARTS, its campus buildings were liquidated through Chapter 7 bankruptcy proceedings. Temple University purchased Terra Hall, now draped with its own banners. Hamilton Hall was acquired by the Philadelphia development firm Scout, which announced plans to convert it into an artist residence. The fate of the remaining buildings remains uncertain as of September 2025, though speculation suggests that some may be redeveloped into condominiums.

There had been discussions of a possible merger with Temple University, but the ongoing civil rights case of *John K.A. Doe v. UARTS* likely influenced Temple's decision to walk away. A merger would have meant assuming both the financial and legal liabilities of UARTS. Instead, Temple's most prudent option was simply to purchase property—which is precisely what they did.

The employment status of the 700 employees laid off in June 2024 is difficult to trace, partly because many UARTS faculty held secondary jobs. What is clear, however, is that by the fall of 2024, the social media presence of many former professors had sharply declined. Several faculty privately estimated that only about 30 colleagues secured new academic positions. The outcome for staff remains even harder to determine. Journalist Violet Comber-Wilen of Billy Penn at WHYY briefly chronicled the careers of a handful of administrators and staff in her "Where Are They Now" series, though updates ended in spring 2025.

For students, the picture is clearer. Out of roughly 1,150 students, about 750 successfully transferred to other institutions, according to reporting by Susan Snyder and Kristen A. Graham of *The Philadelphia Inquirer*. Temple University accepted 300 students, Moore College of Art and Design admitted 114, Drexel University 90, and Bennington College 73. The remaining 263 dispersed across numerous universities. This transfer rate is unusually high; government officials I spoke with noted that in similar closures, only about one-third of students typically continue their studies elsewhere.

One academic program, however, did survive: the UARTS dance program. It was transferred to Bennington College in summer 2024, with plans to eventually return to Philadelphia once the Pennsylvania Department of Education authorizes it to grant degrees again.

Meanwhile, UARTS' last two presidents have receded from public life. David Yager maintains only a limited social media presence, while Kerry Walk has not been heard from since the days leading up to the collapse.

The UARTS alumni community, however, remains active, if modest. A Facebook group of over 2,000 members keeps the school's legacy alive in the digital sphere, a small but meaningful reminder of the institution that once stood at the center of Philadelphia's arts education.

Afterword

I began this report with the intention of overcoming a challenge. Years ago, when I first moved to Philadelphia, I set myself a similar test: to face my fear of dark alleyways by walking through them in the middle of the night. Writing this report carried its own kind of challenge.

I approached it with the tools I know best—engineering and mathematics. In engineering, models are used to represent both existing and hypothetical structures. I created a mental model of UARTS' collapse in much the same way one might analyze an airplane crash or a bridge failure. The first step was to identify the underpinnings that held the university together. From there, I asked the critical question: what caused those supports to give way?

Answering that question meant combing through countless financial records, legal documents, school reports, and databases. There were many long nights. After tutoring engineering students during the evening, I would begin my research at 11 p.m. and often work until 3 a.m. This routine began in July 2024 and carried on for a full year.

Through it all, I found myself asking why the alarm bells hadn't been sounded earlier. Where was the executive board while the university slid closer to oblivion? From my vantage point, it appears as though both trustees and the board were absent, leaving the administration free to act without accountability.

The lessons of UARTS' collapse highlight a truth that applies to higher education broadly: universities need leaders with a wide range of skills, not just administrators. Missing from UARTS were the innovators. As I argued in *Missed Opportunities in Outreach, Branding, and Digital Strategy*, even modest, low-cost, high-impact strategies could have shifted the outcome. Had they been implemented, this report might have been about resilience and rebirth rather than collapse.

It is my hope that anyone in arts administration who reads this report will take the warnings seriously. Remember that structures, whether physical or institutional, always emit signals before they fail. To ignore them is to court disaster. Those who remain blind or deaf to the warning signs will one day find their own institution reduced to another cautionary case study.

As with any investigation, this report could not capture everything. Choices had to be made about focus, and certain threads—though important—remain outside its scope. Each of these areas holds its own story, and together they could provide a more complete understanding of how UARTS came undone.

The collapse of UARTS is also not a closed chapter. The ongoing civil rights lawsuit and the uncertain future of its relocated dance program suggest that this story is still unfolding. The legacy of UARTS is being shaped even now—through courtrooms, real estate developments, and the digital gathering spaces where alumni keep its memory alive.

For me, what matters is that the lessons do not get lost. Collapse rarely comes as a surprise to those who look closely; the warning signs are almost always there. The test is whether leaders recognize them in time, or whether future historians will find themselves writing yet another case study of an institution that could have been saved.

Writing this report has shown me that collapse is never sudden—it is the sum of choices, ignored warnings, and missed opportunities. That lesson is one I will carry with me far beyond UARTS.

Appendix A: Simplified Piecewise Arithmetic Formula for Faculty Step Increases

The pay steps outlined in the UARTS 2024 faculty labor agreement are presented in a line-by-line format. To simplify the structure and enable quantitative analysis, the following piecewise arithmetic sequence was derived. This function approximates the increase in salary based on step number and applies separately to defined intervals.

Full Time Faculty Scale – FY2024	
Sequence	Bounds
$a_0 = 57850 + (n-1)*1000$	$1 \leq n \leq 8$
$a_0 = 69850 + (n-9)*1000$	$9 \leq n \leq 20$
$a_0 = 81850 + (n-21)*1000$	$21 \leq n \leq 25$

Appendix B: Simplified Piecewise Arithmetic Formula for Adjunct Step Increases

The pay steps outlined in the UARTS 2024 faculty labor agreement are presented in a line-by-line format. To simplify the structure and enable quantitative analysis, the following piecewise arithmetic sequence was derived. This function approximates the increase in salary based on step number and applies separately to defined intervals.

Adjunct Pay Scale – FY2024	
Sequence	**Bounds**
$a_0 = 1275 + (n-1)*30$	$1 \le n \le 20$
$a_0 = 1870 + (n-21)*25$	$21 \le n \le 22$
$a_0 = 1915 + (n-23)*20$	$23 \le n \le 30$

Appendix C: Table Listing UARTS Donations to External Organizations (2011-2022)

Recipient Organization	Donation ($)
The University of Pennsylvania	4,760,692
Temple University	2,689,499
Philadelphia Museum of Art	2,601,917
Fabric Workshop and Museum	2,048,270
People's Light & Theatre Company	2,008,328
Opera Company of Philadelphia	1,799,250
Mann Center for the Performing Arts	1,719,556
Pig Iron Theatre Company	1,665,898
Institute of Contemporary Art Philly	1,612,740
The Wilma Theater	1,601,025
Philadelphia Fringe Arts	1,597,128
Bryn Mawr College Performing Arts Series	1,448,628
Drexel University	1,434,957
Asian Arts Initiative	1,356,225
Philadelphia Chamber Music Society	1,311,640
Please Touch Museum	1,258,890
Philadelphia Mural Arts Advocates	1,157,497
Arcadia University Art Gallery	1,096,565
Curtis Institute of Music	1,046,217
Eastern State Penitentiary	994,354
Swarthmore College	976,080
Cliveden of the National Trust	954,534
The University of the Arts	942,997
Philadelphia Orchestra Association	914,000
Prisim Quartet	903,220
Philadelphia Mural Arts Advocates	896,723
The Crossing	860,000
The Franklin Institute	860,000
Fleisher Art Memorial	856,500

Village of Arts & Humanities	852,000
Philadelphia Photo Arts Center	851,000
College of Physicians Philadelphia	820,884
Painted Bridge Art Center	802,880
The Pennsylvania Horticultural Society	793,780
National Constitution Center	743,764
Christ Church Preservation Trust	730,127
Philadelphia Folklore Porject	728,429
Partners for Sacred Places	723,910
Scribe Video Center	719,729
The Clay Studio	713,750
The Library Company of Philadelphia	699,840
Historical Society of Pennsylvania	691,426
Fund for the Water Works	685,000
Settlement Music School	668,000
James A Michener Art Museum	644,143
Japan America Society of Greater Philadelphia	637,111
Al-Bustan Seeds of Culturs	629,920
Free Library of Philadelphia	604,032
Philadelphia Theatre Company	589,472
William Way Gay Community Center of Philadelphia	585,260
Stenton NSCDA- PA	581,000
Zoological Society of Philadelphia	572,000
The Kimmel Center	547,779
Bowerbird	542,819
Theatre Horizon	526,560
Rosenbach Museum and Library	516,683
Tempestra Di Mare	503,000
New Paradise Laboratories	502,930
Data Arts	500,000
Ars Nova Workshop	465,590
Arden Theater Company	451,650
The Print Center	447,998
African American Museum in Philadelphia	419,980

International House Philadelphia	417,849
Pennsylvania Humanities Council	417,000
Beth Shalom Congregation	375,000
The Academy of Natural Sciences	366,024
Association for Public Art	361,000
Philadelphia Live Arts & Philly Fringe	361,000
Fiarmount Park Conservancy	360,000
Independence Visitor Center	360,000
Thomas Jefferson University	360,000
WHYY	360,000
Philadelphia Art Alliance	350,476
Blackstar Projects	348,651
Sruti	344,750
Philadelphia Contemporary	340,294
Presbyterian Historical Society	334,482
Mendelssohn Club of Philadelphia	329,200
Headlong Dance Theater	320,800
Broad Street Ministry	312,500
Maternity Care Coalition	312,500
John Bartram Association	305,437
Historic Germantown Preserved	293,700
American Philosophical Society	292,500
The Center for Art in Wood	288,000
Girard College	276,816
The Galleries at Moore College	262,000
Nichole Canuso Dance Company	261,480
Piffaro the Renaissance Band	257,000
Vox Populi	256,800
Hurfford Center for the Arts & Humanities	253,650
Rair	250,000
The Trust for Public Land	235,850
Johnson House Historic Site	233,500
Friends of Laurel Hill Cemetery	230,000
Pasion y Arte	229,000

Kun-yang Lindancers	220,716
Montgomery Community College	219,200
Orchestra 2001	211,800
Pennsbury Society	211,200
Bucks County Historical Society	211,095
Friends of the Japanese House & Garden	204,230
Preservation Alliance for Greater Philadelphia	196,208
Musicopia	195,001
Kulu Mele African Dance & Drum Ensemble	175,496
Pennsylvania Ballet	170,000
Wagner Free Institute of Science	167,500
The Woodlands	167,000
Ego Po	163,800
The Barnes Foundation	163,800
Black Lily	163,041
Group Motion Multimedia Dance Theater	162,100
Chemical Heritage Foundation	159,280
Fringe Arts	155,160
Voloshky Ukrainian Dance Ensemble of Philadelphia	154,500
South Asian American Digital Archive	154,000
1812 Productions	152,625
Brandywine Conservancy	152,600
Jazz Bridge Project	144,000
Conservation Center for Art & Historic	143,900
Fairmount Park Art Association	137,000
Museum of Black Joy	135,000
The Academy of Vocal Arts	132,630
Monument Lab	124,000
Pennsylvania Academy of the Fine Arts	120,000
University City Science Center	120,000
Philadanco Company	110,000
First Person Arts	109,768
Haverford College	102,600
Chamber Orchestra of Philadelphia	101,794

Leah Stein Dance Company	101,000
Warriors of the Wonderful Sound	100,400
Intercultural Journeys	96,720
The Trust for Public Land	95,400
Network for New Music	91,000
Karmalux	90,000
Independence Seaport Museum	85,626
University City Arts League	85,032
Susan Hess Modern Dance	82,500
Crossroads Music	82,000
Philadelphia University – Design Center	79,268
Philadelphia Ceili Group	77,000
Philadelphia Dance Projects	77,000
Choral Arts Philadelphia	72,000
Fund for Philadelphia	72,000
Philadelphia Area Consortium of Special Collection Libraries	72,000
Philadelphia Yearly Meeting	72,000
Tiny Dynamite	72,000
Astral Artists	70000
Interact Theater Company	65,545
Greater Philadelphia Cultural Alliance	65,000
Tyler School of Art	60,500
Seventh Ward Projects	60,000
The Mayor's Fund for Philadelphia	60,000
Schuylkill Center for Environmental Education	57,501
Nueva Esperanta	55,049
Geoffrey Sobelle Elephant Room	55,000
West Philadelphia Cultural Alliance	55,000
Jumatatu Poeidosncracy Productions	51,000
Moore College of Art & Design	49,517
Philagrafika	49,336
Dolce Suono Chamber Music Concert Series	42,893
Various Other Assistance	36,963

Taras Lewyckj	35,000
Slought Foundation	33,306
Emily Bat	31,250
Art Reach	30,000
Phila Yung Playwrights	30,000
Wyck Association	30,000
Play Penn New Play Development	29,990
Theatre Exile	29,700
Idosyncrazy Productions	29,000
Philadelphia Cultural Alliance	24,000
Alliance of Artists Communities	16,600
Basekamp	15,218
Dance USA Philadelphia	15,000
Grantmakes in the Arts	15,000
Philadelphia Clef Club of Jazz & Performing Arts	15,000
Woodmere Museum of Arts	15,000
Maschere Dance	14,910
Kyl Dancers	12,202
Balletx	11,253
Common Field	10,000
Five Six Media	10,000
Palgrave MacMillian	10,000
Philadelphia Young Playwrights	10,000
The MacDowell Colony Inc	10,000
11th Hour Theatre	8,500
The Wharton Esherick Museum	8,500
Taller Puertorriqueño	7,500
Tilt Institute for the Contemporary Image	7,500
American Composers Forum	6,000
Art Sanctuary	5,000
Berman Museum of Art at Ursinus College	5,000
Carnegie Museum of Art	5,000
Mother Bethelame Church	5,000
The Athenaeum of Philadelphia	5,000

Arab-American Development Corporation	4,600
Philadelphia Sketch Club	4,000
The Bearded Ladies Cabaret	4,000
Solaris Dance – Theatre & Video	3,666
The Pennsbury Society	3,455
Dustin Hurt Werbird	3,000
Penn Praxis	2,900
Bristol Riverside Theatre	2,750
Creative Capacity	2,500
Mega Words	2,334
Fidget	2,050
Miro Dance Theater	2,000
Theatre Bay Area	1,650
Chester county Historical society	1,513
Green House Media	1,060
Community Design Collaborative	1,000
Pearls Buck International	1,000

Appendix D: Legal Framework for Nonprofit Pass-Through Entities

1. **Internal Revenue Code (IRC) §170(b)(1)(F)(ii) – Conduit Foundations**
    Under IRC §170(b)(1)(F)(ii), a private nonoperating foundation may qualify as a "conduit foundation" if it distributes 100% of the contributions received in a taxable year to other qualifying organizations by the 15th day of the third month following the close of the taxable year. These distributions must be qualifying distributions under IRC §4942(g) and treated as distributions out of corpus under IRC §4942(h). The foundation must have no remaining undistributed income for the taxable year.

2. **IRC §4942 – Qualifying Distributions**
    IRC §4942 requires private nonoperating foundations to distribute income equal to their distributable amount for a taxable year via qualifying distributions within 12 months of the close of the taxable year. Conduit foundations, as defined under IRC §170(b)(1)(F)(ii), must make qualifying distributions in an amount equal to 100% of contributions received in a taxable year within 2 months and 15 days of the close of the taxable year.

3. **IRS Revenue Ruling 62-113 – "Mere Conduit" Doctrine**
    IRS Revenue Ruling 62-113 (1962-1 C.B. 10) establishes that a tax-exempt organization acting as a mere conduit—without discretion or control over the funds—is not considered a legitimate charitable intermediary. In such cases, the transaction is treated as a direct donation from the donor to the ultimate recipient, potentially disqualifying the contribution from being tax-deductible.

4. **IRS Publication 557 – Tax-Exempt Status for 501(c)(3) Organizations**
    IRS Publication 557 outlines the requirements for maintaining tax-exempt status under IRC §501(c)(3). It emphasizes that organizations must operate exclusively for exempt purposes and that no part of their net earnings may inure to the benefit of any private shareholder or

individual. Engaging in pass-through arrangements without proper oversight can jeopardize an organization's tax-exempt status.

5. **Fiscal Sponsorship Guidelines**

    Fiscal sponsorship arrangements allow a tax-exempt organization (the sponsor) to provide administrative and financial oversight to a project or program that lacks its own tax-exempt status. Key requirements include:

    - Discretion and Control: The sponsor must maintain complete discretion and control over the funds, ensuring they are used in furtherance of the sponsor's exempt purposes.
    - Administrative Fees: Sponsors typically charge an administrative fee, often ranging from 5% to 15%, to cover the costs of oversight and management.
    - Legal and Financial Responsibility: The sponsor assumes legal and financial responsibility for the project, including compliance with applicable laws and regulations.

    Sources:
    - Propel Nonprofits – A Board's Guide to Fiscal Sponsorship
    - Council of Nonprofits – Fiscal Sponsorship for Nonprofits

6. **Case Law and Legal Precedents**
    - Rev. Rul. 68-489 (1968-2 C.B. 210): This ruling reinforces the principle that a fiscal sponsorship arrangement must involve active oversight and control by the sponsor. A mere pass-through arrangement without such control is not permissible.
    - Rev. Rul. 64-275 (1964-2 C.B. 142): This ruling discusses the implications of an organization acting as an agent for another and the potential impact on its tax-exempt status.

Appendix E: Enrollment Trends for Sample Universities (2001–2023)

UARTS stood apart as the only American university to house the full spectrum of the arts under one roof. To place its enrollment trajectory in a broader context, thirty comparable institutions were selected for this statistical study (n = 30). The selection criteria were as follows:

- Private, nonprofit universities (501c3)
- Comparable enrollment size to UARTS
- Programs exclusively in the arts
- Institutions offering only visual and performing arts degrees (non-arts programs excluded)

Each graph includes both the Pearson correlation coefficient and the regression equation, measuring the relationship between year and total student enrollment. The results not only identify which demographic shifts influenced total enrollment, but also reveal broader trends in arts university enrollment.

Three broad patterns emerged across the sample:

- 20 universities experienced overall growth
- 7 universities experienced overall decline
- 3 universities remained relatively stable

What stands out most is a striking geographic concentration: of the seven arts universities with declining student enrollment, three were located in Philadelphia. The statistical evidence confirms the severity of this trend:

University/College	Pearson Correlation Coefficient	Regression Equation
Moore College of Art & Design	-0.9187	-13.29x + 27229
Pennsylvania Academy of the Fine Arts	-0.602	-4.983x + 10300
University of the Arts	-0.8039	-39.95x + 82379

The negative coefficients confirm sustained declines over time, with UARTS showing the steepest regression slope among the three.

Beyond Philadelphia, demographic correlations also shaped enrollment trends:

- 16 universities: enrollment correlated with white student enrollment
- 7 universities: enrollment correlated with nonresident (international) student enrollment
- 6 universities: enrollment correlated with both white and nonresident student enrollment
- 1 university: enrollment correlated with Hispanic and nonresident student enrollment

Taken together, the graphs reveal not just isolated institutional struggles but a systemic vulnerability: heavy dependence on specific demographics left many arts universities exposed to enrollment shocks. In Philadelphia, the convergence of three separate declines is especially telling—placing UARTS' collapse within a wider statistical frame and underscoring its role in a regional pattern of contraction.

Art Center College of Design (Pasadena, CA)

Enrollment by Race

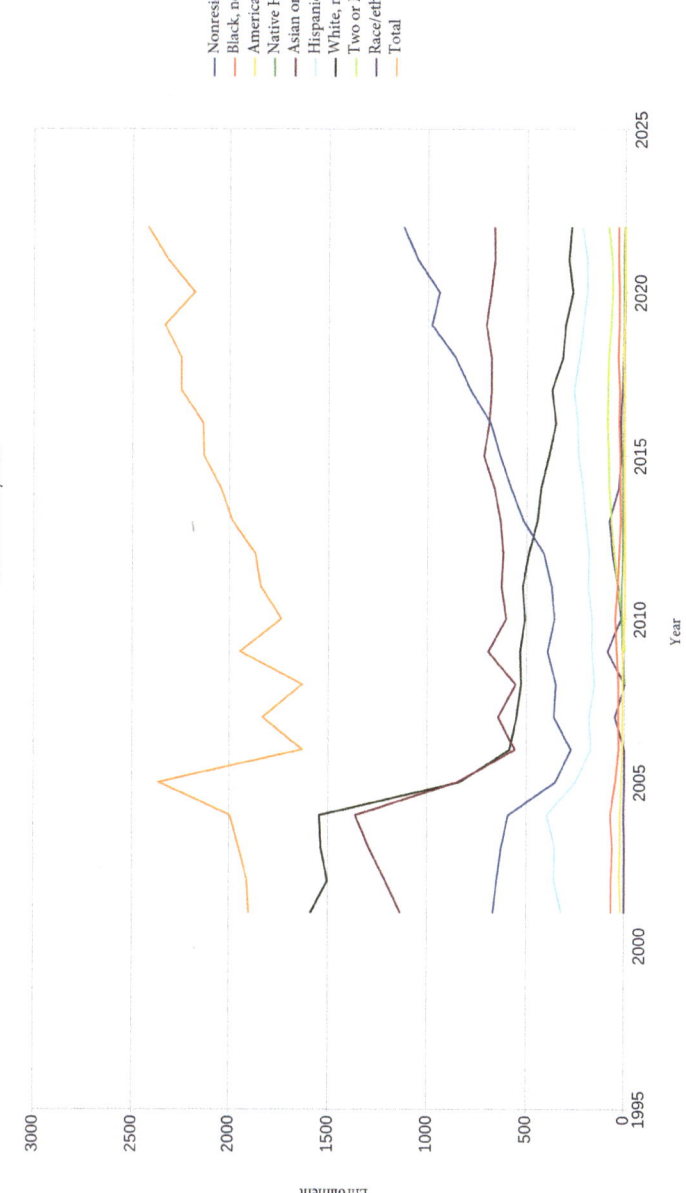

Person Coefficient: 0.6407

Regression: 22.94x - 44104

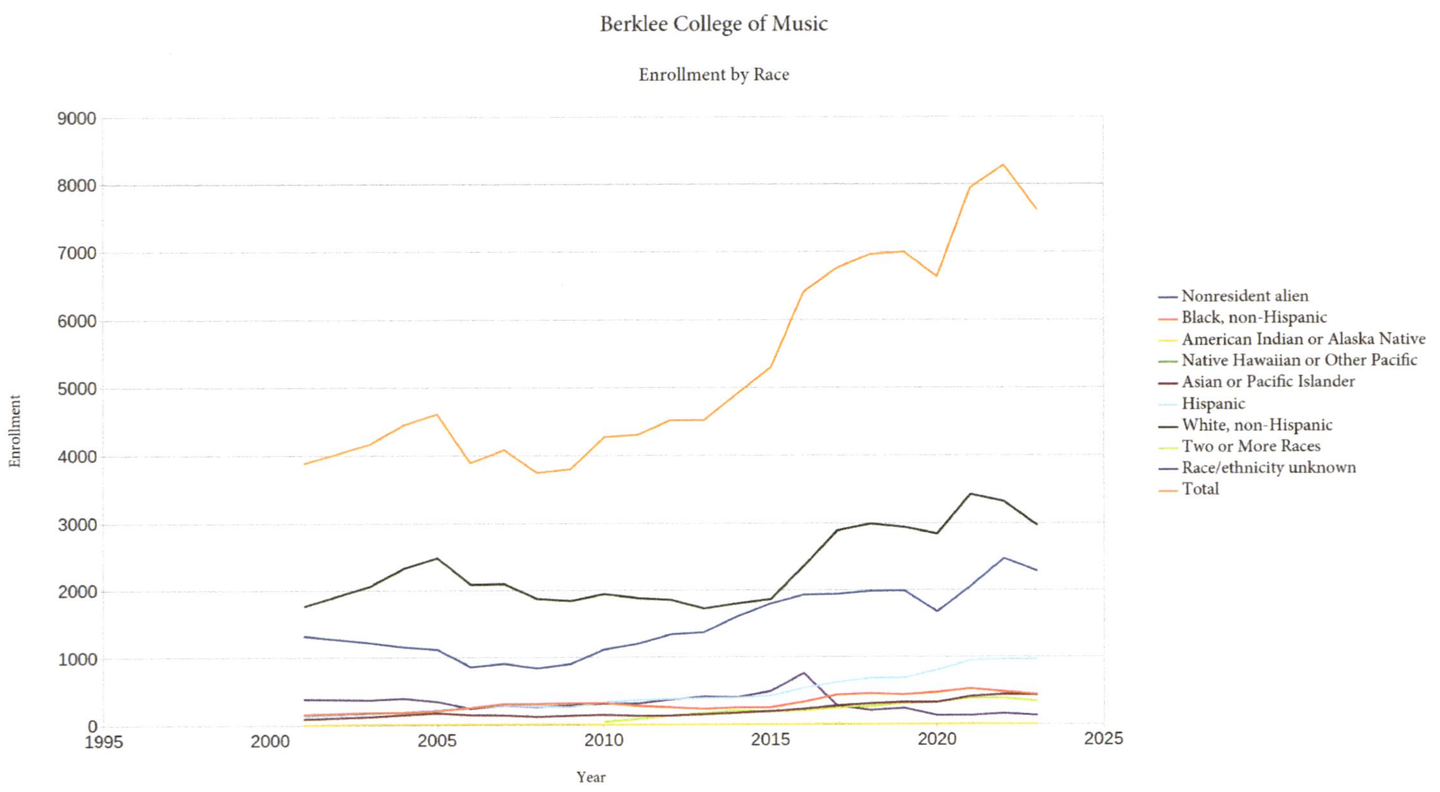

Berklee College of Music

Enrollment by Race

Enrollment

9000
8000
7000
6000
5000
4000
3000
2000
1000
0

1995   2000   2005   2010   2015   2020   2025

Year

— Nonresident alien
— Black, non-Hispanic
— American Indian or Alaska Native
— Native Hawaiian or Other Pacific
— Asian or Pacific Islander
— Hispanic
— White, non-Hispanic
— Two or More Races
— Race/ethnicity unknown
— Total

Person Coefficient: -0.3519

Regression: -3.607x + 7565

California College of the Arts

Enrollment by Race

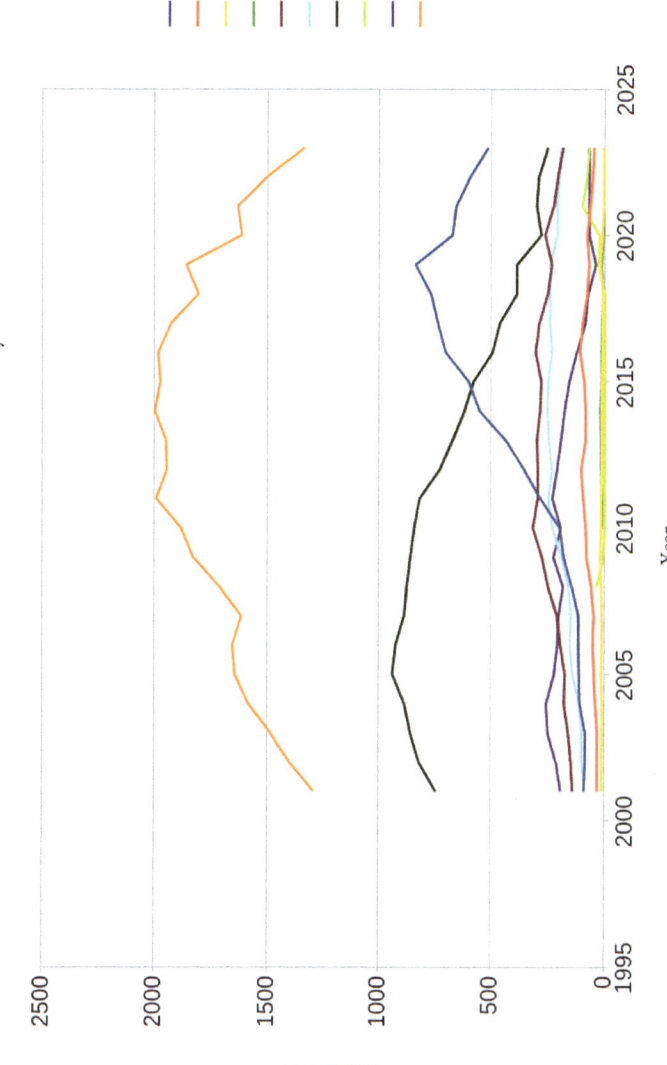

Person Coefficient: 0.2632

Regression: 8.669x - 15721

California Institute of the Arts

Enrollment by Race

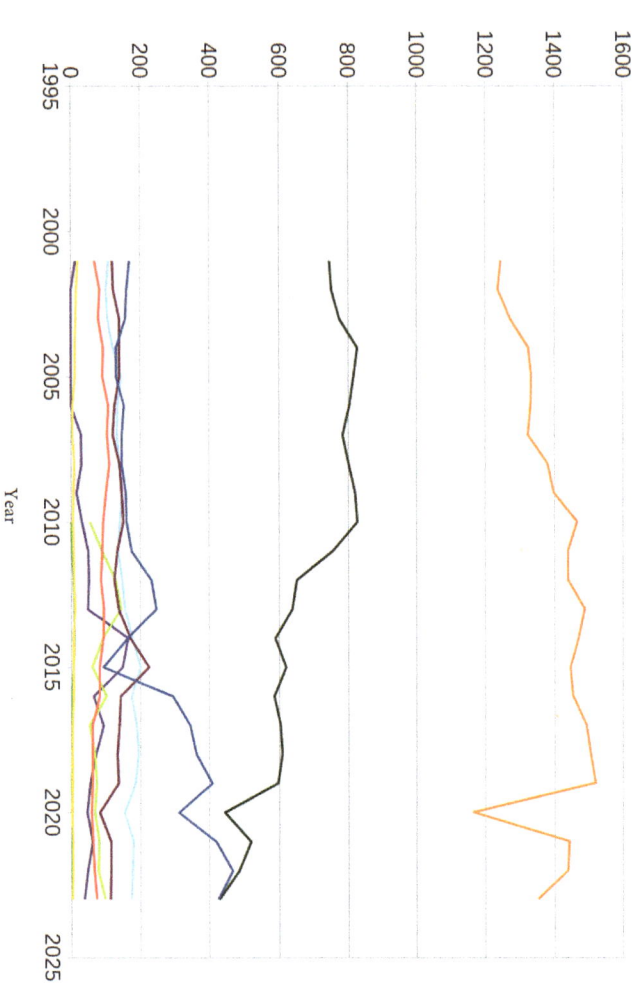

Enrollment

Year

- Nonresident alien
- Black, non-Hispanic
- American Indian or Alaska Native
- Native Hawaiian or Other Pacific
- Asian or Pacific Islander
- Hispanic
- White, non-Hispanic
- Two or More Races
- Race/ethnicity unknown
- Total

Person Coefficient: 0.4962

Regression: 7.084x - 12862

Cleveland Institute of Art (Cleveland, OH)

Enrollment by Race

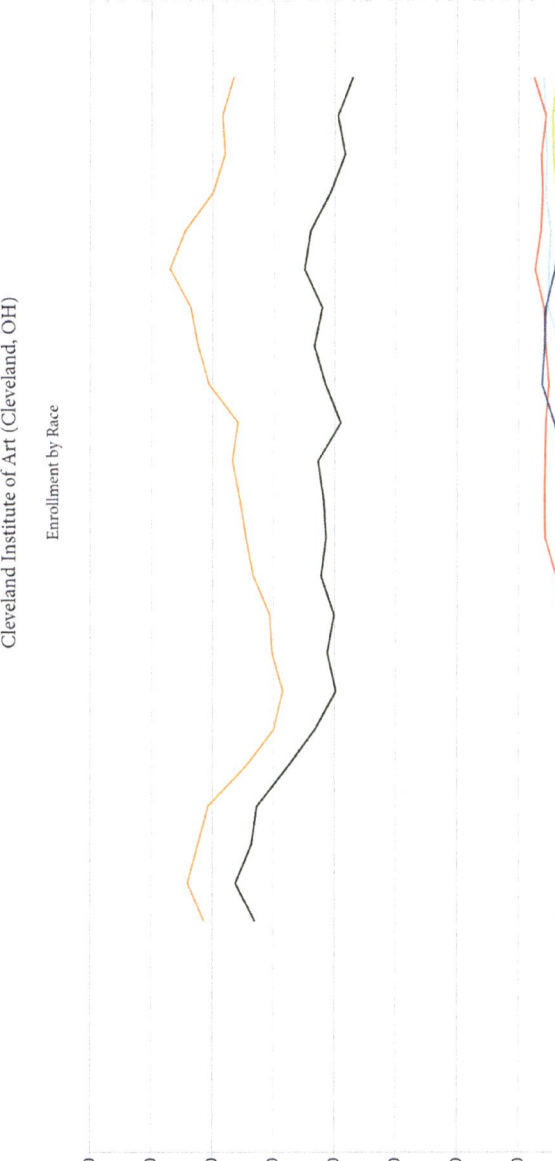

Nonresident alien
Black, non-Hispanic
American Indian or Alaska Native
Native Hawaiian or Other Pacific
Asian or Pacific Islander
Hispanic
White, non-Hispanic
Two or More Races
Race/ethnicity unknown
Total

Person Coefficient: 0.2278

Regression: 1.728x - 2899

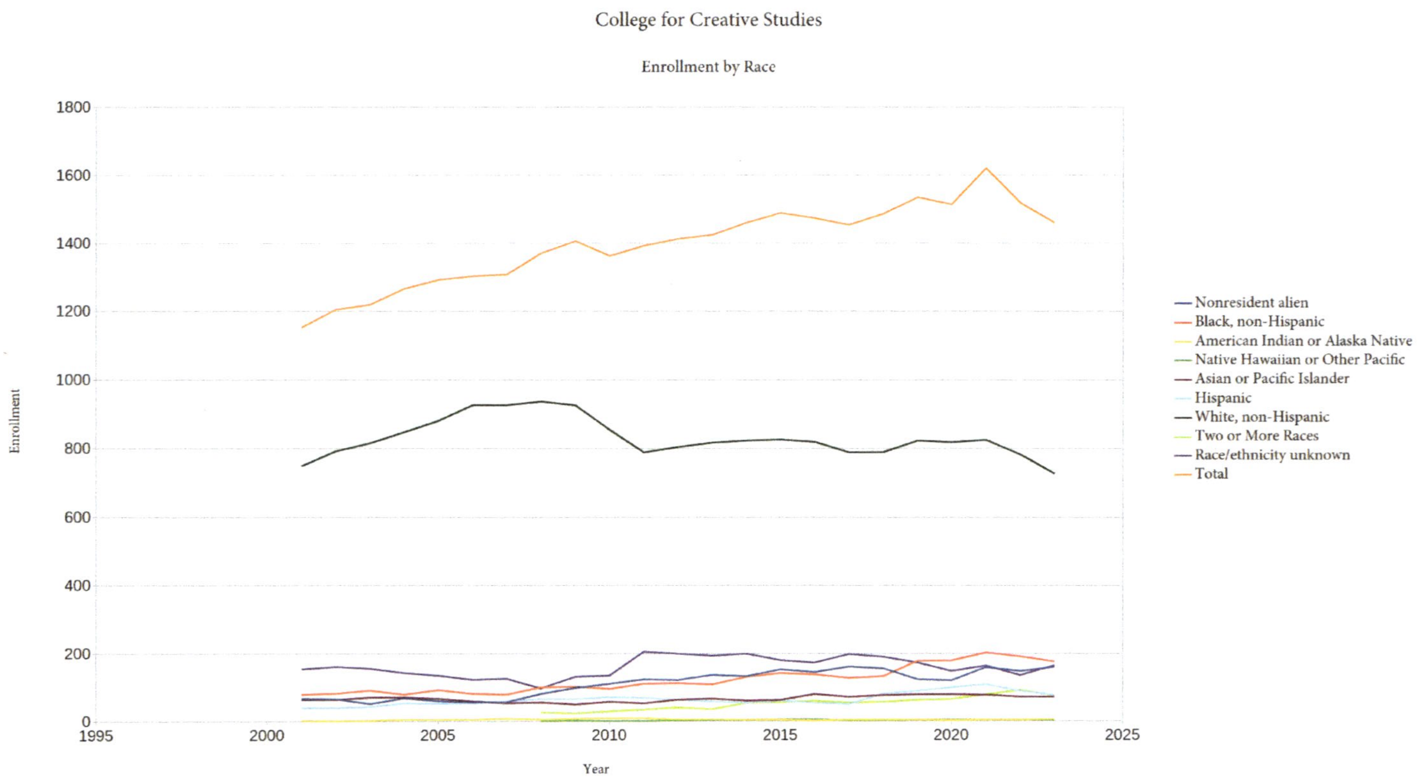

College for Creative Studies

Enrollment by Race

Enrollment

1800
1600
1400
1200
1000
800
600
400
200
0

1995
2000
2005
2010
2015
2020
2025

Year

- Nonresident alien
- Black, non-Hispanic
- American Indian or Alaska Native
- Native Hawaiian or Other Pacific
- Asian or Pacific Islander
- Hispanic
- White, non-Hispanic
- Two or More Races
- Race/ethnicity unknown
- Total

Person Coefficient: 0.9378

Regression: 16.31x - 31427

Columbia College Chicago

Enrollment by Race

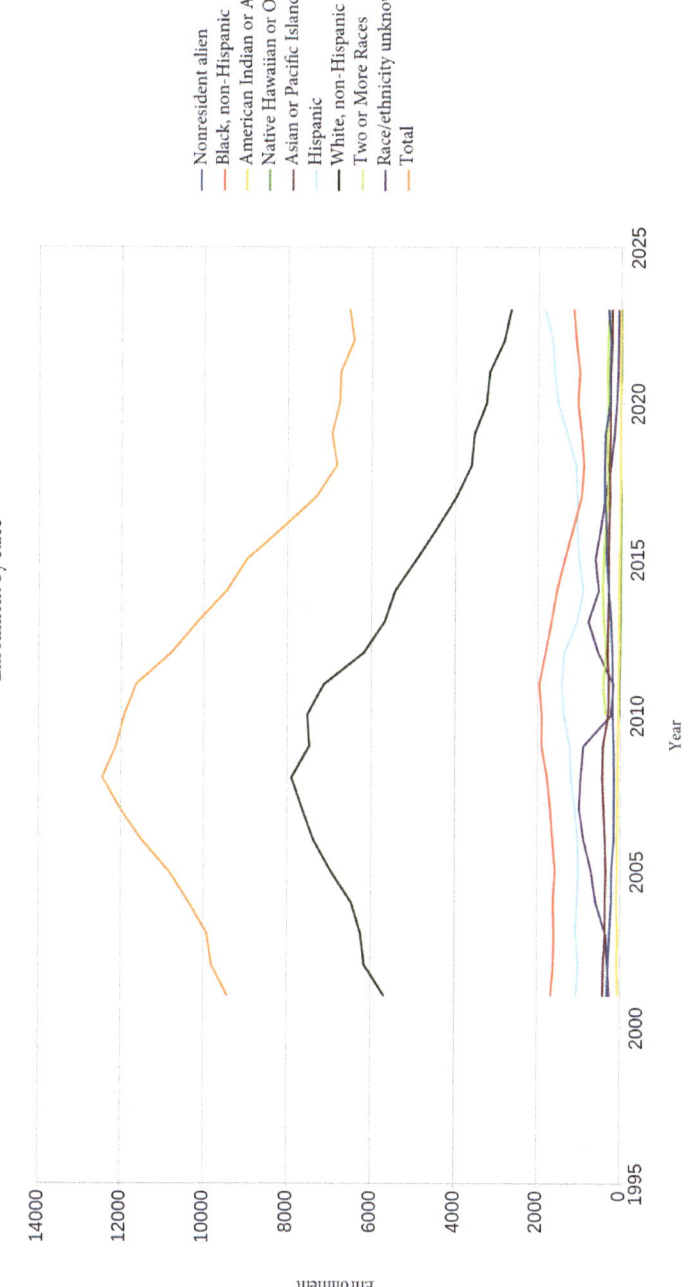

Person Coefficient: -0.7571

Regression: -232.2x + 476673

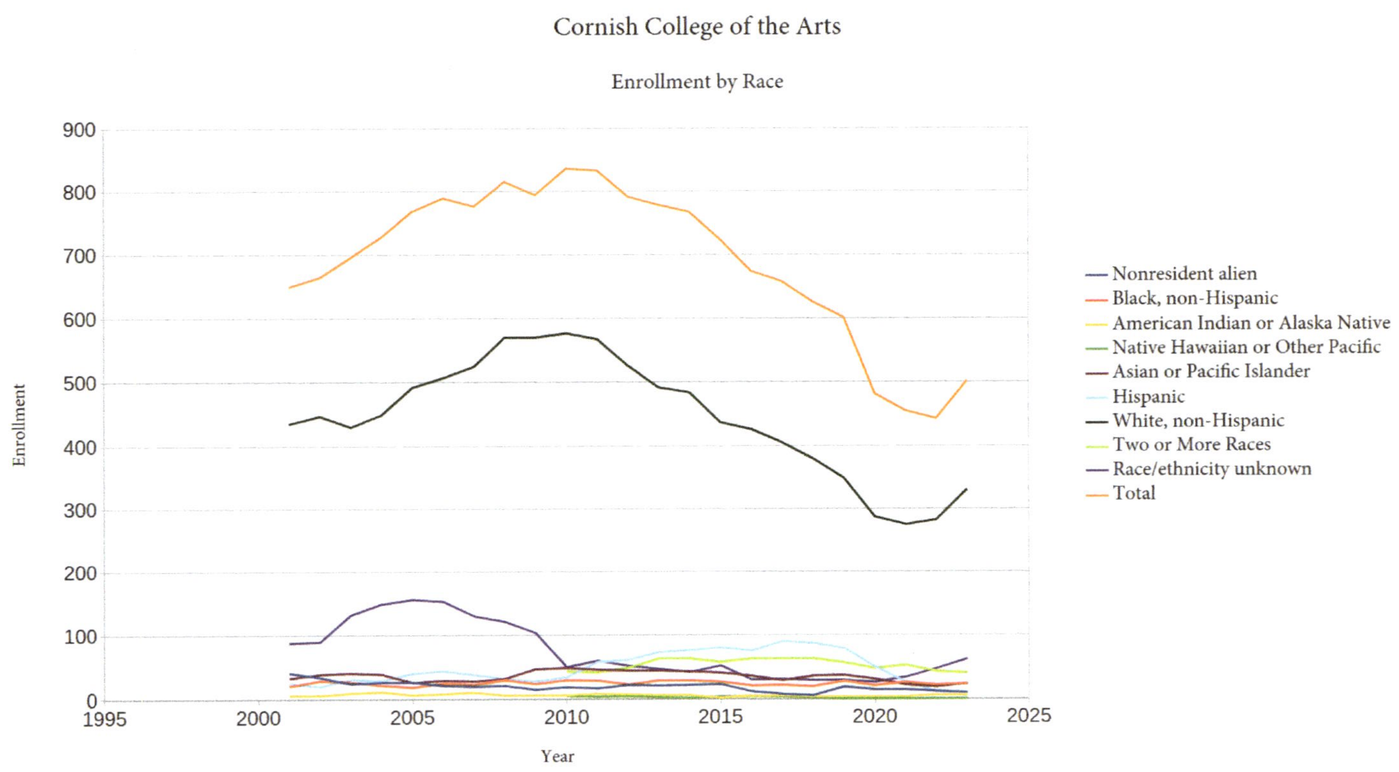

Cornish College of the Arts

Enrollment by Race

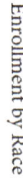

Enrollment

900
800
700
600
500
400
300
200
100
0

1995 2000 2005 2010 2015 2020 2025

Year

- Nonresident alien
- Black, non-Hispanic
- American Indian or Alaska Native
- Native Hawaiian or Other Pacific
- Asian or Pacific Islander
- Hispanic
- White, non-Hispanic
- Two or More Races
- Race/ethnicity unknown
- Total

Person Coefficient: -0.641

Regression: - 11.54x + 23915

Emerson College

Enrollment by Race

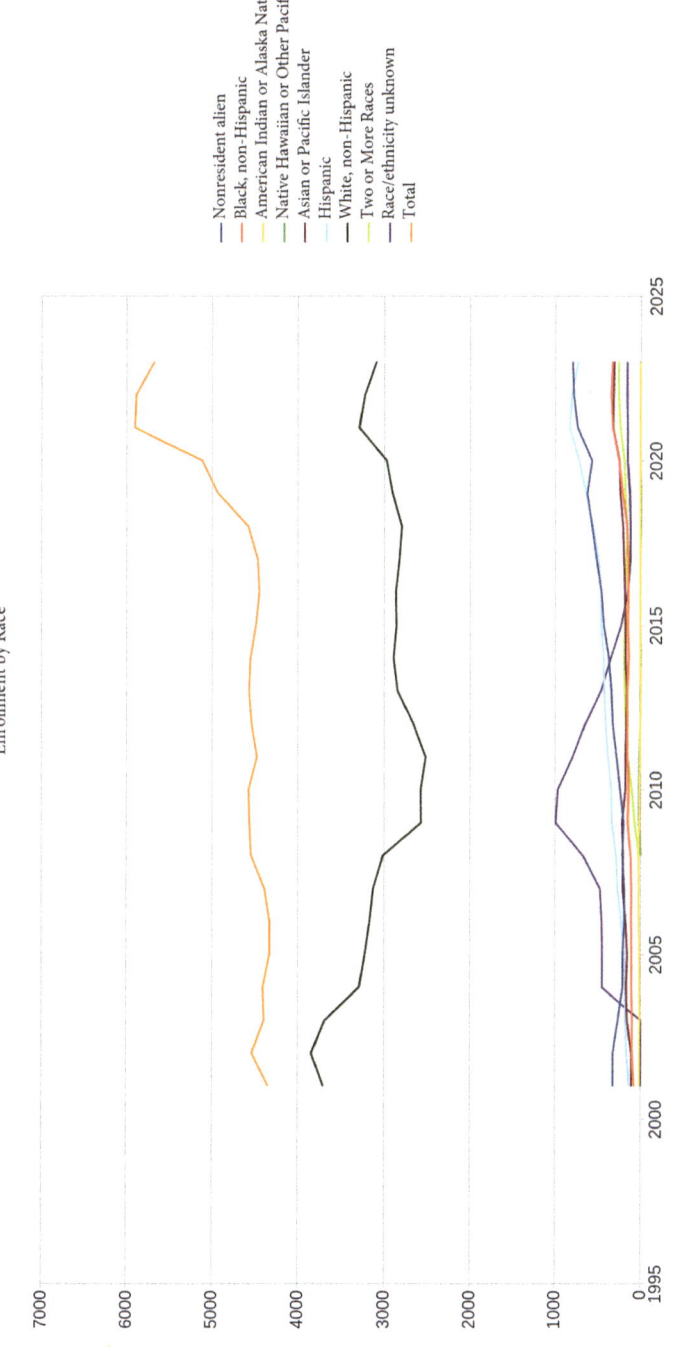

Year

Enrollment

- Nonresident alien
- Black, non-Hispanic
- American Indian or Alaska Native
- Native Hawaiian or Other Pacific
- Asian or Pacific Islander
- Hispanic
- White, non-Hispanic
- Two or More Races
- Race/ethnicity unknown
- Total

Person Coefficient: 0.7374

Regression: 52.61x - 101169

Maine College of Art & Design

Enrollment by Race

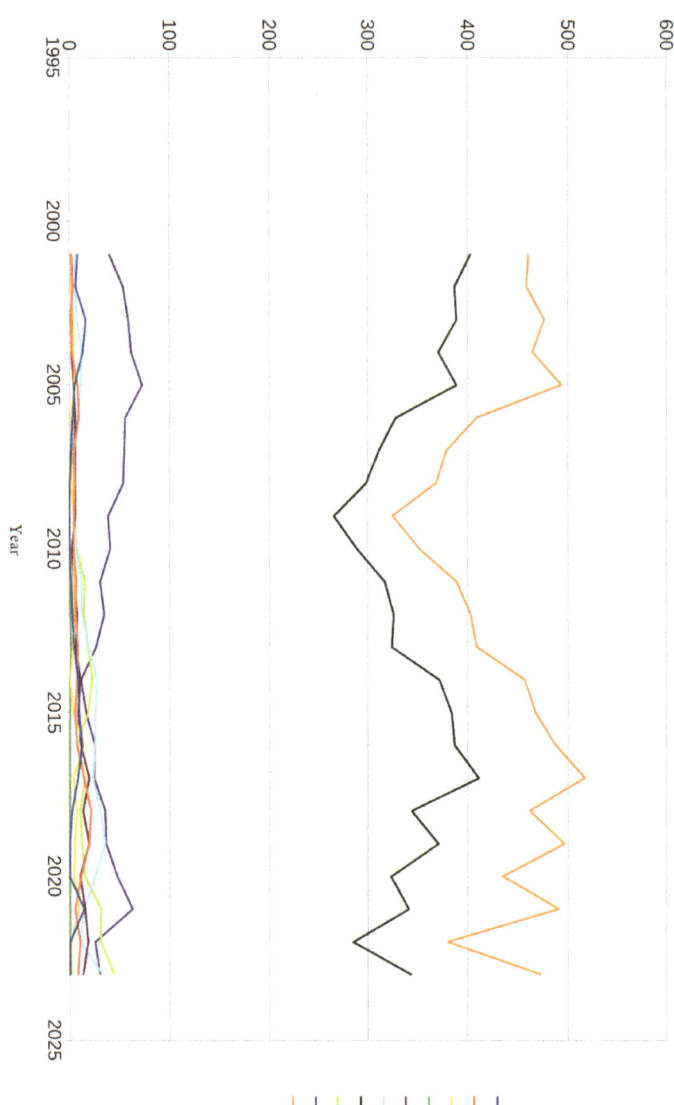

Enrollment

600

500

400

300

200

100

0
1995   2000   2005   2010   2015   2020   2025

Year

— Nonresident alien
— Black, non-Hispanic
— American Indian or Alaska Native
— Native Hawaiian or Other Pacific
— Asian or Pacific Islander
— Hispanic
— White, non-Hispanic
— Two or More Races
— Race/ethnicity unknown
— Total

Person Coefficient: 0.1777

Regression: 1.386x - 2352

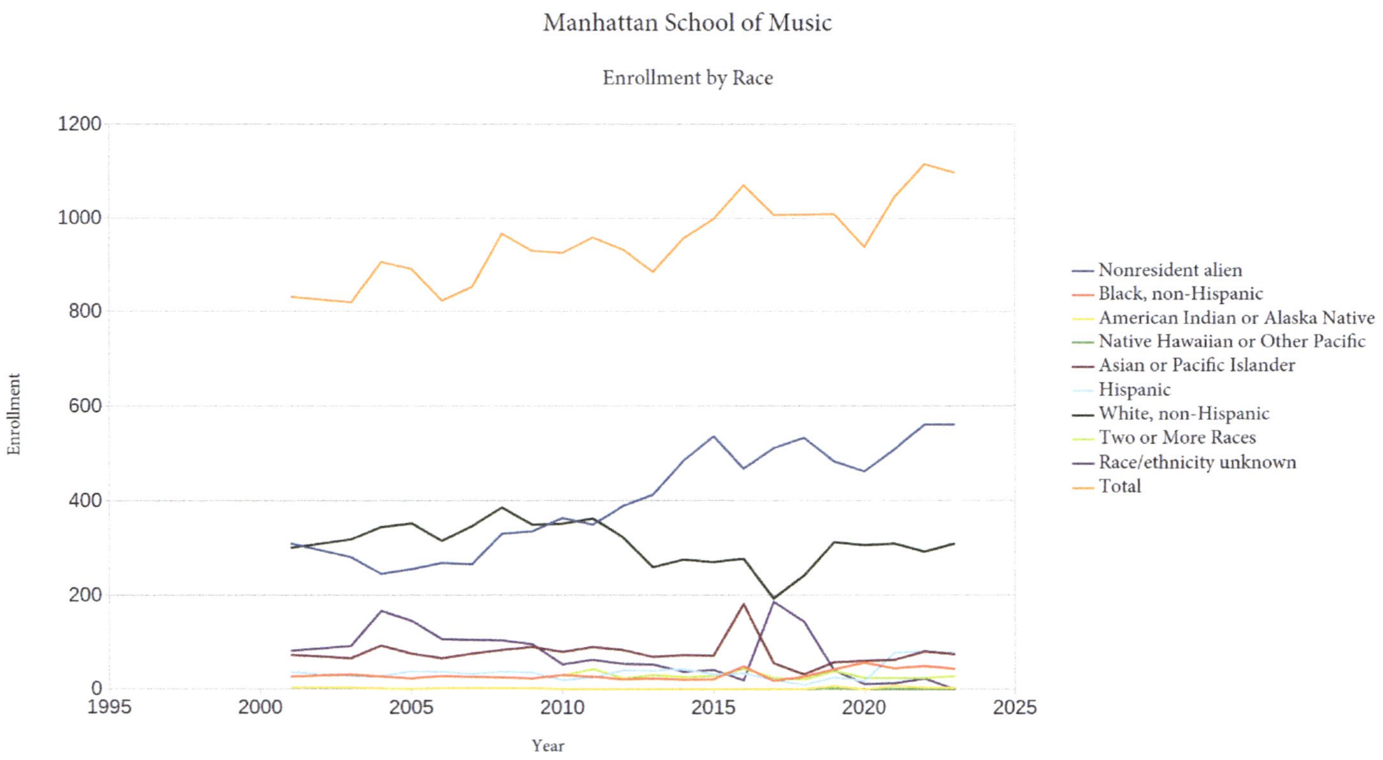
Manhattan School of Music
Enrollment by Race
Enrollment
1200
1000
800
600
400
200
0
1995
2000
2005
2010
2015
2020
2025
Year
Nonresident alien
Black, non-Hispanic
American Indian or Alaska Native
Native Hawaiian or Other Pacific
Asian or Pacific Islander
Hispanic
White, non-Hispanic
Two or More Races
Race/ethnicity unknown
Total

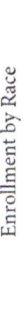

Person Coefficient: 0.8624

Regression: 19.47x - 38267

Maryland Institute College of Art

Enrollment by Race

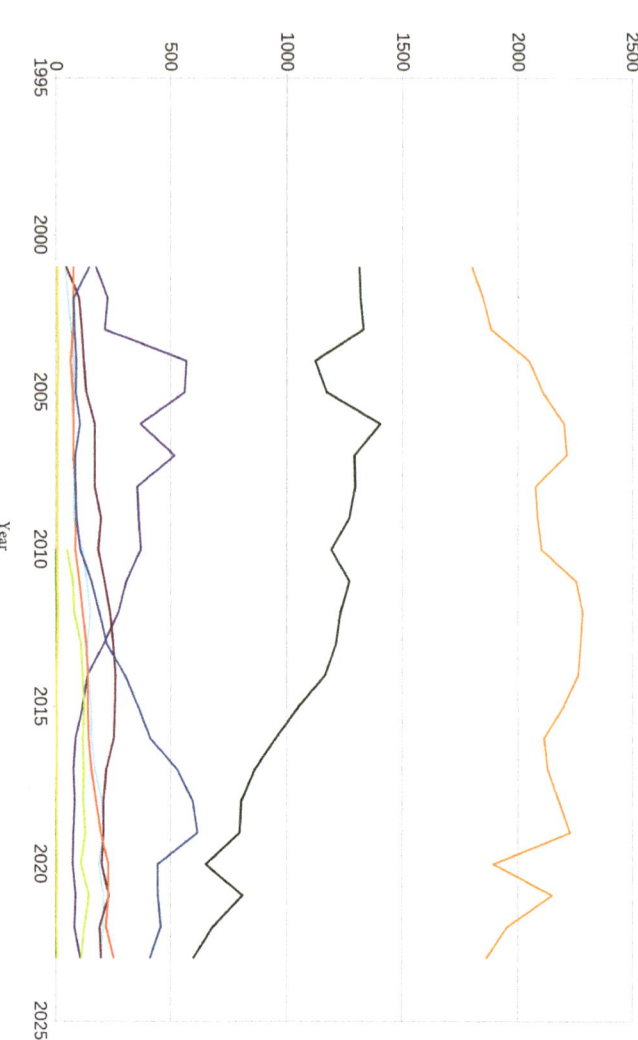

Enrollment

2500

2000

1500

1000

500

0
1995   2000   2005   2010   2015   2020   2025

Year

— Nonresident alien
— Black, non-Hispanic
— American Indian or Alaska Native
— Native Hawaiian or Other Pacific
— Asian or Pacific Islander
— Hispanic
— White, non-Hispanic
— Two or More Races
— Race/ethnicity unknown
— Total

Person Coefficient: 0.1775

Regression: 3.938x - 5831

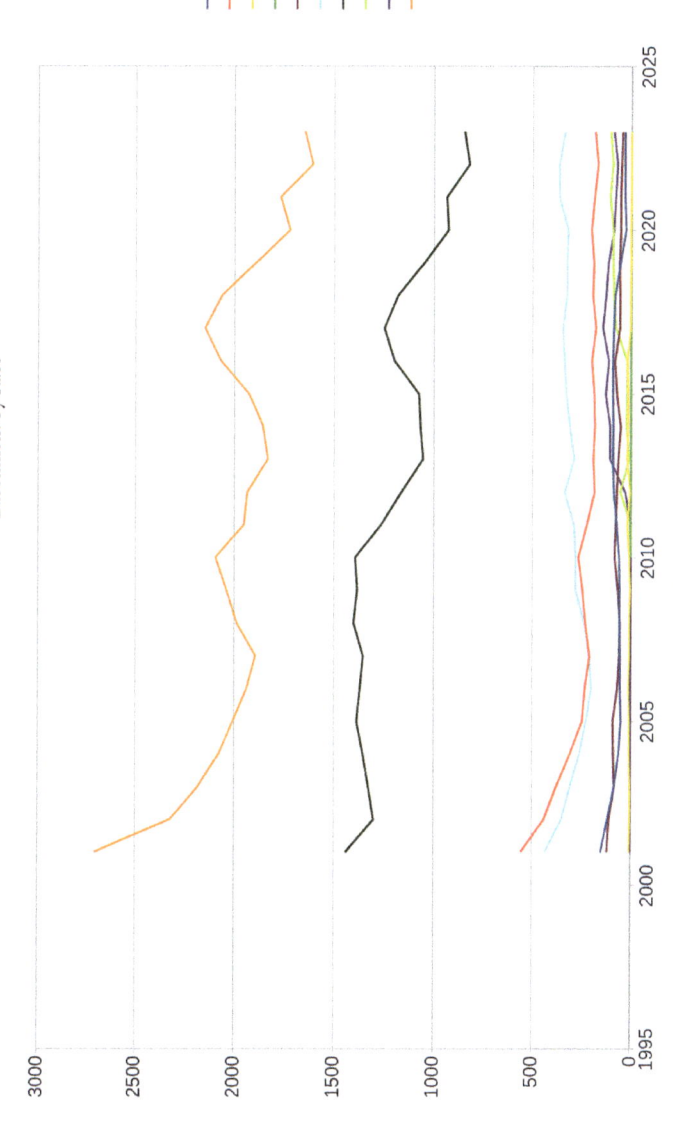

Marymount Manhattan College

Enrollment by Race

— Nonresident alien
— Black, non-Hispanic
— American Indian or Alaska Native
— Native Hawaiian or Other Pacific
— Asian or Pacific Islander
— Hispanic
— White, non-Hispanic
— Two or More Races
— Race/ethnicity unknown
— Total

Person Coefficient: -0.7175

Regression: -24.45*X + 51177

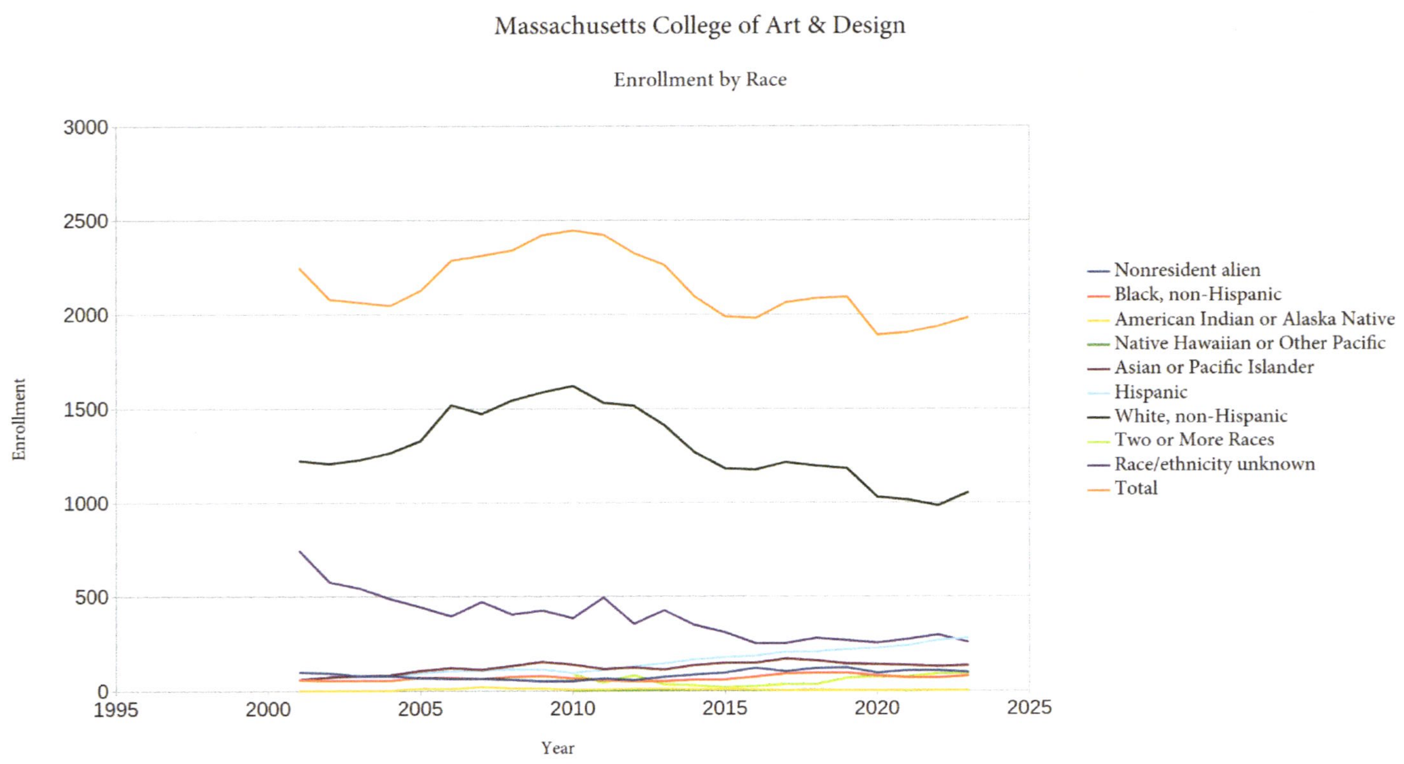

Massachusetts College of Art & Design

Enrollment by Race

Enrollment

3000
2500
2000
1500
1000
500
0

1995 2000 2005 2010 2015 2020 2025

Year

Legend:
— Nonresident alien
— Black, non-Hispanic
— American Indian or Alaska Native
— Native Hawaiian or Other Pacific
— Asian or Pacific Islander
— Hispanic
— White, non-Hispanic
— Two or More Races
— Race/ethnicity unknown
— Total

Person Coefficient: -0.5107

Regression: -13.05x + 28406

Minneapolis College of Art and Design

Enrollment by Race

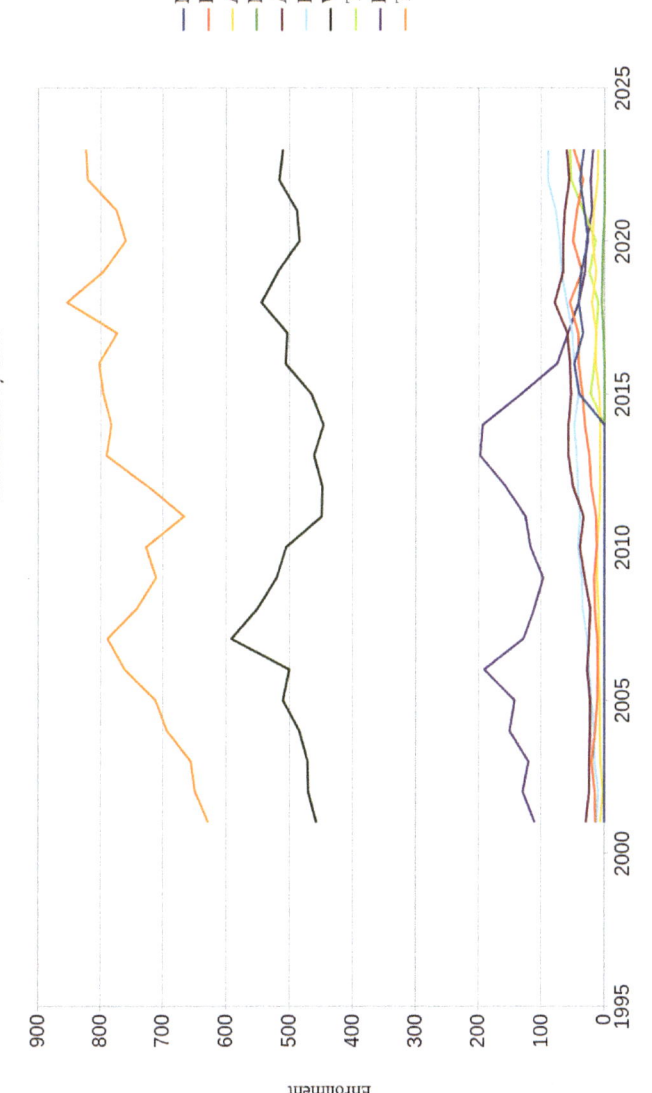

- Nonresident alien
- Black, non-Hispanic
- American Indian or Alaska Native
- Native Hawaiian or Other Pacific
- Asian or Pacific Islander
- Hispanic
- White, non-Hispanic
- Two or More Races
- Race/ethnicity unknown
- Total

Person Coefficient: 0.7986

Regression: 7.199*X - 13734

Montserrat College of Art

Enrollment of Race

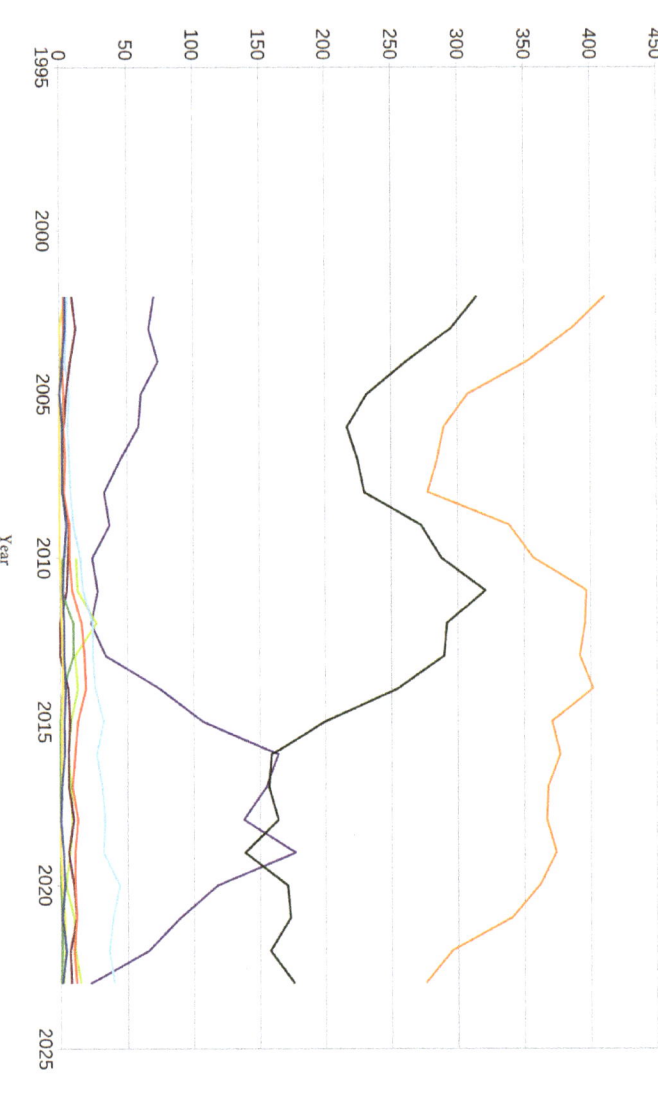

Enrollment

450
400
350
300
250
200
150
100
50
0

1995   2000   2005   2010   2015   2020   2025

Year

Nonresident alien
Black, non-Hispanic
American Indian or Alaska Native
Native Hawaiian or Other Pacific
Asian or Pacific Islander
Hispanic
White, non-Hispanic
Two or More Races
Race/ethnicity unknown
Total

Person Coefficient: -0.06811

Regression: -0.4568*X + 1271

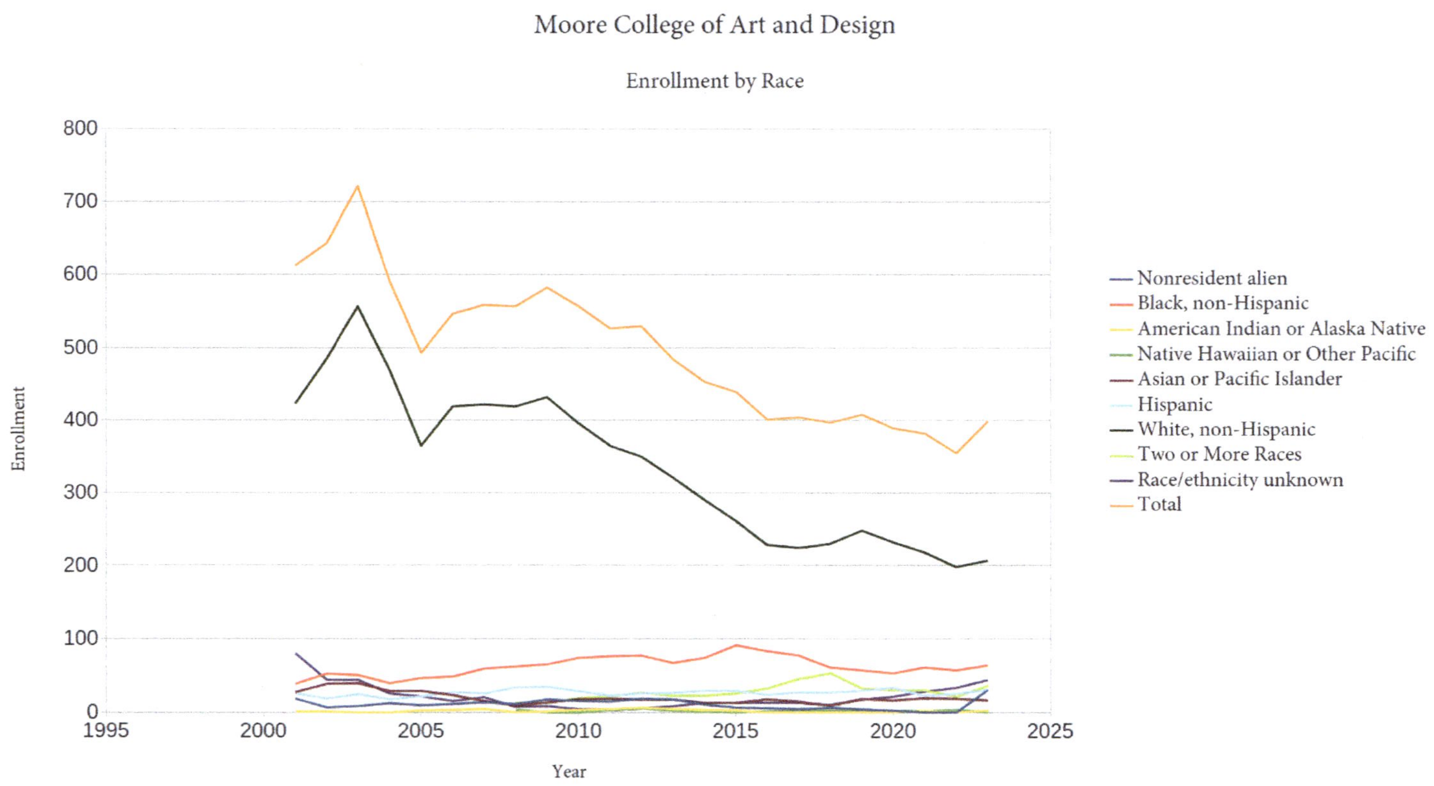

Moore College of Art and Design

Enrollment by Race

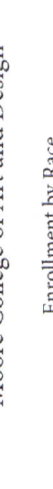

Legend:
- Nonresident alien
- Black, non-Hispanic
- American Indian or Alaska Native
- Native Hawaiian or Other Pacific
- Asian or Pacific Islander
- Hispanic
- White, non-Hispanic
- Two or More Races
- Race/ethnicity unknown
- Total

Y-axis: Enrollment (0, 100, 200, 300, 400, 500, 600, 700, 800)

X-axis: Year (1995, 2000, 2005, 2010, 2015, 2020, 2025)

Person Coefficient: -0.9187

Regression: -13.29x + 27229

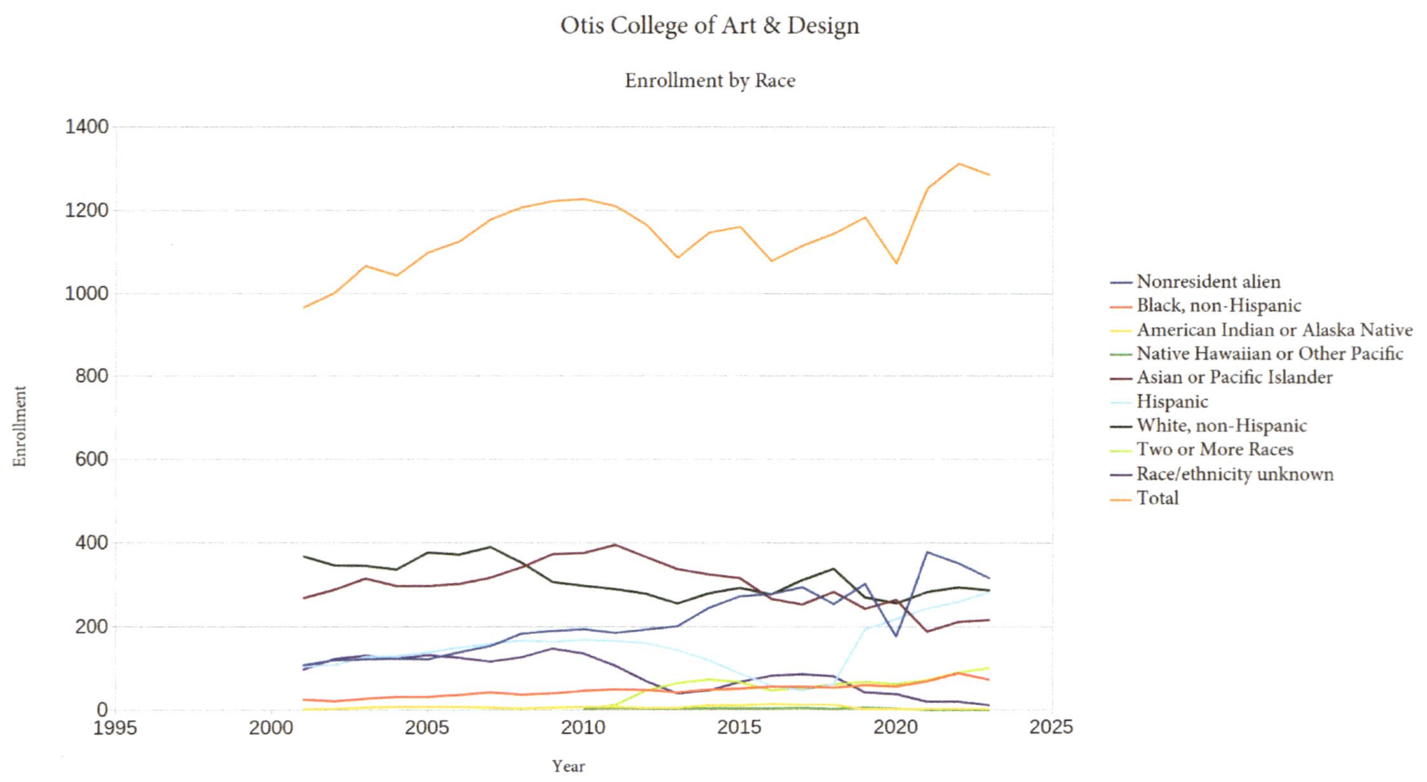

Otis College of Art & Design

Enrollment by Race

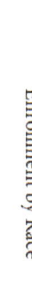

Enrollment

1400
1200
1000
800
600
400
200
0

1995   2000   2005   2010   2015   2020   2025

Year

— Nonresident alien
— Black, non-Hispanic
— American Indian or Alaska Native
— Native Hawaiian or Other Pacific
— Asian or Pacific Islander
— Hispanic
— White, non-Hispanic
— Two or More Races
— Race/ethnicity unknown
— Total

Person Coefficient: 0.6094

Regression: 7.860x - 14669

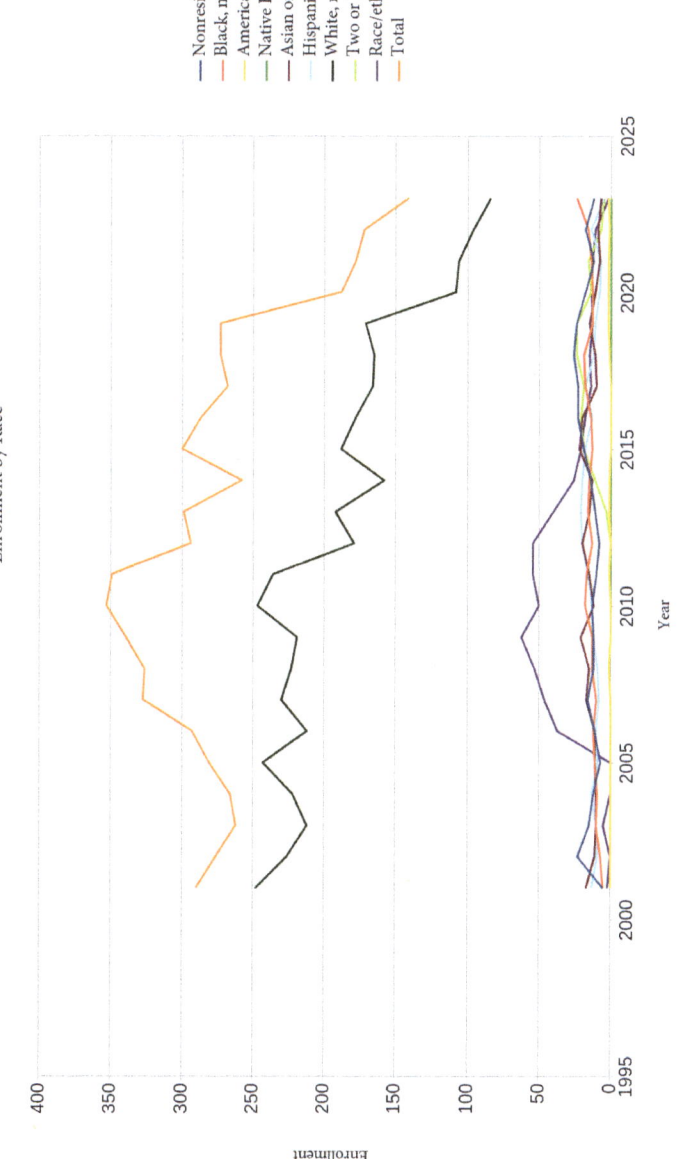

Pennsylvania Academy of the Fine Arts

Enrollment by Race

Legend:
- Nonresident alien
- Black, non-Hispanic
- American Indian or Alaska Native
- Native Hawaiian or Other Pacific
- Asian or Pacific Islander
- Hispanic
- White, non-Hispanic
- Two or More Races
- Race/ethnicity unknown
- Total

Person Coefficient: -0.602

Regression: -4.983x + 10300

Pennsylvania College of Art & Design

Enrollment by Race

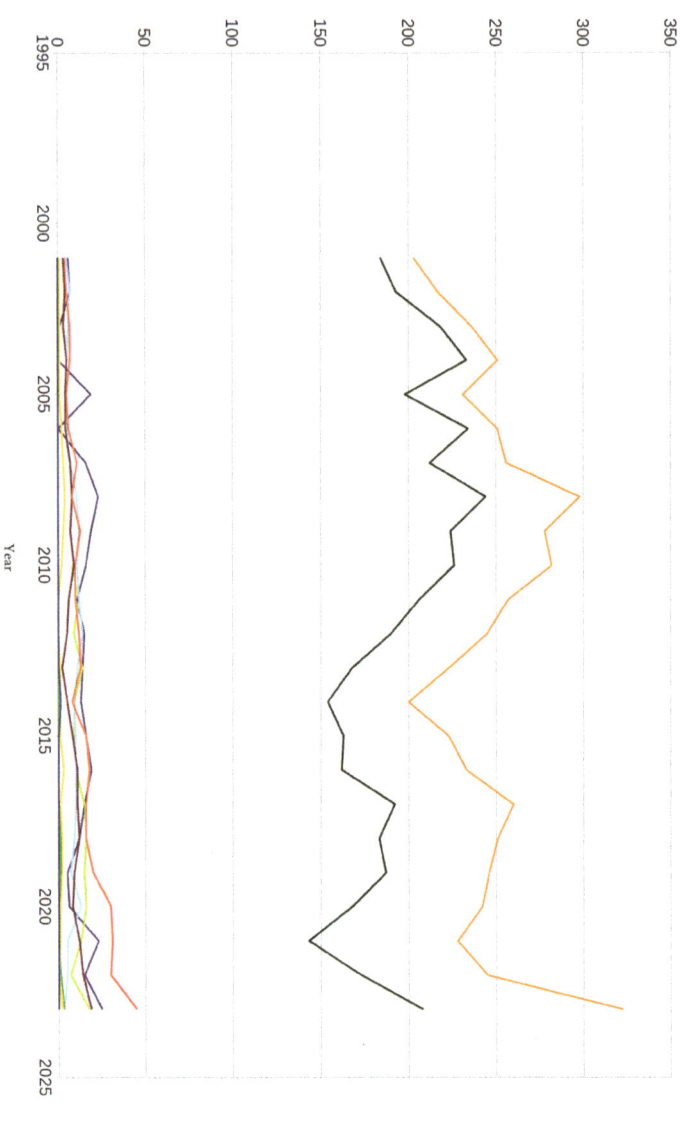

Enrollment

Year

Legend:
- Nonresident alien
- Black, non-Hispanic
- American Indian or Alaska Native
- Native Hawaiian or Other Pacific
- Asian or Pacific Islander
- Hispanic
- White, non-Hispanic
- Two or More Races
- Race/ethnicity unknown
- Total

Person Coefficient: 0.2237

Regression: 0.9466x - 1658

Point Park University

Enrollment by Race

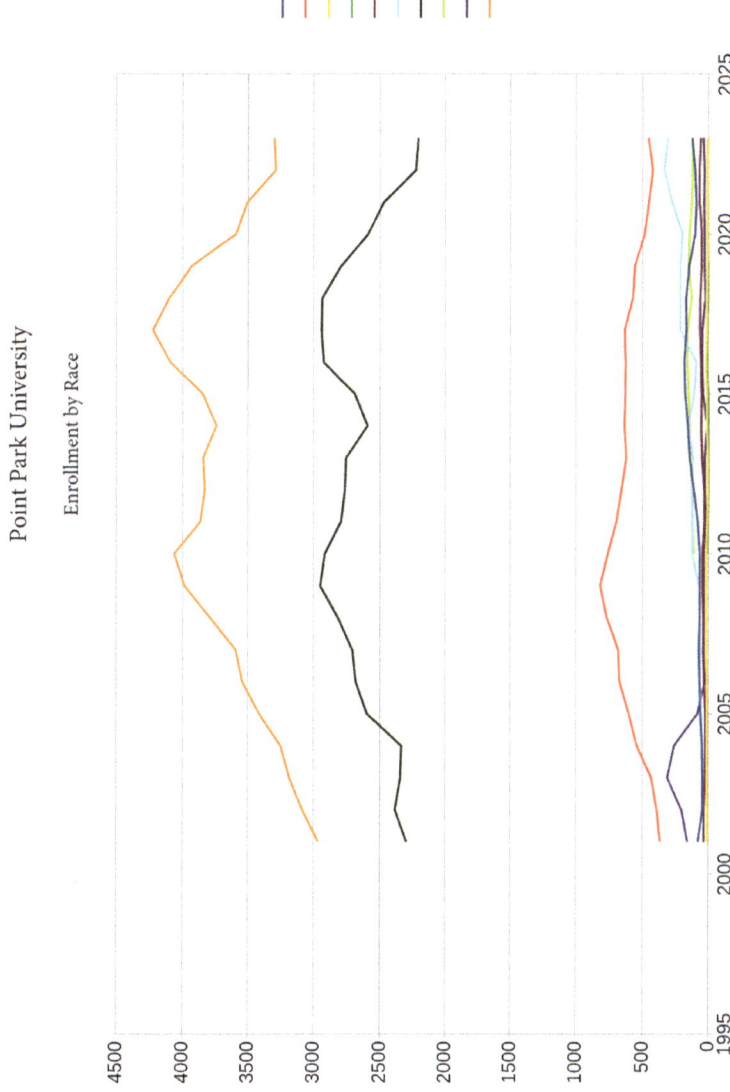

Person Coefficient: 0.4073

Regression: 21.35x - 39302

Pratt Institute-Main

Enrollment by Race

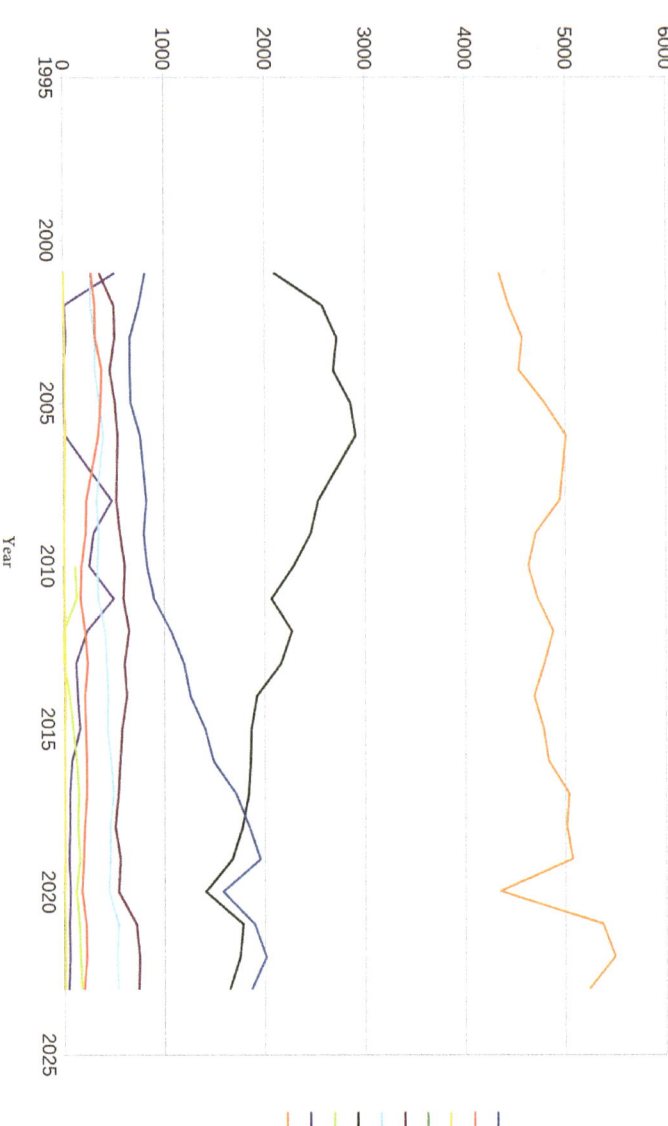

Person Coefficient: 0.6629

Regression: 52.45x - 100905

Legend:
— Nonresident alien
— Black, non-Hispanic
— American Indian or Alaska Native
— Native Hawaiian or Other Pacific
— Asian or Pacific Islander
— Hispanic
— White, non-Hispanic
— Two or More Races
— Race/ethnicity unknown
— Total

Rhode Island School of Design

Enrollment by Race

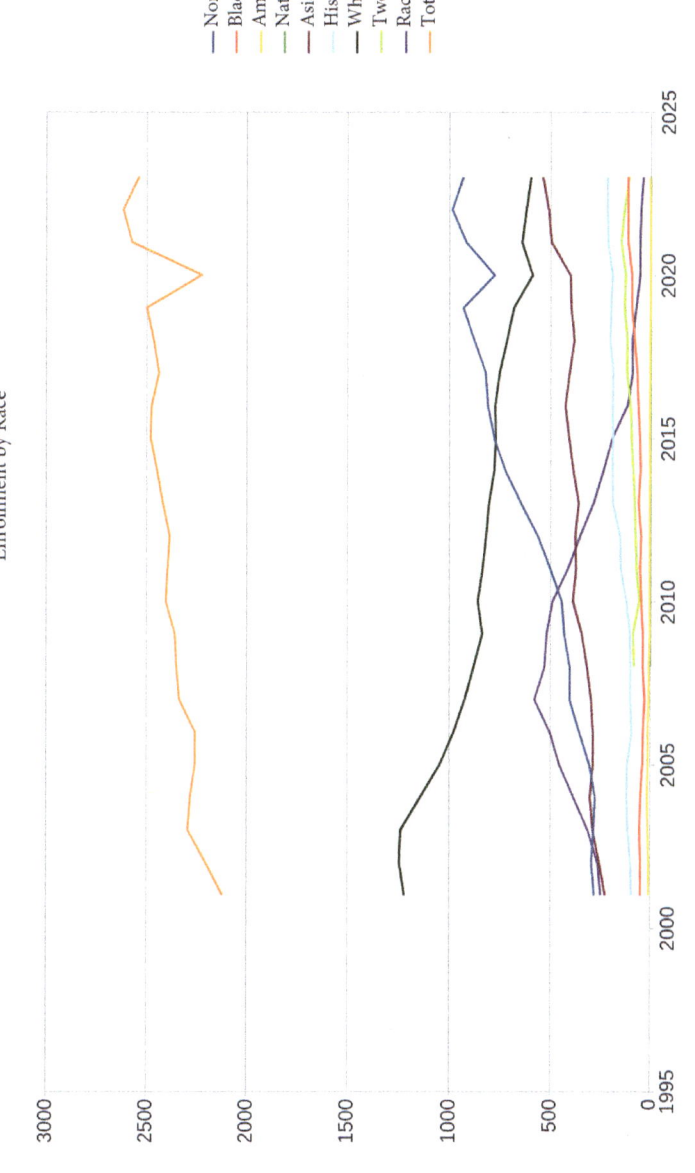

Person Coefficient: 0.8192

Regression: 15.14x - 28085

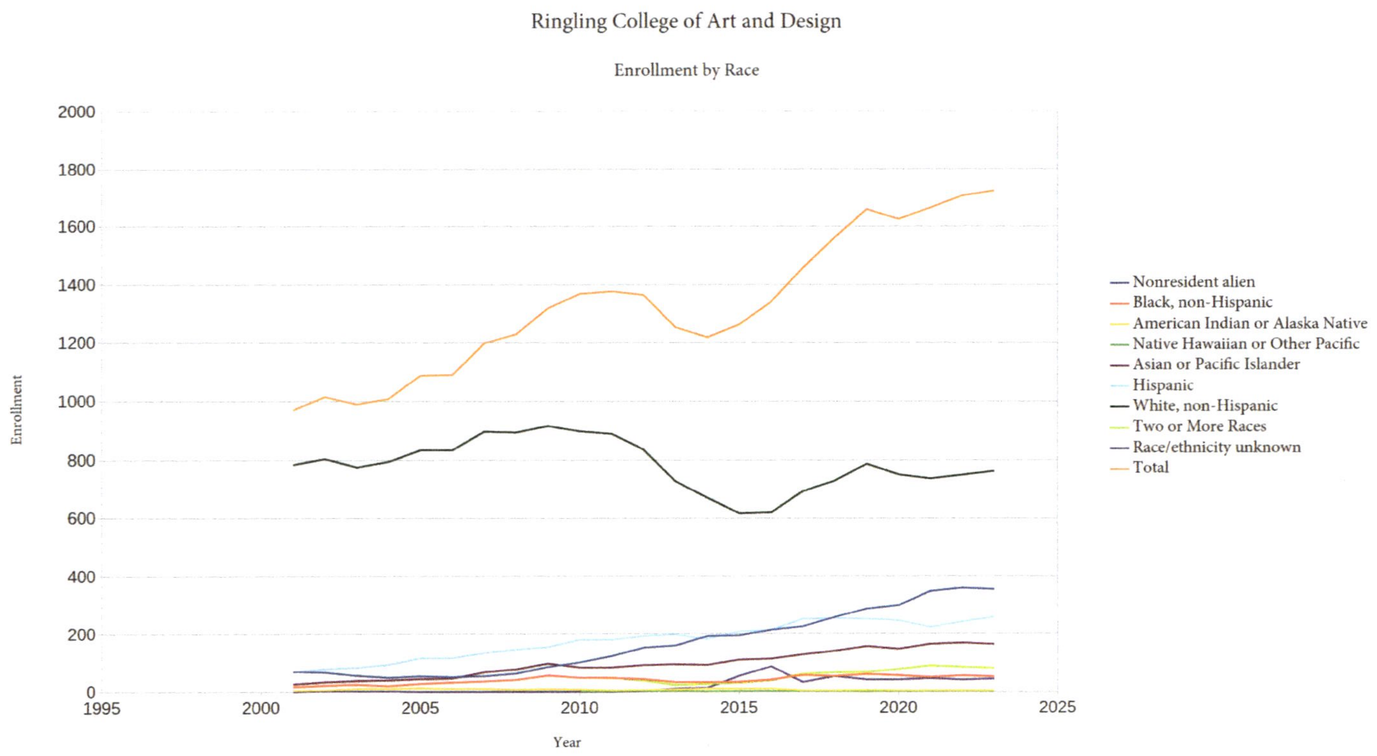
Ringling College of Art and Design
Enrollment by Race
Enrollment
2000
1800
1600
1400
1200
1000
800
600
400
200
0
1995
2000
2005
2010
2015
2020
2025
Year
Nonresident alien
Black, non-Hispanic
American Indian or Alaska Native
Native Hawaiian or Other Pacific
Asian or Pacific Islander
Hispanic
White, non-Hispanic
Two or More Races
Race/ethnicity unknown
Total

Person Coefficient: 0.9452

Regression: 33.73x - 66536

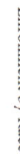

Savannah College of Art and Design

Enrollment by Race

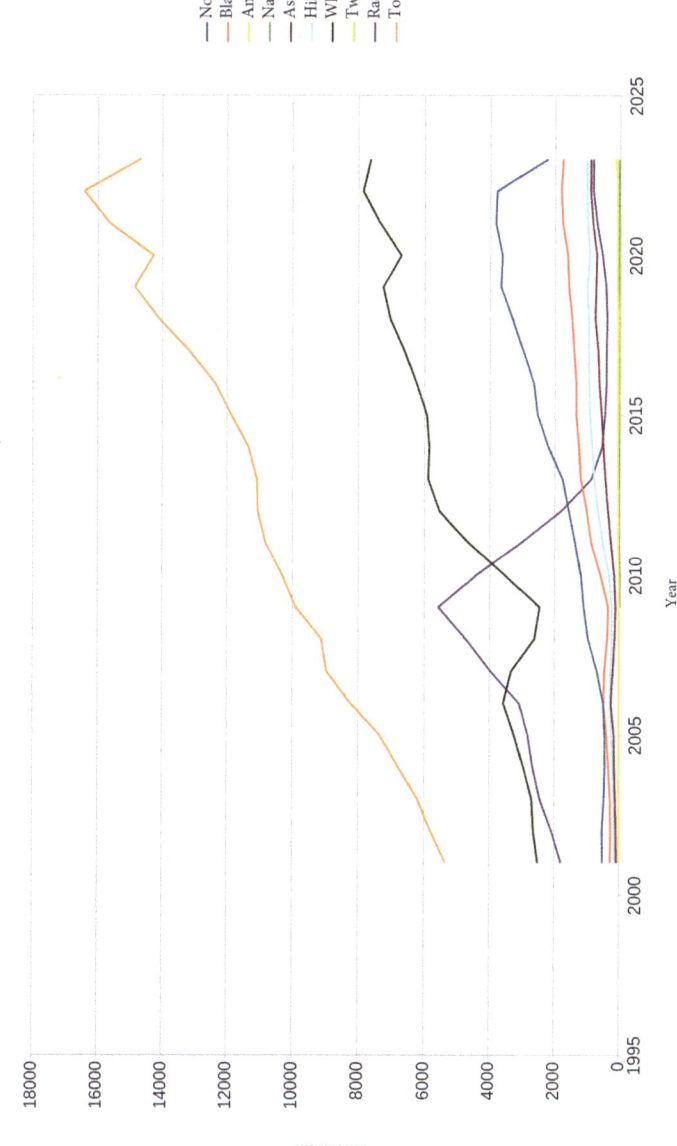

Legend:
- Nonresident alien
- Black, non-Hispanic
- American Indian or Alaska Native
- Native Hawaiian or Other Pacific
- Asian or Pacific Islander
- Hispanic
- White, non-Hispanic
- Two or More Races
- Race/ethnicity unknown
- Total

X-axis: Year (1995, 2000, 2005, 2010, 2015, 2020, 2025)

Y-axis: Enrollment (0, 2000, 4000, 6000, 8000, 10000, 12000, 14000, 16000, 18000)

Person Coefficient: 0.988

Regression: 477.5x - 949817

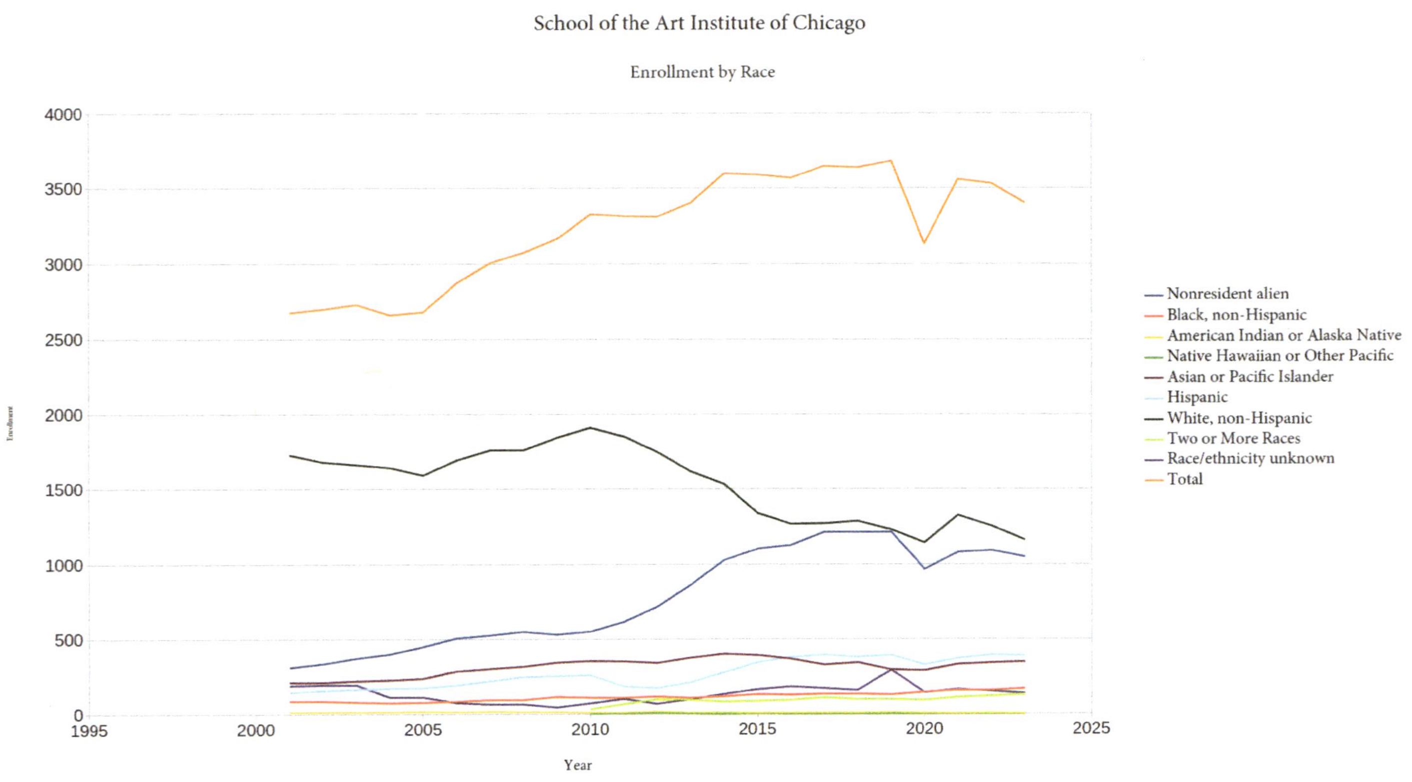
School of the Art Institute of Chicago
Enrollment by Race
Enrollment
4000
3500
3000
2500
2000
1500
1000
500
0
1995
2000
2005
2010
2015
2020
2025
Year
Nonresident alien
Black, non-Hispanic
American Indian or Alaska Native
Native Hawaiian or Other Pacific
Asian or Pacific Islander
Hispanic
White, non-Hispanic
Two or More Races
Race/ethnicity unknown
Total

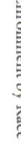

Person Coefficient: 0.8551

Regression: 45.75x - 88826

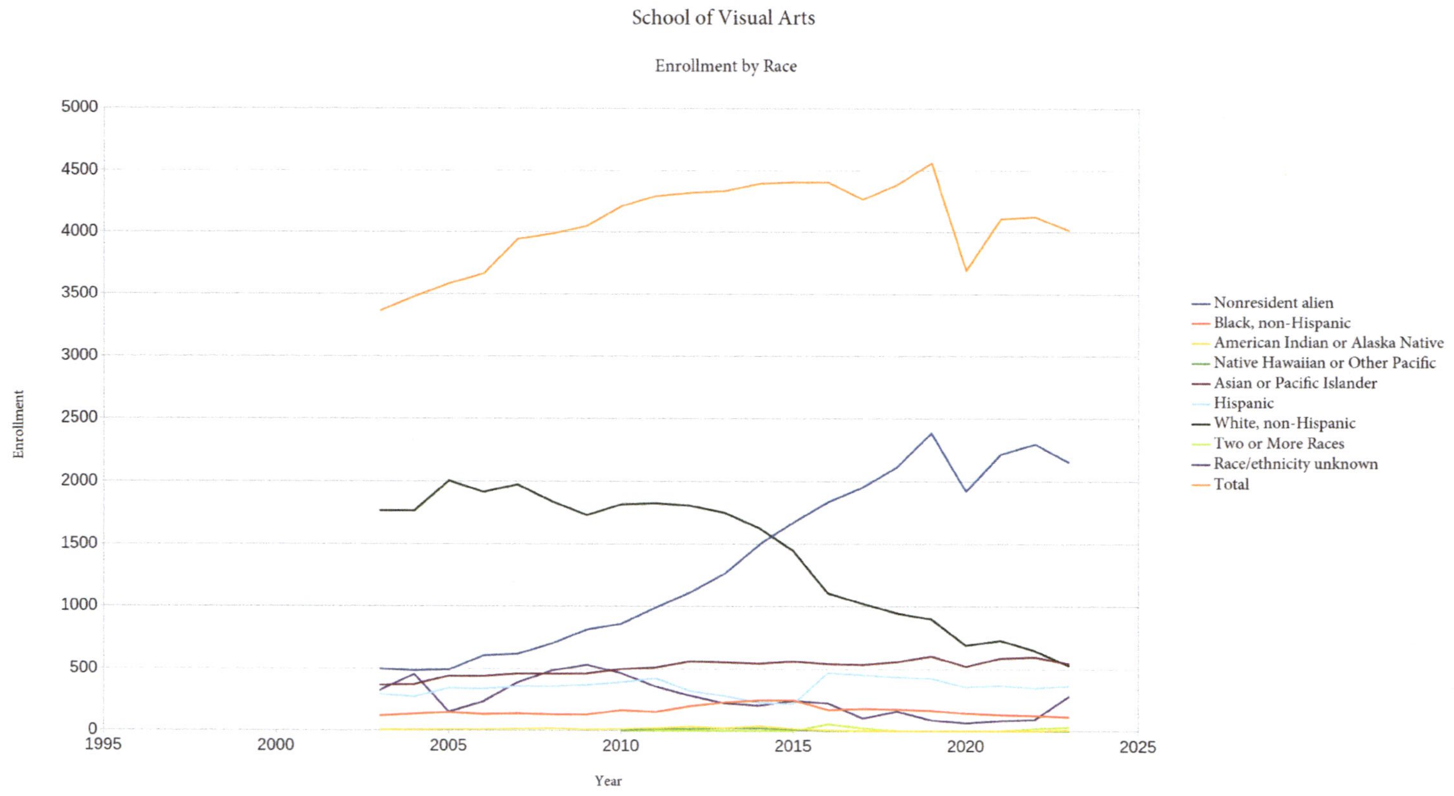

School of Visual Arts

Enrollment by Race

Legend:
- Nonresident alien
- Black, non-Hispanic
- American Indian or Alaska Native
- Native Hawaiian or Other Pacific
- Asian or Pacific Islander
- Hispanic
- White, non-Hispanic
- Two or More Races
- Race/ethnicity unknown
- Total

X-axis: Year (1995, 2000, 2005, 2010, 2015, 2020, 2025)

Y-axis: Enrollment (0, 500, 1000, 1500, 2000, 2500, 3000, 3500, 4000, 4500, 5000)

Person Coefficient: 0.5701

Regression: 31.53x - 59398

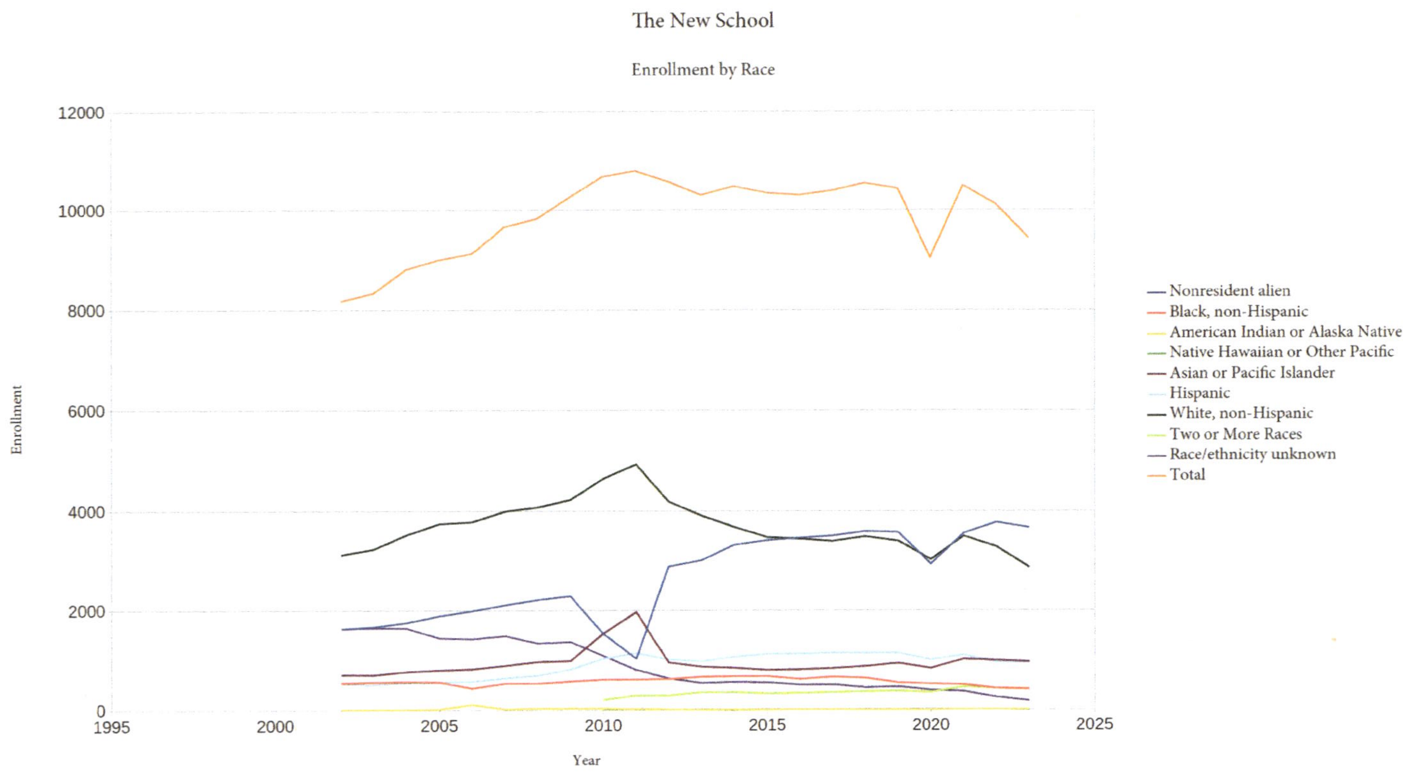

The New School

Enrollment by Race

Enrollment

1200	
1000	
8000	
6000	
4000	
2000	
0	

1995 2000 2005 2010 2015 2020 2025

Year

— Nonresident alien
— Black, non-Hispanic
— American Indian or Alaska Native
— Native Hawaiian or Other Pacific
— Asian or Pacific Islander
— Hispanic
— White, non-Hispanic
— Two or More Races
— Race/ethnicity unknown
— Total

Person Coefficient: 0.5487

Regression: 66.90x - 124770

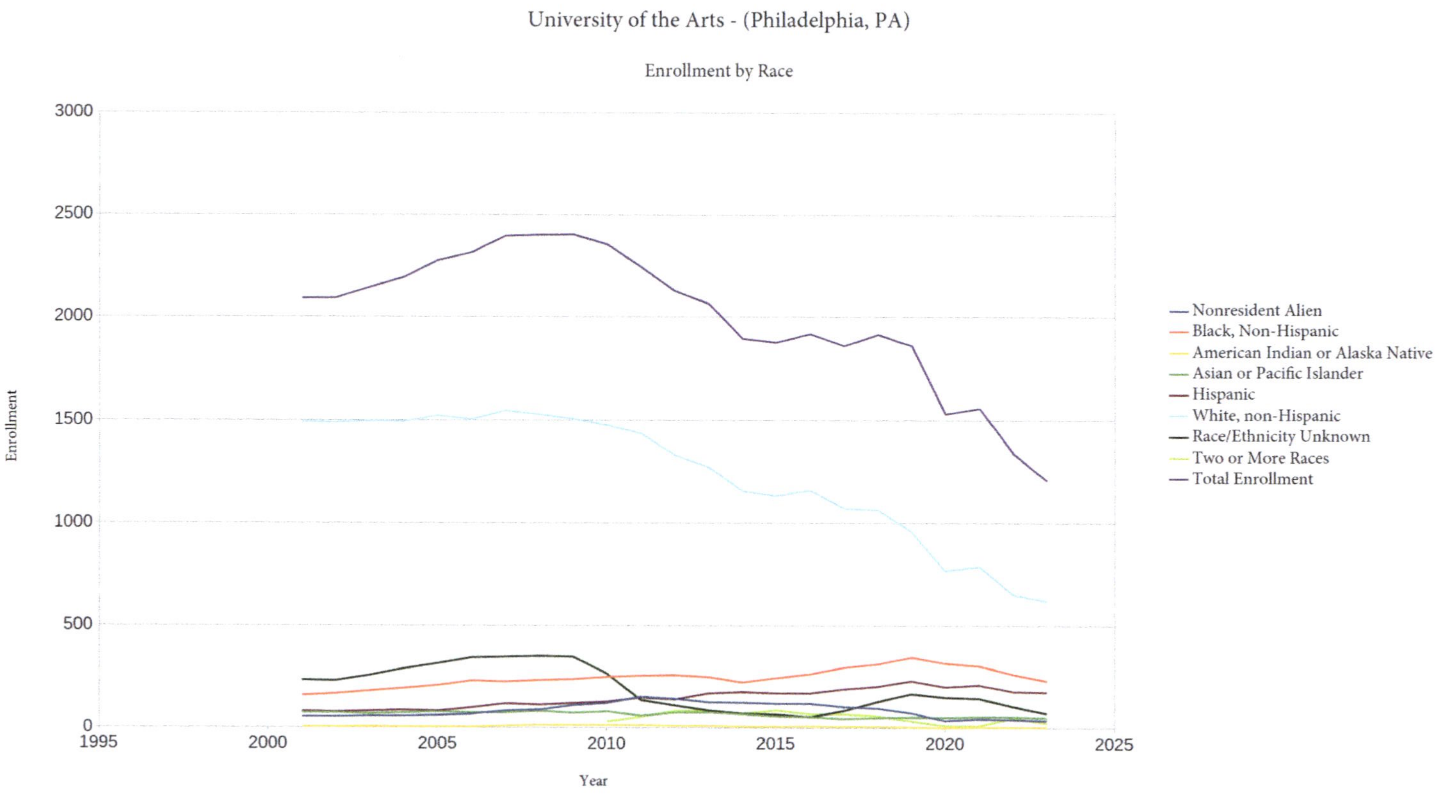
University of the Arts - (Philadelphia, PA)
Enrollment by Race
3000
2500
2000
1500
1000
500
0
Enrollment
1995
2000
2005
2010
2015
2020
2025
Year
Nonresident Alien
Black, Non-Hispanic
American Indian or Alaska Native
Asian or Pacific Islander
Hispanic
White, non-Hispanic
Race/Ethnicity Unknown
Two or More Races
Total Enrollment

Person Coefficient: -0.8039

Regression: -39.95x + 82379

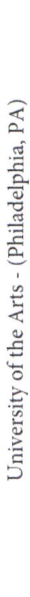

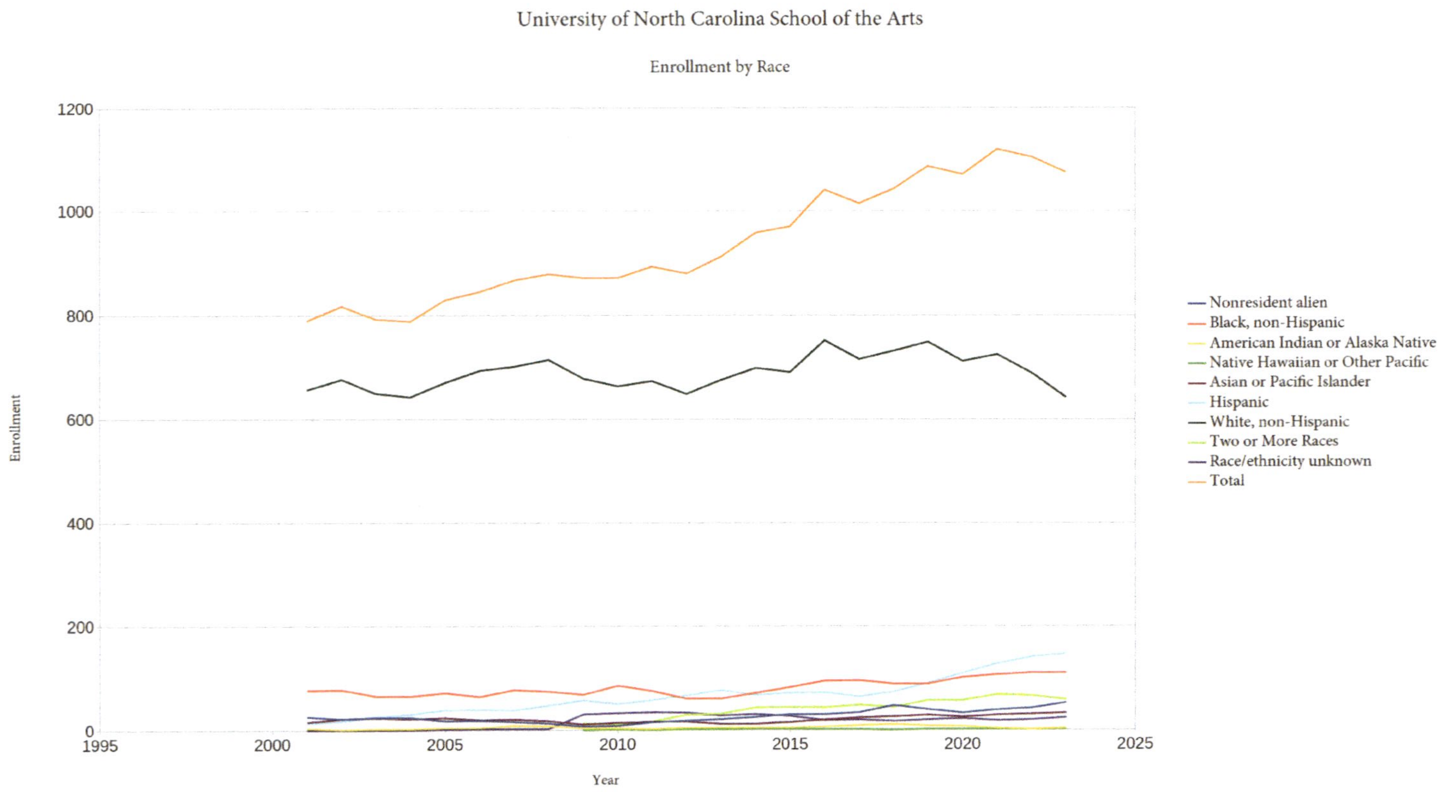

University of North Carolina School of the Arts

Enrollment by Race

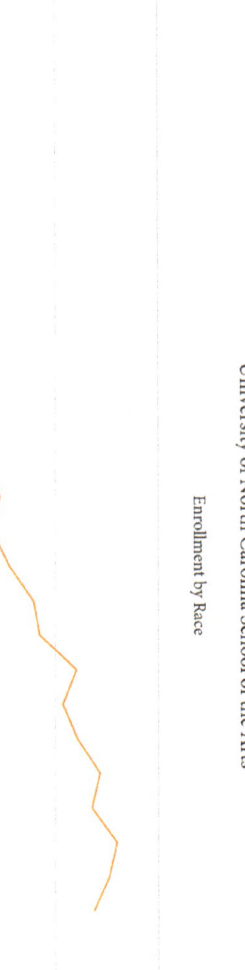

Enrollment

1200
1000
800
600
400
200
0

1995   2000   2005   2010   2015   2020   2025

Year

— Nonresident alien
— Black, non-Hispanic
— American Indian or Alaska Native
— Native Hawaiian or Other Pacific
— Asian or Pacific Islander
— Hispanic
— White, non-Hispanic
— Two or More Races
— Race/ethnicity unknown
— Total

Person Coefficient: 0.9693

Regression: 15.86x - 30972

Appendix F: Foundation Grants to UARTS – (2016-2023)

Year/ Foundation	Neubauer Family Foundation	William Penn Foundation	Hamilton Family Foundation	Wyncote Foundation	William B. Dietrich Foundation
2016	0	0	43,000	0	0
2017	0	0	17,500	50,000	0
2018	23,125	0	13,000	50,000	0
2019	0	0	0	0	0
2020	35,867	0	0	100,000	625,428
2021	7,142	65,000	0	0	0
2022	0	50,000	0	0	0
2023	0	36,745	0	0	0

Year/ Foundation	Presser Foundation	Greenfield Foundation	The W W Smith Charitable Trust	Zeldin Family Foundation	T/W Mary F Lindback Residuary Tr Nect
2016	4,000	0	0	5,310	2,000
2017	4,000	0	0	9,620	0
2018	104,000	100,000	78,000	0	0
2019	104,000	100,000	0	3,000	6,500
2020	104,000	100,000	73,000	10,000	2,500
2021	104,000	100,000	108,000	NA	4,000
2022	104,000	0	91,000	0	3,500
2023	3,000	0	0	0	3,500

Year/ Foundation	The Charlotte Cushman Foundation	Howard A & Martha R Wolf Fund	Richard And Jean Coyne Family Foundation	Jeff & Jenifer Westphal Foundation	Henry Nias Foundation
2016	2,500	0	18,000	0	0
2017	2,500	12,500	19,000	0	0
2018	2,500	12,500	19,000	0	0
2019	2,500	12,500	19,000	0	0
2020	2,500	6,250	19,000	20,000	0
2021	2,500	6,250	19,000	30,000	15,000
2022	2,500	12,000	24,000	10,000	0
2023	2,500	12,000	24,000	0	0

Sources

UARTS: Granting Organization or University?

Schedule I (External Grants & Contributions)

- • 2009 – UARTS Form 990, Schedule I – https://projects.propublica.org/nonprofits/display_990/231639911/2011_04_EO%2F23-1639911_990_201006
- • 2010 – UARTS Form 990, Schedule I – https://projects.propublica.org/nonprofits/display_990/231639911/2012_06_EO%2F23-1639911_990_201106
- • 2011 – UARTS Form 990, Schedule I – https://projects.propublica.org/nonprofits/display_990/231639911/2013_07_EO%2F23-1639911_990_201206
- • 2012 – UARTS Form 990, Schedule I – https://projects.propublica.org/nonprofits/organizations/231639911/201411329349302366/full
- • 2013 – UARTS Form 990, Schedule I – https://projects.propublica.org/nonprofits/organizations/231639911/201510909349300771/full
- • 2014 – UARTS Form 990, Schedule I – https://projects.propublica.org/nonprofits/organizations/231639911/201621189349300642/full
- • 2015 – UARTS Form 990, Schedule I – https://projects.propublica.org/nonprofits/organizations/231639911/201711359349309761/full
- • 2016 – UARTS Form 990, Schedule I – https://projects.propublica.org/nonprofits/organizations/231639911/201831349349303133/full
- • 2017 – UARTS Form 990, Part VII – https://projects.propublica.org/nonprofits/organizations/231639911/201941349349302784/full
- • 2018 – UARTS Form 990, Part VII – https://projects.propublica.org/nonprofits/organizations/231639911/202041359349302699/full
- • 2019 – UARTS Form 990, Part VII – https://projects.propublica.org/nonprofits/organizations/231639911/202111049349301466/full
- • 2020 – UARTS Form 990, Part VII – https://projects.propublica.org/nonprofits/organizations/231639911/202221299349301942/full
- • 2021 – UARTS Form 990, Part VII – https://projects.propublica.org/nonprofits/organizations/231639911/202311039349301001/full
- • 2022 – UARTS Form 990, Part VII – https://projects.propublica.org/nonprofits/organizations/231639911/202401169349300700/full

The Curious Case of Paula Marincola & Her Relationship with UARTS

Schedule A, Part I

- 2000 – UARTS Form 990, Schedule A, Part I – https://projects.propublica.org/nonprofits/display_990/231639911/2002_07_EO%2F23-1639911_990_200106
- 2002 – UARTS Form 990, Schedule A, Part I – https://projects.propublica.org/nonprofits/display_990/231639911/2004_07_EO%2F23-1639911_990_200306
- 2003 – UARTS Form 990, Schedule A, Part I – [link not available]

Part VII (Compensation of Officers, Directors, Trustees, Key Employees, etc.)

- 2008 – UARTS Form 990, Part VII – https://projects.propublica.org/nonprofits/display_990/231639911/2010_03_EO%2F23-1639911_990_200906
- 2009 – UARTS Form 990, Part VII – https://projects.propublica.org/nonprofits/display_990/231639911/2011_04_EO%2F23-1639911_990_201006
- 2010 – UARTS Form 990, Part VII – https://projects.propublica.org/nonprofits/display_990/231639911/2012_06_EO%2F23-1639911_990_201106
- 2011 – UARTS Form 990, Part VII – https://projects.propublica.org/nonprofits/display_990/231639911/2013_07_EO%2F23-1639911_990_201206
- 2012 – UARTS Form 990, Part VII – https://projects.propublica.org/nonprofits/organizations/231639911/201411329349302366/full
- 2013 – UARTS Form 990, Part VII – https://projects.propublica.org/nonprofits/organizations/231639911/201510909349300771/full
- 2014 – UARTS Form 990, Part VII – https://projects.propublica.org/nonprofits/organizations/231639911/201621189349300642/full
- 2015 – UARTS Form 990, Part VII – https://projects.propublica.org/nonprofits/organizations/231639911/201711359349309761/full
- 2016 – UARTS Form 990, Part VII – https://projects.propublica.org/nonprofits/organizations/231639911/201831349349303133/full
- 2017 – UARTS Form 990, Part VII – https://projects.propublica.org/nonprofits/organizations/231639911/201941349349302784/full
- 2018 – UARTS Form 990, Part VII – https://projects.propublica.org/nonprofits/organizations/231639911/202041359349302699/full
- 2019 – UARTS Form 990, Part VII – https://projects.propublica.org/nonprofits/organizations/231639911/202111049349301466/full
- 2020 – UARTS Form 990, Part VII – https://projects.propublica.org/nonprofits/organizations/231639911/202221299349301942/full
- 2021 – UARTS Form 990, Part VII – https://projects.propublica.org/nonprofits/organizations/231639911/202311039349301001/full
- 2022 – UARTS Form 990, Part VII – https://projects.propublica.org/nonprofits/organizations/231639911/202401169349300700/full

Pew Charitable Trust Donations to UARTS

Form 990 – Schedule I / Relevant Pages

- 2003 – Form 990, p. 19 – https://projects.propublica.org/nonprofits/display_990/562307147/2004_11_EO%2F56-2307147_990_200406
- 2004 – Form 990, pp. 33–34 – https://projects.propublica.org/nonprofits/display_990/562307147/2006_03_EO%2F56-2307147_990_200506
- 2005 – Form 990, p. 19 – https://projects.propublica.org/nonprofits/display_990/562307147/2008_01_EO%2F56-2307147_990_200606
- 2006 – Form 990, p. 22 – https://projects.propublica.org/nonprofits/display_990/562307147/2008_11_EO%2F56-2307147_990_200706
- 2007 – Form 990, pp. 22–42 – https://projects.propublica.org/nonprofits/display_990/562307147/2009_05_EO%2F56-2307147_990_200806
- 2008 – Form 990, Schedule I, Part II – https://projects.propublica.org/nonprofits/display_990/562307147/2010_05_EO%2F56-2307147_990_200906
- 2009 – Form 990, Schedule I, Part II – https://projects.propublica.org/nonprofits/display_990/562307147/2010_05_EO%2F56-2307147_990_200906
- 2010 – Form 990, Schedule I, Part II – https://projects.propublica.org/nonprofits/display_990/562307147/2012_05_EO%2F56-2307147_990_201106
- 2011 – Form 990, Schedule I, Part II – https://projects.propublica.org/nonprofits/display_990/562307147/2013_05_EO%2F56-2307147_990_201206
- 2012 – Form 990, Schedule I, Part II – https://projects.propublica.org/nonprofits/organizations/562307147/201420999349300532/full
- 2013 – Form 990, Schedule I, Part II – https://projects.propublica.org/nonprofits/organizations/562307147/201541069349300534/full
- 2014 – Form 990, Schedule I, Part II – https://projects.propublica.org/nonprofits/organizations/562307147/201601069349300625/full
- 2015 – Form 990, Schedule I, Part II – https://projects.propublica.org/nonprofits/organizations/562307147/201741009349300904/full
- 2016 – Form 990, Schedule I, Part II – https://projects.propublica.org/nonprofits/organizations/562307147/201841109349300819/full
- 2017 – Form 990, Schedule I, Part II – https://projects.propublica.org/nonprofits/organizations/562307147/201941069349300334/full
- 2018 – Form 990, Schedule I, Part II – https://projects.propublica.org/nonprofits/organizations/562307147/202021129349300042/full
- 2019 – Form 990, Schedule I, Part II – https://projects.propublica.org/nonprofits/organizations/562307147/202111059349301696/full
- 2020 – Form 990, Schedule I, Part II – https://projects.propublica.org/nonprofits/organizations/562307147/202221029349301247/full
- 2021 – Form 990, Schedule I, Part II – https://projects.propublica.org/nonprofits/organizations/562307147/202340889349301359/full
- 2022 – Form 990, Schedule I, Part II – https://projects.propublica.org/nonprofits/organizations/562307147/202440829349300334/full
- 2023 – Form 990, Schedule I, Part II – https://projects.propublica.org/nonprofits/organizations/562307147/202520859349300727/full

2009: The Year Enrollment Declines

University of the Arts

IPEDS - Enrollment by race/ethnicity and gender

- 2001 - https://nces.ed.gov/ipeds/reported-data/215105?year=2001&surveyNumber=2
- 2002 - https://nces.ed.gov/ipeds/reported-data/215105?year=2002&surveyNumber=2
- 2003 - https://nces.ed.gov/ipeds/reported-data/215105?year=2003&surveyNumber=2
- 2004 - https://nces.ed.gov/ipeds/reported-data/215105?year=2004&surveyNumber=2

IPEDS – Part A - Fall Enrollment - Summary by race/ethnicity

- 2005 - https://nces.ed.gov/ipeds/reported-data/215105?year=2005&surveyNumber=2
- 2006 - https://nces.ed.gov/ipeds/reported-data/215105?year=2006&surveyNumber=2
- 2007 - https://nces.ed.gov/ipeds/reported-data/215105?year=2007&surveyNumber=2
- 2008 - https://nces.ed.gov/ipeds/reported-data/215105?year=2008&surveyNumber=15

IPEDS – Part A - Fall Enrollment – Summary

- 2009 - https://nces.ed.gov/ipeds/reported-data/215105?year=2009&surveyNumber=15
- 2010 - https://nces.ed.gov/ipeds/reported-data/215105?year=2010&surveyNumber=15
- 2011 - https://nces.ed.gov/ipeds/reported-data/215105?year=2011&surveyNumber=15
- 2011 - https://nces.ed.gov/ipeds/reported-data/215105?year=2012&surveyNumber=15
- 2012 - https://nces.ed.gov/ipeds/reported-data/215105?year=2013&surveyNumber=15
- 2013 - https://nces.ed.gov/ipeds/reported-data/215105?year=2014&surveyNumber=15
- 2014 - https://nces.ed.gov/ipeds/reported-data/215105?year=2015&surveyNumber=15
- 2015 - https://nces.ed.gov/ipeds/reported-data/215105?year=2016&surveyNumber=15
- 2016 - https://nces.ed.gov/ipeds/reported-data/215105?year=2017&surveyNumber=15
- 2017 - https://nces.ed.gov/ipeds/reported-data/215105?year=2018&surveyNumber=15
- 2018 - https://nces.ed.gov/ipeds/reported-data/215105?year=2019&surveyNumber=15
- 2019 - https://nces.ed.gov/ipeds/reported-data/215105?year=2020&surveyNumber=15
- 2020 - https://nces.ed.gov/ipeds/reported-data/215105?year=2021&surveyNumber=15

IPEDS – Part A - Fall Enrollment – Summary – Grand Totals

- 2021 - https://nces.ed.gov/ipeds/reported-data/215105?year=2022&surveyNumber=15
- 2022 - https://nces.ed.gov/ipeds/reported-data/215105?year=2023&surveyNumber=15

Moore College of Art & Design

IPEDS - Enrollment by race/ethnicity and gender

- 2001 - https://nces.ed.gov/ipeds/reported-data/214148?year=2001&surveyNumber=2
- 2002 - https://nces.ed.gov/ipeds/reported-data/214148?year=2002&surveyNumber=2
- 2003 - https://nces.ed.gov/ipeds/reported-data/214148?year=2003&surveyNumber=2
- 2004 - https://nces.ed.gov/ipeds/reported-data/214148?year=2004&surveyNumber=2

IPEDS - Part A - Fall Enrollment - Summary by race/ethnicity

- 2005 - https://nces.ed.gov/ipeds/reported-data/214148?year=2005&surveyNumber=2
- 2006 - https://nces.ed.gov/ipeds/reported-data/214148?year=2006&surveyNumber=2
- 2007 - https://nces.ed.gov/ipeds/reported-data/214148?year=2007&surveyNumber=2
- 2008 - https://nces.ed.gov/ipeds/reported-data/214148?year=2008&surveyNumber=15

IPEDS - Part A - Fall Enrollment - Summary

- 2009 - https://nces.ed.gov/ipeds/reported-data/214148?year=2009&surveyNumber=15
- 2010 - https://nces.ed.gov/ipeds/reported-data/214148?year=2010&surveyNumber=15
- 2011 - https://nces.ed.gov/ipeds/reported-data/214148?year=2011&surveyNumber=15
- 2012 - https://nces.ed.gov/ipeds/reported-data/214148?year=2012&surveyNumber=15
- 2013 - https://nces.ed.gov/ipeds/reported-data/214148?year=2013&surveyNumber=15
- 2014 - https://nces.ed.gov/ipeds/reported-data/214148?year=2014&surveyNumber=15
- 2015 - https://nces.ed.gov/ipeds/reported-data/214148?year=2015&surveyNumber=15
- 2016 - https://nces.ed.gov/ipeds/reported-data/214148?year=2016&surveyNumber=15
- 2017 - https://nces.ed.gov/ipeds/reported-data/214148?year=2017&surveyNumber=15
- 2018 - https://nces.ed.gov/ipeds/reported-data/214148?year=2018&surveyNumber=15
- 2019 - https://nces.ed.gov/ipeds/reported-data/214148?year=2019&surveyNumber=15
- 2020 - https://nces.ed.gov/ipeds/reported-data/214148?year=2020&surveyNumber=15
- 2021 - https://nces.ed.gov/ipeds/reported-data/214148?year=2021&surveyNumber=15

IPEDS - Part A - Fall Enrollment - Fall 2022 – Grand Totals

- 2022 - https://nces.ed.gov/ipeds/reported-data/214148?year=2022&surveyNumber=15
- 2023 - https://nces.ed.gov/ipeds/reported-data/214148?year=2023&surveyNumber=15

Pennsylvania Academy of the Fine Arts

IPEDS - Enrollment by race/ethnicity and gender

- 2001 - https://nces.ed.gov/ipeds/reported-data/214971?year=2001&surveyNumber=2
- 2002 - https://nces.ed.gov/ipeds/reported-data/214971?year=2002&surveyNumber=2
- 2003 - https://nces.ed.gov/ipeds/reported-data/214971?year=2003&surveyNumber=2
- 2004 - https://nces.ed.gov/ipeds/reported-data/214971?year=2004&surveyNumber=2

IPEDS - Part A - Fall Enrollment - Summary by race/ethnicity

- 2005 - https://nces.ed.gov/ipeds/reported-data/214971?year=2005&surveyNumber=2
- 2006 - https://nces.ed.gov/ipeds/reported-data/214971?year=2006&surveyNumber=2
- 2007 - https://nces.ed.gov/ipeds/reported-data/214971?year=2007&surveyNumber=2
- 2008 - https://nces.ed.gov/ipeds/reported-data/214971?year=2008&surveyNumber=15

IPEDS - Part A - Fall Enrollment - Summary

- 2009 - https://nces.ed.gov/ipeds/reported-data/214971?year=2009&surveyNumber=15
- 2010 - https://nces.ed.gov/ipeds/reported-data/214971?year=2010&surveyNumber=15
- 2011 - https://nces.ed.gov/ipeds/reported-data/214971?year=2011&surveyNumber=15
- 2012 - https://nces.ed.gov/ipeds/reported-data/214971?year=2012&surveyNumber=15
- 2013 - https://nces.ed.gov/ipeds/reported-data/214971?year=2013&surveyNumber=15
- 2014 - https://nces.ed.gov/ipeds/reported-data/214971?year=2014&surveyNumber=15
- 2015 - https://nces.ed.gov/ipeds/reported-data/214971?year=2015&surveyNumber=15
- 2016 - https://nces.ed.gov/ipeds/reported-data/214971?year=2016&surveyNumber=15
- 2017 - https://nces.ed.gov/ipeds/reported-data/214971?year=2017&surveyNumber=15
- 2018 - https://nces.ed.gov/ipeds/reported-data/214971?year=2018&surveyNumber=15
- 2019 - https://nces.ed.gov/ipeds/reported-data/214971?year=2019&surveyNumber=15
- 2020 - https://nces.ed.gov/ipeds/reported-data/214971?year=2020&surveyNumber=15
- 2021 - https://nces.ed.gov/ipeds/reported-data/214971?year=2021&surveyNumber=15

IPEDS - Part A - Fall Enrollment - Fall 2022 – Grand Totals

- 2022 - https://nces.ed.gov/ipeds/reported-data/214971?year=2022&surveyNumber=15
- 2023 - https://nces.ed.gov/ipeds/reported-data/214971?year=2023&surveyNumber=15

Donating While in Debt: UARTS' Morally Bankrupt Fundraising Strategy

UARTS Form 990 Part VIII 8c, Schedule G Part II

- 2008 – https://projects.propublica.org/nonprofits/display_990/562307147/2010_05_EO%2F56-2307147_990_200906
- 2009 – https://projects.propublica.org/nonprofits/display_990/562307147/2010_05_EO%2F56-2307147_990_200906
- 2010 – https://projects.propublica.org/nonprofits/display_990/562307147/2012_05_EO%2F56-2307147_990_201106
- 2011 – https://projects.propublica.org/nonprofits/display_990/562307147/2013_05_EO%2F56-2307147_990_201206
- 2012 - https://projects.propublica.org/nonprofits/organizations/562307147/201420999349300532/full
- 2013 – https://projects.propublica.org/nonprofits/organizations/562307147/201541069349300534/full
- 2014 – https://projects.propublica.org/nonprofits/organizations/562307147/201601069349300625/full
- 2015 – https://projects.propublica.org/nonprofits/organizations/562307147/201741009349300904/full
- 2016 – https://projects.propublica.org/nonprofits/organizations/562307147/201841109349300819/full
- 2017 – https://projects.propublica.org/nonprofits/organizations/562307147/201941069349300334/full
- 2018 – https://projects.propublica.org/nonprofits/organizations/562307147/202021129349300042/full
- 2019 – https://projects.propublica.org/nonprofits/organizations/562307147/202111059349301696/full
- 2020 – https://projects.propublica.org/nonprofits/organizations/562307147/202221029349301247/full
- 2021 – https://projects.propublica.org/nonprofits/organizations/562307147/202340889349301359/full
- 2022 – https://projects.propublica.org/nonprofits/organizations/562307147/202440829349300334/full
- 2023 – https://projects.propublica.org/nonprofits/organizations/562307147/202520859349300727/full

Day of Giving

- 2020 - https://www.givecampus.com/schools/UniversityoftheArts/uartist-day-of-giving#updates
- 2021 - https://www.givecampus.com/schools/UniversityoftheArts/uartist-day-of-giving-2021/
- 2022 - https://www.givecampus.com/schools/UniversityoftheArts/uartist-day-of-giving-2022/?trk=public_post_share-update_update-text
- 2023 - https://www.givecampus.com/schools/UniversityoftheArts/2023-uartist-day-of-giving
- 2024 - https://www.givecampus.com/schools/UniversityoftheArts/2024-uartist-day-of-giving

2020: The Year UARTS Ignored the Alarm Bells

Accountability and Transparency Concerns Surrounding UARTS' HEERF Grants

- U.S. Department of Education. (2020, April). Allocations for Section 18004(a)(1) of the CARES Act. https://www.ed.gov/sites/ed/files/about/offices/list/ope/allocationsforsection18004a1ofcaresact.pdf
- U.S. Department of Education. (2021, January 13). HEERF II allocations for public and nonprofit institutions under CRRSAA section 314(a)(1). https://www.ed.gov/sites/ed/files/about/offices/list/ope/314a1allocationtableheerfii.pdf
- U.S. Department of Education. (2021, July). HEERF III allocations for public and nonprofit institutions under ARP section 2003(a)(1). https://www.ed.gov/sites/ed/files/about/offices/list/ope/arpa1allocationtable.pdf

UARTS Bond: From Junk Bond to Default

- Fitch Ratings. (2018, December 3). Fitch affirms University of the Arts, PA Revs 'BB+'; Outlook Stable. Fitch Ratings. https://www.fitchratings.com/research/us-public-finance/fitch-affirms-university-of-arts-pa-revs-bb-outlook-stable-03-12-2018

- Fitch Ratings. (2021, March 1). Fitch downgrades University of the Arts, PA Revs to 'BB'; Outlook Negative. Fitch Ratings. https://www.fitchratings.com/research/us-public-finance/fitch-downgrades-university-of-arts-pa-revs-to-bb-outlook-negative-01-03-2021

- Fitch Ratings. (2023, February 14). Fitch downgrades University of the Arts, PA Revs to 'BB-'; Outlook Remains Negative. Fitch Ratings. https://www.fitchratings.com/research/us-public-finance/fitch-downgrades-university-of-arts-pa-revs-to-bb-outlook-remains-negative-14-02-2023

- Fitch Ratings. (2024, January 23). Fitch downgrades University of the Arts, PA's Revs to 'B+'; Outlook Negative. Fitch Ratings. https://www.fitchratings.com/research/us-public-finance/fitch-downgrades-university-of-arts-pa-revs-to-b-outlook-negative-23-01-2024

- Fitch Ratings. (2024, June 4). Fitch downgrades University of the Arts (PA) Revs to 'C'; Rating Watch Negative. Fitch Ratings. https://www.fitchratings.com/research/us-public-finance/fitch-downgrades-university-of-arts-pa-revs-to-c-rating-watch-negative-04-06-2024

- Fitch Ratings. (2024, August 28). Fitch downgrades The University of the Arts to 'D' and withdraws ratings. Fitch Ratings. https://www.fitchratings.com/research/us-public-finance/fitch-downgrades-the-university-of-arts-to-d-withdraws-ratings-28-08-2024

Changes in Faculty Wages & Job Positions

IPEDS – Human Resources

- 2010 - https://nces.ed.gov/ipeds/reported-data/215105?year=2010&surveyNumber=9
- 2011 - https://nces.ed.gov/ipeds/reported-data/215105?year=2011&surveyNumber=9
- 2012 - https://nces.ed.gov/ipeds/reported-data/215105?year=2012&surveyNumber=9
- 2013 - https://nces.ed.gov/ipeds/reported-data/215105?year=2013&surveyNumber=9
- 2014 - https://nces.ed.gov/ipeds/reported-data/215105?year=2014&surveyNumber=9
- 2015 - https://nces.ed.gov/ipeds/reported-data/215105?year=2015&surveyNumber=9
- 2016 - https://nces.ed.gov/ipeds/reported-data/215105?year=2016&surveyNumber=9
- 2017 - https://nces.ed.gov/ipeds/reported-data/215105?year=2017&surveyNumber=9
- 2018 - https://nces.ed.gov/ipeds/reported-data/215105?year=2018&surveyNumber=9
- 2019 - https://nces.ed.gov/ipeds/reported-data/215105?year=2019&surveyNumber=9
- 2020 - https://nces.ed.gov/ipeds/reported-data/215105?year=2020&surveyNumber=9
- 2021 - https://nces.ed.gov/ipeds/reported-data/215105?year=2021&surveyNumber=9
- 2022 - https://nces.ed.gov/ipeds/reported-data/215105?year=2022&surveyNumber=9
- 2023 - https://nces.ed.gov/ipeds/reported-data/215105?year=2023&surveyNumber=9

A Labor Contract That Set Faculty Back

- University of the Arts & United Academics of Philadelphia. (2024). Faculty contract

A Mounting Legal Crisis: Lawsuits from Students and Faculty

- Fogel v. University of the Arts, No. (E.D. Pa. 2018).
- Czarnota v. University of the Arts, No. (E.D. Pa. 2020).
- Doe, J. K. A. v. University of the Arts, No. (E.D. Pa. 2022).

UARTS Presidential Compensation

Form 990 Schedule A

- 2000 – https://projects.propublica.org/nonprofits/display_990/231639911/2002_07_EO%2F23-1639911_990_200106
- 2001 - https://projects.propublica.org/nonprofits/display_990/231639911/2003_06_EO%2F23-1639911_990_200206

Form 990 Schedule A Part V

- 2002 – https://projects.propublica.org/nonprofits/display_990/231639911/2004_07_EO%2F23-1639911_990_200306
- 2003 – UARTS Form 990, Schedule A, Part I – [link not available]
- 2004 - https://projects.propublica.org/nonprofits/display_990/231639911/2006_03_EO%2F23-1639911_990_200506
- 2005 - https://projects.propublica.org/nonprofits/display_990/231639911/2008_01_EO%2F23-1639911_990_200606
- 2006 - https://projects.propublica.org/nonprofits/display_990/231639911/2008_11_EO%2F23-1639911_990_200706
- 2007 - https://projects.propublica.org/nonprofits/display_990/231639911/2009_06_EO%2F23-1639911_990_200806

Form 990 Schedule J Part II

- 2008 – UARTS Form 990, Part VII – https://projects.propublica.org/nonprofits/display_990/231639911/2010_03_EO%2F23-1639911_990_200906
- 2009 – https://projects.propublica.org/nonprofits/display_990/231639911/2011_04_EO%2F23-1639911_990_201006
- 2010 – https://projects.propublica.org/nonprofits/display_990/231639911/2012_06_EO%2F23-1639911_990_201106
- 2011 – https://projects.propublica.org/nonprofits/display_990/231639911/2013_07_EO%2F23-1639911_990_201206
- 2012 – https://projects.propublica.org/nonprofits/organizations/231639911/201411329349302366/full
- 2013 – https://projects.propublica.org/nonprofits/organizations/231639911/201510909349300771/full
- 2014 – https://projects.propublica.org/nonprofits/organizations/231639911/201621189349300642/full
- 2015 – https://projects.propublica.org/nonprofits/organizations/231639911/201711359349309761/full
- 2016 – https://projects.propublica.org/nonprofits/organizations/231639911/201831349349303133/full
- 2017 – https://projects.propublica.org/nonprofits/organizations/231639911/201941349349302784/full
- 2018 – https://projects.propublica.org/nonprofits/organizations/231639911/202041359349302699/full
- 2019 – https://projects.propublica.org/nonprofits/organizations/231639911/202111049349301466/full
- 2020 - https://projects.propublica.org/nonprofits/organizations/231639911/202221299349301942/full
- 2021 – https://projects.propublica.org/nonprofits/organizations/231639911/202311039349301001/full
- 2022 – https://projects.propublica.org/nonprofits/organizations/231639911/202401169349300700/full

Dangerously Low Student-to-Employee Ratios Undermined Financial Stability

University of the Arts Enrollment

IPEDS - Enrollment by race/ethnicity and gender

- 2001 - https://nces.ed.gov/ipeds/reported-data/215105?year=2001&surveyNumber=2
- 2002 - https://nces.ed.gov/ipeds/reported-data/215105?year=2002&surveyNumber=2
- 2003 - https://nces.ed.gov/ipeds/reported-data/215105?year=2003&surveyNumber=2
- 2004 - https://nces.ed.gov/ipeds/reported-data/215105?year=2004&surveyNumber=2

IPEDS – Part A - Fall Enrollment - Summary by race/ethnicity

- 2005 - https://nces.ed.gov/ipeds/reported-data/215105?year=2005&surveyNumber=2
- 2006 - https://nces.ed.gov/ipeds/reported-data/215105?year=2006&surveyNumber=2
- 2007 - https://nces.ed.gov/ipeds/reported-data/215105?year=2007&surveyNumber=2
- 2008 - https://nces.ed.gov/ipeds/reported-data/215105?year=2008&surveyNumber=15

IPEDS – Part A - Fall Enrollment – Summary

- 2009 - https://nces.ed.gov/ipeds/reported-data/215105?year=2009&surveyNumber=15
- 2010 - https://nces.ed.gov/ipeds/reported-data/215105?year=2010&surveyNumber=15
- 2011 - https://nces.ed.gov/ipeds/reported-data/215105?year=2011&surveyNumber=15
- 2011 - https://nces.ed.gov/ipeds/reported-data/215105?year=2012&surveyNumber=15
- 2012 - https://nces.ed.gov/ipeds/reported-data/215105?year=2013&surveyNumber=15
- 2013 - https://nces.ed.gov/ipeds/reported-data/215105?year=2014&surveyNumber=15
- 2014 - https://nces.ed.gov/ipeds/reported-data/215105?year=2015&surveyNumber=15
- 2015 - https://nces.ed.gov/ipeds/reported-data/215105?year=2016&surveyNumber=15
- 2016 - https://nces.ed.gov/ipeds/reported-data/215105?year=2017&surveyNumber=15
- 2017 - https://nces.ed.gov/ipeds/reported-data/215105?year=2018&surveyNumber=15
- 2018 - https://nces.ed.gov/ipeds/reported-data/215105?year=2019&surveyNumber=15
- 2019 - https://nces.ed.gov/ipeds/reported-data/215105?year=2020&surveyNumber=15
- 2020 - https://nces.ed.gov/ipeds/reported-data/215105?year=2021&surveyNumber=15

IPEDS – Part A - Fall Enrollment – Summary – Grand Totals

- 2021 - https://nces.ed.gov/ipeds/reported-data/215105?year=2022&surveyNumber=15
- 2022 - https://nces.ed.gov/ipeds/reported-data/215105?year=2023&surveyNumber=15

University of the Arts Employee Headcounts

IPEDS – Fall Staff – Part E
- 2001 - https://nces.ed.gov/ipeds/reported-data/215105?year=2001&surveyNumber=5

IPEDS - Employees by Assigned Position
- 2002 - https://nces.ed.gov/ipeds/reported-data/215105?year=2002&surveyNumber=11

IPEDS – Fall Staff – Part E
- 2003 - https://nces.ed.gov/ipeds/reported-data/215105?year=2003&surveyNumber=5

IPEDS - Employees by Assigned Position
- 2004 - https://nces.ed.gov/ipeds/reported-data/215105?year=2004&surveyNumber=11

IPEDS – Human Resources Part E
- 2005 - https://nces.ed.gov/ipeds/reported-data/215105?year=2005&surveyNumber=9

IPEDS – Human Resources Part C
- 2006 - https://nces.ed.gov/ipeds/reported-data/215105?year=2006&surveyNumber=9

IPEDS – Fall Staff - Part K
- 2007 - https://nces.ed.gov/ipeds/reported-data/215105?year=2007&surveyNumber=9

IPEDS – Human Resources Part C
- 2008 - https://nces.ed.gov/ipeds/reported-data/215105?year=2008&surveyNumber=9

IPEDS – Human Resources Part K
- 2009 - https://nces.ed.gov/ipeds/reported-data/215105?year=2009&surveyNumber=9

IPEDS – Human Resources Part C
- 2010 - https://nces.ed.gov/ipeds/reported-data/215105?year=2010&surveyNumber=9

IPEDS – Human Resources Part K
- 2011 - https://nces.ed.gov/ipeds/reported-data/215105?year=2011&surveyNumber=9

IPEDS – Human Resources
- 2012 - https://nces.ed.gov/ipeds/reported-data/215105?year=2012&surveyNumber=9
- 2013 - https://nces.ed.gov/ipeds/reported-data/215105?year=2013&surveyNumber=9
- 2014 - https://nces.ed.gov/ipeds/reported-data/215105?year=2014&surveyNumber=9
- 2015 - https://nces.ed.gov/ipeds/reported-data/215105?year=2015&surveyNumber=9
- 2016 - https://nces.ed.gov/ipeds/reported-data/215105?year=2016&surveyNumber=9
- 2017 - https://nces.ed.gov/ipeds/reported-data/215105?year=2017&surveyNumber=9
- 2018 - https://nces.ed.gov/ipeds/reported-data/215105?year=2018&surveyNumber=9
- 2019 - https://nces.ed.gov/ipeds/reported-data/215105?year=2019&surveyNumber=9
- 2020 - https://nces.ed.gov/ipeds/reported-data/215105?year=2020&surveyNumber=9
- 2021 - https://nces.ed.gov/ipeds/reported-data/215105?year=2021&surveyNumber=9
- 2022 - https://nces.ed.gov/ipeds/reported-data/215105?year=2022&surveyNumber=9
- 2023 - https://nces.ed.gov/ipeds/reported-data/215105?year=2023&surveyNumber=9

Controversial Union Demands & Questionable Tactics During Negotiations

- Doe v. Washington University, No. 4:22-cv-01007-SRC (E.D. Mo. Jan. 20, 2023).
- University of Pennsylvania v. EEOC, 493 U.S. 182 (1990).
- Jew v. University of Iowa, 749 F. Supp. 946 (S.D. Iowa 1990).
- Faculty, Alumni, and Students Opposed to Racial Preferences v. Northwestern University, No. 1:24-cv-05558 (N.D. Ill. July 2, 2024).
- Fogel v. University of the Arts, (E.D. Pa. 2018).
- Czarnota v. University of the Arts, (E.D. Pa. 2020).
- United Academics of Philadelphia. (2021, April, 28). Session 8 – Bargaining notes. UARTS Union Blog. [No longer available online; screenshot in author's possession].
- United Academics of Philadelphia. (2021, July 14). Session 9 – Bargaining notes. UARTS Union Blog. [No longer available online; screenshot in author's possession].

Missed Opportunities in Outreach, Branding, and Digital Strategy

- University of the Arts. (2018, May 1). Large building size banner on front of Anderson Hall [Photograph]. X. https://x.com/UArts/status/991311294031593472

Academic Inbreeding: How Insularity Stifled Innovation

- University of the Arts. (2006). 2006–2007 course catalog. University of the Arts. Retrieved September 21, 2025, from https://archive.org/details/2006-07-uarts-catalog
- University of the Arts. (2007). 2007–2008 course catalog. University of the Arts. Retrieved September 21, 2025, from https://archive.org/details/2007-08-university-catalog
- University of the Arts. (2008). 2008–2009 course catalog. University of the Arts. Retrieved September 21, 2025, from https://archive.org/details/2008-09-uarts-catalog
- University of the Arts. (2011). 2011–2012 course catalog. University of the Arts. Retrieved September 21, 2025, from https://archive.org/details/university-of-the-arts-2011-12-catalog
- University of the Arts. (2013). 2013–2014 course catalog. University of the Arts. Retrieved September 21, 2025, from https://archive.org/details/university-of-the-arts-2013-14-catalog
- University of the Arts. (2014). 2014–2015 course catalog. University of the Arts. Retrieved September 21, 2025, from https://archive.org/details/2008-09-uarts-catalog
- University of the Arts. (2015). 2015–2016 course catalog. University of the Arts. Retrieved September 21, 2025, from https://archive.org/details/university-of-the-arts-2015-16-catalog
- University of the Arts. (2016). 2016–2017 course catalog. University of the Arts. Retrieved September 21, 2025, from https://archive.org/details/university-of-the-

arts-2016-17-catalog

  • University of the Arts. (2017). 2017–2018 course catalog. University of the Arts. Retrieved September 21, 2025, from https://archive.org/details/university-of-the-arts-2017-18-catalog

  • University of the Arts. (2022). 2022–2023 course catalog. University of the Arts. Retrieved September 21, 2025, from https://archive.org/details/university-of-the-arts-2022-23-catalog

  • University of the Arts. (2023). 2023–2024 course catalog. University of the Arts. Retrieved September 21, 2025, from https://archive.org/details/university-of-the-arts-2023-24-catalog

A Phantom Capital Campaign Masked Financial Collapse

  • Dobrin, P. (2022, April 26). University of the Arts raises $67 million in its first capital campaign. The Philadelphia Inquirer. https://www.inquirer.com/arts/university-arts-philadelphia-fundraising-scholarships-20220426.html

Capital Campaign Expenditures

  • 2016 – https://projects.propublica.org/nonprofits/organizations/231639911/201831349349303133/full• 2017 – https://projects.propublica.org/nonprofits/organizations/231639911/201941349349302784/full• 2018 – https://projects.propublica.org/nonprofits/organizations/231639911/202041359349302699/full• 2019 – https://projects.propublica.org/nonprofits/organizations/231639911/202111049349301466/full• 2020 – https://projects.propublica.org/nonprofits/organizations/231639911/202221299349301942/full• 2021 – https://projects.propublica.org/nonprofits/organizations/231639911/202311039349301001/full• 2022 – https://projects.propublica.org/nonprofits/organizations/231639911/202401169349300700/full

"The biggest chunk, about $24 million, will be kept in perpetuity in endowment."

UARTS Schedule D Part V

  • 2015 – https://projects.propublica.org/nonprofits/organizations/231639911/201711359349309761/full• 2016 – https://projects.propublica.org/nonprofits/organizations/231639911/201831349349303133/full• 2017 – https://projects.propublica.org/nonprofits/organizations/231639911/201941349349302784/full• 2018 – https://projects.propublica.org/nonprofits/organizations/231639911/202041359349302699/full• 2019 – https://projects.propublica.org/nonprofits/organizations/231639911/202111049349301466/full• 2020 - https://projects.propublica.org/nonprofits/organizations/231639911/202221299349301942/full• 2021 – https://projects.propublica.org/nonprofits/organizations/231639911/202311039349301001/full• 2022 – https://projects.propublica.org/nonprofits/organizations/231639911/202401169349300700/full

"$5.5 Million for Scholarships & $5 Million in Discretionary Funds"

- U.S. Department of Education. (2020, April). Allocations for Section 18004(a)(1) of the CARES Act. https://www.ed.gov/sites/ed/files/about/offices/list/ope/allocationsforsection18004a1ofcaresact.pdf
- U.S. Department of Education. (2021, January 13). HEERF II allocations for public and nonprofit institutions under CRRSAA section 314(a)(1). https://www.ed.gov/sites/ed/files/about/offices/list/ope/314a1allocationtableheerfii.pdf
- U.S. Department of Education. (2021, July). HEERF III allocations for public and nonprofit institutions under ARP section 2003(a)(1). https://www.ed.gov/sites/ed/files/about/offices/list/ope/arpa1allocationtable.pdf

No Grand Foundational Grants

Neubauer Foundation – 990 PF Form Part XIV

- 2016 - https://projects.propublica.org/nonprofits/display_990/256627704/IRS%2F256627704_201611_990PF_2017102014870279• 2017 -https://projects.propublica.org/nonprofits/display_990/256627704/11_2019_prefixes_23-26%2F256627704_201811_990PF_2019111916865306• 2018 -https://projects.propublica.org/nonprofits/display_990/256627704/05_2021_prefixes_25-26%2F256627704_201911_990PF_2021051118086632• 2020 -https://projects.propublica.org/nonprofits/organizations/256627704/202232509349100203/full• 2021 -https://projects.propublica.org/nonprofits/organizations/256627704/202312879349100416/fullWilliamPennFoundationDonations-990PFFormPartXIV•2021-https://projects.propublica.org/nonprofits/organizations/231503488/202223189349106592/full• 2021 - https://projects.propublica.org/nonprofits/organizations/231503488/202323199349105797/full• 2023 - https://projects.propublica.org/nonprofits/organizations/231503488/202433199349103223/full

Hamilton Family Foundation

- Hamilton Family Foundation. (2016). Form 990-PF: Return of private foundation [IRS Form 990-PF]. ProPublica Nonprofit Explorer. https://projects.propublica.org/nonprofits/organizations/232684976/201713069349101311/full
- Hamilton Family Foundation. (2017). Form 990-PF: Return of private foundation [IRS Form 990-PF]. ProPublica Nonprofit Explorer. https://projects.propublica.org/nonprofits/organizations/232684976/201801309349102030/full
- Hamilton Family Foundation. (2018). Form 990-PF: Return of private foundation [IRS Form 990-PF]. ProPublica Nonprofit Explorer. https://projects.propublica.org/nonprofits/organizations/232684976/201941089349100209/full
- Hamilton Family Foundation. (2019). Form 990-PF: Return of private foundation [IRS Form 990-PF]. ProPublica Nonprofit Explorer. https://projects.propublica.org/nonprofits/organizations/232684976/202003169349102650/full
- Hamilton Family Foundation. (2020). Form 990-PF: Return of private foundation [IRS Form 990-PF]. ProPublica Nonprofit Explorer. https://projects.propublica.org/nonprofits/organizations/232684976/202101369349100735/full
- Hamilton Family Foundation. (2021). Form 990-PF: Return of private foundation

[IRS Form 990-PF]. ProPublica Nonprofit Explorer. https://projects.propublica.org/
nonprofits/organizations/232684976/202201449349101100/full
• Hamilton Family Foundation. (2022). Form 990-PF: Return of private foundation
[IRS Form 990-PF]. ProPublica Nonprofit Explorer. https://projects.propublica.org/
nonprofits/organizations/232684976/202333199349104658/full
• Hamilton Family Foundation. (2023). Form 990-PF: Return of private foundation
[IRS Form 990-PF]. ProPublica Nonprofit Explorer. https://projects.propublica.org/
nonprofits/organizations/232684976/202443199349102839/full

Wyncote Foundation

• Wyncote Foundation. (2016). Form 990-PF: Return of private foundation
[IRS Form 990-PF]. ProPublica Nonprofit Explorer. https://projects.propublica.
org/nonprofits/display_990/263535044/IRS%2F263535044_201612_990
PF_2017112914985471
• Wyncote Foundation. (2017). Form 990-PF: Return of private foundation [IRS
Form 990-PF]. ProPublica Nonprofit Explorer. https://projects.propublica.org/
nonprofits/display_990/263535044/02_2019_prefixes_25-26%2F263535044_20171
2_990PF_2019022716131559
• Wyncote Foundation. (2018). Form 990-PF: Return of private foundation [IRS
Form 990-PF]. ProPublica Nonprofit Explorer. https://projects.propublica.org/
nonprofits/display_990/263535044/01_2020_prefixes_26-26%2F263535044_20181
2_990PF_2020011517034388
• Wyncote Foundation. (2019). Form 990-PF: Return of private foundation
[IRS Form 990-PF]. ProPublica Nonprofit Explorer. https://projects.propublica.
org/nonprofits/display_990/263535044/download990pdf_01_2022_prefixes_25-
34%2F263535044_201912_990PF_2022013119582803
• Wyncote Foundation. (2020). Form 990-PF: Return of private foundation [IRS
Form 990-PF]. ProPublica Nonprofit Explorer. https://projects.propublica.org/
nonprofits/organizations/263535044/202123199349100347/full
• Wyncote Foundation. (2021). Form 990-PF: Return of private foundation [IRS
Form 990-PF]. ProPublica Nonprofit Explorer. https://projects.propublica.org/
nonprofits/organizations/263535044/202223189349103507/full
• Wyncote Foundation. (2022). Form 990-PF: Return of private foundation [IRS
Form 990-PF]. ProPublica Nonprofit Explorer. https://projects.propublica.org/
nonprofits/organizations/263535044/202303199349100040/full
• Wyncote Foundation. (2023). Form 990-PF: Return of private foundation [IRS
Form 990-PF]. ProPublica Nonprofit Explorer. https://projects.propublica.org/
nonprofits/organizations/263535044/202423199349102017/full

William B. Dietrich Foundation

• William B. Dietrich Foundation. (2017). Form 990-PF: Return of private
foundation [IRS Form 990-PF]. ProPublica Nonprofit Explorer. https://projects.
propublica.org/nonprofits/organizations/900628306/201731959349100753/full
• William B. Dietrich Foundation. (2019). Form 990-PF: Return of private
foundation [IRS Form 990-PF]. ProPublica Nonprofit Explorer. https://projects.
propublica.org/nonprofits/organizations/900628306/201832429349100118/full

- William B. Dietrich Foundation. (2019). Form 990-PF: Return of private foundation [IRS Form 990-PF]. ProPublica Nonprofit Explorer. https://projects.propublica.org/nonprofits/organizations/900628306/201931339349103353/full
- William B. Dietrich Foundation. (2020). Form 990-PF: Return of private foundation [IRS Form 990-PF]. ProPublica Nonprofit Explorer. https://projects.propublica.org/nonprofits/organizations/900628306/202011419349100401/full
- William B. Dietrich Foundation. (2022). Form 990-PF: Return of private foundation [IRS Form 990-PF]. ProPublica Nonprofit Explorer. https://projects.propublica.org/nonprofits/organizations/900628306/202131949349100653/full
- William B. Dietrich Foundation. (2023). Form 990-PF: Return of private foundation [IRS Form 990-PF]. ProPublica Nonprofit Explorer. https://projects.propublica.org/nonprofits/organizations/900628306/202231539349100323/full
- William B. Dietrich Foundation. (2023). Form 990-PF: Return of private foundation [IRS Form 990-PF]. ProPublica Nonprofit Explorer. https://projects.propublica.org/nonprofits/organizations/900628306/202331929349100818/full
- William B. Dietrich Foundation. (2024). Form 990-PF: Return of private foundation [IRS Form 990-PF]. ProPublica Nonprofit Explorer. https://projects.propublica.org/nonprofits/organizations/900628306/202430449349100008/full

Presser Foundation

- Presser Foundation. (2016). Form 990-PF: Return of private foundation [IRS Form 990-PF]. ProPublica Nonprofit Explorer. https://projects.propublica.org/nonprofits/organizations/232164013/201623499349100202/full
- Presser Foundation. (2017). Form 990-PF: Return of private foundation [IRS Form 990-PF]. ProPublica Nonprofit Explorer. https://projects.propublica.org/nonprofits/organizations/232164013/201840109349100014/full
- Presser Foundation. (2018). Form 990-PF: Return of private foundation [IRS Form 990-PF]. ProPublica Nonprofit Explorer. https://projects.propublica.org/nonprofits/organizations/232164013/201940159349100109/full
- Presser Foundation. (2019). Form 990-PF: Return of private foundation [IRS Form 990-PF]. ProPublica Nonprofit Explorer. https://projects.propublica.org/nonprofits/organizations/232164013/202031849349101333/full
- Presser Foundation. (2020). Form 990-PF: Return of private foundation [IRS Form 990-PF]. ProPublica Nonprofit Explorer. https://projects.propublica.org/nonprofits/organizations/232164013/202120269349101407/full
- Presser Foundation. (2021). Form 990-PF: Return of private foundation [IRS Form 990-PF]. ProPublica Nonprofit Explorer. https://projects.propublica.org/nonprofits/organizations/232164013/202210209349100401/full
- Presser Foundation. (2022). Form 990-PF: Return of private foundation [IRS Form 990-PF]. ProPublica Nonprofit Explorer. https://projects.propublica.org/nonprofits/organizations/232164013/202320269349100107/full
- Presser Foundation. (2024). Form 990-PF: Return of private foundation [IRS Form 990-PF]. ProPublica Nonprofit Explorer. https://projects.propublica.org/nonprofits/organizations/232164013/202440259349100004/full
- Presser Foundation. (2023). Form 990-PF: Return of private foundation [IRS Form 990-PF]. ProPublica Nonprofit Explorer. https://projects.propublica.org/nonprofits/organizations/232164013/202520439349101007/full

The W W Smith Charitable Trust

• W. W. Smith Charitable Trust. (2016). Form 990-PF: Return of private foundation [IRS Form 990-PF]. ProPublica Nonprofit Explorer. https://projects.propublica.org/nonprofits/display_990/236648841/06_2018%2F236648841_201706_990PF_2018060715378571• W. W. Smith Charitable Trust. (2017). Form 990-PF: Return of private foundation [IRS Form 990-PF]. ProPublica Nonprofit Explorer. https://projects.propublica.org/nonprofits/display_990/236648841/07_2019_prefixes_20-23%2F236648841_201806_9 90PF_2019072516523336• W. W. Smith Charitable Trust. (2018). Form 990-PF: Return of private foundation [IRS Form 990-PF]. ProPublica Nonprofit Explorer. https://projects.propublica.org/nonprofits/display_990/236648841/09_2020_prefixes_22-23%2F236648841_201906_990PR_2020090817284995• W. W. Smith Charitable Trust. (2019). Form 990-PF: Return of private foundation [IRS Form 990-PF]. ProPublica Nonprofit Explorer. https://projects.propublica.org/nonprofits/display_990/236648841/download990pdf_03_2022_prefixes_22-26%2F236648841_202006_990 PF_2022030719701897• W. W. Smith Charitable Trust. (2020). Form 990-PF: Return of private foundation [IRS Form 990-PF]. ProPublica Nonprofit Explorer. https://projects.propublica.org/nonprofits/organizations/236648841/202201229349101500/full• W. W. Smith Charitable Trust. (2021). Form 990-PF: Return of private foundation [IRS Form 990-PF]. Internal Revenue Service. https://apps.irs.gov/pub/epostcard/cor/236648841_202 106_990PF_2022051320043614.pdf• W. W. Smith Charitable Trust. (2022). Form 990-PF: Return of private foundation [IRS Form 990-PF]. Internal Revenue Service. https://apps.irs.gov/pub/epostcard/cor/236648841_202306_990PF_2024040522340219.pdf

Zeldin Family Foundation

• Zeldin Family Foundation. (2017). Form 990-PF: Return of private foundation [IRS Form 990-PF]. Internal Revenue Service. https://apps.irs.gov/pub/epostcard/cor/236861835_201612_990PF_2017061514526560.pdf
• Zeldin Family Foundation. (2018). Form 990-PF: Return of private foundation [IRS Form 990-PF]. Internal Revenue Service. https://apps.irs.gov/pub/epostcard/cor/236861835_201712_990PF_2018062115457123.pdf
• Zeldin Family Foundation. (2019). Form 990-PF: Return of private foundation [IRS Form 990-PF]. Internal Revenue Service. https://apps.irs.gov/pub/epostcard/cor/236861835_201812_990PF_2019071516487178.pdf
• Zeldin Family Foundation. (2020). Form 990-PF: Return of private foundation [IRS Form 990-PF]. Internal Revenue Service. https://apps.irs.gov/pub/epostcard/cor/236861835_201912_990PR_2020102317404838.pdf
• Zeldin Family Foundation. (2021). Form 990-PF: Return of private foundation [IRS Form 990-PF]. Internal Revenue Service. https://apps.irs.gov/pub/epostcard/cor/236861835_202012_990PF_2021061718377603.pdf
• Zeldin Family Foundation. (2022). Form 990-PF: Return of private foundation [IRS Form 990-PF]. Internal Revenue Service. https://apps.irs.gov/pub/epostcard/cor/236861835_202112_990PF_2022061512345678.pdf
• Zeldin Family Foundation. (2023). Form 990-PF: Return of private foundation [IRS Form 990-PF]. Internal Revenue Service. https://projects.propublica.org/nonprofits/organizations/236861835/202411369349103981/full

T/W Mary F Lindback Residuary Tr Nect

• T/W Mary F. Lindback Residuary Trust Nect. (2016). Form 990-PF: Return of private foundation [IRS Form 990-PF]. Internal Revenue Service. https://projects.propublica.org/nonprofits/display_990/236290348/2017_05_PF%2F23-6290348_990PF_201612

• T/W Mary F. Lindback Residuary Trust Nect. (2017). Form 990-PF: Return of private foundation [IRS Form 990-PF]. Internal Revenue Service. https://apps.irs.gov/pub/epostcard/cor/236290348_201712_990PF_2018071115505561.pdf

• T/W Mary F. Lindback Residuary Trust Nect. (2018). Form 990-PF: Return of private foundation [IRS Form 990-PF]. Internal Revenue Service. https://projects.propublica.org/nonprofits/display_990/236290348/03_2021_prefixes_21-23%2F236290348_201812_990PA_2021030217775665

• T/W Mary F. Lindback Residuary Trust Nect. (2019). Form 990-PF: Return of private foundation [IRS Form 990-PF]. Internal Revenue Service. https://projects.propublica.org/nonprofits/organizations/236290348/202043159349100209/full

• T/W Mary F. Lindback Residuary Trust Nect. (20200). Form 990-PF: Return of private foundation [IRS Form 990-PF]. Internal Revenue Service. https://projects.propublica.org/nonprofits/organizations/236290348/202133139349102688/full

• T/W Mary F. Lindback Residuary Trust Nect. (2021). Form 990-PF: Return of private foundation [IRS Form 990-PF]. Internal Revenue Service. https://projects.propublica.org/nonprofits/organizations/236290348/202201319349103255/full

• T/W Mary F. Lindback Residuary Trust Nect. (2022). Form 990-PF: Return of private foundation [IRS Form 990-PF]. Internal Revenue Service. https://projects.propublica.org/nonprofits/organizations/236290348/202311989349101101/full

• T/W Mary F. Lindback Residuary Trust Nect. (2023). Form 990-PF: Return of private foundation [IRS Form 990-PF]. Internal Revenue Service. https://projects.propublica.org/nonprofits/organizations/236290348/202431289349101703/full

The Charlotte Cushman Foundation

• The Charlotte Cushman Foundation. (2025). Form 990 for 2017. ProPublica Nonprofit Explorer. https://projects.propublica.org/nonprofits/organizations/231280780/201742429349100114/full

• Charlotte Cushman Foundation. (2018). Form 990-PF: Return of private foundation. ProPublica Nonprofit Explorer. https://projects.propublica.org/nonprofits/organizations/231280780/201843199349104809/full

• Charlotte Cushman Foundation. (2019). Form 990-PF: Return of private foundation. ProPublica Nonprofit Explorer. https://projects.propublica.org/nonprofits/organizations/231280780/201922879349100432/full

• Charlotte Cushman Foundation. (2020). Form 990-PF: Return of private foundation. ProPublica Nonprofit Explorer. https://projects.propublica.org/nonprofits/organizations/231280780/202003039349100500/full

• Charlotte Cushman Foundation. (2021). Form 990-PF: Return of private foundation. ProPublica Nonprofit Explorer. https://projects.propublica.org/nonprofits/organizations/231280780/202123149349101012/full

• Charlotte Cushman Foundation. (2022). Form 990-PF: Return of private foundation. ProPublica Nonprofit Explorer. https://projects.propublica.org/

nonprofits/organizations/231280780/202222979349100052/full
- Charlotte Cushman Foundation. (2023). Form 990-PF: Return of private foundation. ProPublica Nonprofit Explorer. https://projects.propublica.org/nonprofits/organizations/231280780/202311679349100006/full
- Charlotte Cushman Foundation. (2024). Form 990-PF: Return of private foundation. ProPublica Nonprofit Explorer. https://projects.propublica.org/nonprofits/organizations/231280780/202422979349100507/full

Howard A & Martha R Wolf Fund

- Howard A. & Martha R. Wolf Fund. (2016). Form 990-PF: Return of private foundation. ProPublica Nonprofit Explorer. https://projects.propublica.org/nonprofits/display_990/236207349/2017_03_PF%2F23-6207349_990PF_201612
- Howard A. & Martha R. Wolf Fund. (2017). Form 990-PF: Return of private foundation. ProPublica Nonprofit Explorer. https://projects.propublica.org/nonprofits/display_990/236207349/07_2018_prefixes_22-23%2F236207349_201712_990PF_2018071015502935
- Howard A. & Martha R. Wolf Fund. (2017). Form 990-PF: Return of private foundation. ProPublica Nonprofit Explorer. https://projects.propublica.org/nonprofits/display_990/236207349/07_2018_prefixes_22-23%2F236207349_201712_990PF_2018071015502935
- Howard A. & Martha R. Wolf Fund. (2018). Form 990-PF: Return of private foundation. ProPublica Nonprofit Explorer. https://projects.propublica.org/nonprofits/display_990/236207349/06_2019_prefixes_22-23%2F236207349_201812_990PF_2019061016397395
- Howard A. & Martha R. Wolf Fund. (2019). Form 990-PF: Return of private foundation. ProPublica Nonprofit Explorer. https://projects.propublica.org/nonprofits/display_990/236207349/download990pdf_02_2022_prefixes_23-34%2F236207349_201912_990PF_2022020219621783
- Howard A. & Martha R. Wolf Fund. (2020). Form 990-PF: Return of private foundation. ProPublica Nonprofit Explorer. https://projects.propublica.org/nonprofits/organizations/236207349/202101179349102800/full
- Howard A. & Martha R. Wolf Fund. (2021). Form 990-PF: Return of private foundation. ProPublica Nonprofit Explorer. https://projects.propublica.org/nonprofits/organizations/236207349/202241239349100509/full
- Howard A. & Martha R. Wolf Fund. (2022). Form 990-PF: Return of private foundation. ProPublica Nonprofit Explorer. https://projects.propublica.org/nonprofits/organizations/236207349/202311229349100431/full
- Howard A. & Martha R. Wolf Fund. (2023). Form 990-PF: Return of private foundation. ProPublica Nonprofit Explorer. https://projects.propublica.org/nonprofits/organizations/236207349/202401229349102350/full

Richard And Jean Coyne Family Foundation

- Richard And Jean Coyne Family Foundation. (2017). Form 990-PF: Return of private foundation. ProPublica Nonprofit Explorer. https://projects.propublica.org/nonprofits/organizations/770259860/201713199349104571/full
- Richard And Jean Coyne Family Foundation. (2018). Form 990-PF: Return of

private foundation. ProPublica Nonprofit Explorer. https://projects.propublica.org/nonprofits/organizations/770259860/201833199349104878/full

- Richard And Jean Coyne Family Foundation. (2019). Form 990-PF: Return of private foundation. ProPublica Nonprofit Explorer. https://projects.propublica.org/nonprofits/organizations/770259860/201923179349101622/full
- Richard And Jean Coyne Family Foundation. (2020). Form 990-PF: Return of private foundation. ProPublica Nonprofit Explorer. https://projects.propublica.org/nonprofits/organizations/770259860/202013189349103916/full
- Richard And Jean Coyne Family Foundation. (2021). Form 990-PF: Return of private foundation. ProPublica Nonprofit Explorer. https://projects.propublica.org/nonprofits/organizations/770259860/202133199349109853/full
- Richard And Jean Coyne Family Foundation. (2022). Form 990-PF: Return of private foundation. ProPublica Nonprofit Explorer. https://projects.propublica.org/nonprofits/organizations/770259860/202213269349100221/full
- Richard And Jean Coyne Family Foundation. (2023). Form 990-PF: Return of private foundation. ProPublica Nonprofit Explorer. https://projects.propublica.org/nonprofits/organizations/770259860/202332919349100213/full
- Richard And Jean Coyne Family Foundation. (2024). Form 990-PF: Return of private foundation. ProPublica Nonprofit Explorer. https://projects.propublica.org/nonprofits/organizations/770259860/202540349349100019/full

Jeff & Jenifer Westphal Foundation

- Jeff & Jenifer Westphal Foundation. (2017). Form 990-PF: Return of private foundation. ProPublica Nonprofit Explorer. https://projects.propublica.org/nonprofits/organizations/200251341/201713109349100036/full
- Jeff & Jenifer Westphal Foundation. (2018). Form 990-PF: Return of private foundation. ProPublica Nonprofit Explorer. https://projects.propublica.org/nonprofits/organizations/200251341/201803199349101105/full
- Jeff & Jenifer Westphal Foundation. (2019). Form 990-PF: Return of private foundation. ProPublica Nonprofit Explorer. https://projects.propublica.org/nonprofits/organizations/200251341/201903199349100415/full
- Jeff & Jenifer Westphal Foundation. (2020). Form 990-PF: Return of private foundation. ProPublica Nonprofit Explorer. https://projects.propublica.org/nonprofits/organizations/200251341/202033219349106118/full
- Jeff & Jenifer Westphal Foundation. (2022). Form 990-PF: Return of private foundation. ProPublica Nonprofit Explorer. https://projects.propublica.org/nonprofits/organizations/200251341/202230489349100703/full
- Jeff & Jenifer Westphal Foundation. (2022). Form 990-PF: Return of private foundation. ProPublica Nonprofit Explorer. https://projects.propublica.org/nonprofits/organizations/200251341/202203199349103265/full
- Jeff & Jenifer Westphal Foundation. (2023). Form 990-PF: Return of private foundation. ProPublica Nonprofit Explorer. https://projects.propublica.org/nonprofits/organizations/200251341/202313179349102566/full
- Jeff & Jenifer Westphal Foundation. (2024). Form 990-PF: Return of private foundation. ProPublica Nonprofit Explorer. https://projects.propublica.org/nonprofits/organizations/200251341/202431369349102643/full

Henry Nias Foundation

- Henry Nias Foundation. (2018). Form 990-PF: Return of private foundation. ProPublica Nonprofit Explorer. https://projects.propublica.org/nonprofits/organizations/136075785/201801939349100405/full
- Henry Nias Foundation. (2019). Form 990-PF: Return of private foundation. ProPublica Nonprofit Explorer. https://projects.propublica.org/nonprofits/organizations/136075785/201932839349100703/full
- Henry Nias Foundation. (2020). Form 990-PF: Return of private foundation. ProPublica Nonprofit Explorer. https://projects.propublica.org/nonprofits/organizations/136075785/202000729349100500/full
- Henry Nias Foundation. (2021). Form 990-PF: Return of private foundation. ProPublica Nonprofit Explorer. https://projects.propublica.org/nonprofits/organizations/136075785/202140899349100614/full
- Henry Nias Foundation. (2022). Form 990-PF: Return of private foundation. ProPublica Nonprofit Explorer. https://projects.propublica.org/nonprofits/organizations/136075785/202210979349100121/full
- Henry Nias Foundation. (2022). Form 990-PF: Return of private foundation. Internal Revenue Service. https://apps.irs.gov/pub/epostcard/cor/136075785_2022 11_990PF_2023060621377436.pdf
- Henry Nias Foundation. (2023). Form 990-PF: Return of private foundation. Internal Revenue Service. https://apps.irs.gov/pub/epostcard/cor/136075785_2023 11_990PF_2024042322366972.pdf

UARTS Pledges Form 990 – Part X

- 2015 – https://projects.propublica.org/nonprofits/organizations/231639911/201711359349309761/full• 2016 – https://projects.propublica.org/nonprofits/organizations/231639911/201831349349303133/full
- 2017 – https://projects.propublica.org/nonprofits/organizations/231639911/201941349349302784/full• 2018 – https://projects.propublica.org/nonprofits/organizations/231639911/202041359349302699/full
- 2019 – https://projects.propublica.org/nonprofits/organizations/231639911/202111049349301466/full• 2020 - https://projects.propublica.org/nonprofits/organizations/231639911/202221299349301942/full
- 2021 – https://projects.propublica.org/nonprofits/organizations/231639911/202311039349301001/full• 2022 – https://projects.propublica.org/nonprofits/organizations/231639911/202401169349300700/full

The Cohort Default Rate: An Overlooked Crisis at UARTS

- National Student Loan Data System. (n.d.). CDR searchable database: School detail. U.S. Department of Education. Retrieved September 21, 2025, from https://nsldsfap.ed.gov/cdr-searchable-database/school/detail/view

- USAspending.gov. (n.d.). Recipient details: 9f11680c-e296-d6de-ac54-76b7cfb4e362-C. U.S. Department of the Treasury. Retrieved September 21, 2025, from https://www.usaspending.gov/recipient/9f11680c-e296-d6de-ac54-76b7cfb4e362-C/latest

2023: UARTS' Slide Into Oblivion

- Walk, K., & Aaron, J. (2024, May 31). Letter to the UArts community announcing closure. In 6ABC. Reproduced in "The University of the Arts in Philadelphia announces sudden closure." 6ABC. https://www.6abc.com/post/university-of-the-arts-philadelphia-closing-letter-accreditation-president-kerry-walk/14897571
- ProPublica. (2025, August 21). University of the Arts – Audit for period ending June 2016. Nonprofit Explorer. https://projects.propublica.org/nonprofits/display_audit/2610820161
- ProPublica. (2025, August 21). University of the Arts – Audit for period ending June 2017. Nonprofit Explorer. https://projects.propublica.org/nonprofits/display_audit/2610820171
- ProPublica. (2025, August 21). University of the Arts – Audit for period ending June 2018. Nonprofit Explorer. https://projects.propublica.org/nonprofits/display_audit/2610820181
- ProPublica. (2025, August 21). University of the Arts – Audit for period ending June 2019. Nonprofit Explorer. https://projects.propublica.org/nonprofits/display_audit/2610820192
- ProPublica. (2025, August 21). University of the Arts – Audit for period ending June 2020. Nonprofit Explorer. https://projects.propublica.org/nonprofits/display_audit/2610820201
- ProPublica. (2025, August 21). University of the Arts – Audit for period ending June 2021. Nonprofit Explorer. https://projects.propublica.org/nonprofits/display_audit/2610820211
- ProPublica. (2025, August 21). University of the Arts – Audit for period ending June 2022. Nonprofit Explorer. https://projects.propublica.org/nonprofits/display_audit/2610820221
- ProPublica. (2025, August 21). University of the Arts – Audit for period ending June 2023. Nonprofit Explorer. https://projects.propublica.org/nonprofits/display_audit/2023-06-GSAFAC-0000003827

Appendix E: Enrollment Trends for Sample Universities (2001–2023)

Art Center College of Design Pasadena, CA

IPEDS - Enrollment by race/ethnicity and gender – Fall

- 2001 - https://nces.ed.gov/ipeds/reported-data/109651?year=2001&surveyNumber=2
- 2002 - https://nces.ed.gov/ipeds/reported-data/109651?year=2002&surveyNumber=2
- 2003 - https://nces.ed.gov/ipeds/reported-data/109651?year=2003&surveyNumber=2
- 2004 - https://nces.ed.gov/ipeds/reported-data/109651?year=2004&surveyNumber=2

IPEDS - Part A - Fall Enrollment - Summary by race/ethnicity – Fall

- 2005 - https://nces.ed.gov/ipeds/reported-data/109651?year=2005&surveyNumber=2
- 2006 - https://nces.ed.gov/ipeds/reported-data/109651?year=2006&surveyNumber=2
- 2007 - https://nces.ed.gov/ipeds/reported-data/109651?year=2007&surveyNumber=2
- 2008 - https://nces.ed.gov/ipeds/reported-data/109651?year=2008&surveyNumber=15

IPEDS - Part A - Fall Enrollment Summary

- 2009 - https://nces.ed.gov/ipeds/reported-data/109651?year=2009&surveyNumber=15
- 2010 - https://nces.ed.gov/ipeds/reported-data/109651?year=2010&surveyNumber=15
- 2011 - https://nces.ed.gov/ipeds/reported-data/109651?year=2011&surveyNumber=15
- 2012 - https://nces.ed.gov/ipeds/reported-data/109651?year=2012&surveyNumber=15
- 2013 - https://nces.ed.gov/ipeds/reported-data/109651?year=2013&surveyNumber=15
- 2014 - https://nces.ed.gov/ipeds/reported-data/109651?year=2014&surveyNumber=15
- 2015 - https://nces.ed.gov/ipeds/reported-data/109651?year=2015&surveyNumber=15
- 2016 - https://nces.ed.gov/ipeds/reported-data/109651?year=2016&surveyNumber=15
- 2017 - https://nces.ed.gov/ipeds/reported-data/109651?year=2017&surveyNumber=15
- 2018 - https://nces.ed.gov/ipeds/reported-data/109651?year=2018&surveyNumber=15
- 2019 - https://nces.ed.gov/ipeds/reported-data/109651?year=2019&surveyNumber=15
- 2020 - https://nces.ed.gov/ipeds/reported-data/109651?year=2020&surveyNumber=15
- 2021 - https://nces.ed.gov/ipeds/reported-data/109651?year=2021&surveyNumber=15

IPEDS - Part A - Fall Enrollment - Grand Totals

- 2022 - https://nces.ed.gov/ipeds/reported-data/109651?year=2022&surveyNumber=15

Berklee College of Music

IPEDS - Enrollment by race/ethnicity and gender: Fall

- 2001 - https://nces.ed.gov/ipeds/reported-data/164748?year=2001&surveyNumber=2
- 2002 - NA
- 2003 - https://nces.ed.gov/ipeds/reported-data/164748?year=2003&surveyNumber=2
- 2004 - https://nces.ed.gov/ipeds/reported-data/164748?year=2004&surveyNumber=2

IPEDS - Part A - Fall Enrollment - Summary by race/ethnicity

- 2005 - https://nces.ed.gov/ipeds/reported-data/164748?year=2005&surveyNumber=2
- 2006 - https://nces.ed.gov/ipeds/reported-data/164748?year=2006&surveyNumber=2
- 2007 - https://nces.ed.gov/ipeds/reported-data/164748?year=2007&surveyNumber=2
- 2008 - https://nces.ed.gov/ipeds/reported-data/164748?year=2008&surveyNumber=15

IPEDS - Part A - Fall Enrollment Summary

- 2000 - https://nces.ed.gov/ipeds/reported-data/164748?year=2009&surveyNumber=15
- 2010 - https://nces.ed.gov/ipeds/reported-data/164748?year=2010&surveyNumber=15
- 2011 - https://nces.ed.gov/ipeds/reported-data/164748?year=2011&surveyNumber=15
- 2012 - https://nces.ed.gov/ipeds/reported-data/164748?year=2012&surveyNumber=15
- 2013 - https://nces.ed.gov/ipeds/reported-data/164748?year=2013&surveyNumber=15
- 2014 - https://nces.ed.gov/ipeds/reported-data/164748?year=2014&surveyNumber=15
- 2015 - https://nces.ed.gov/ipeds/reported-data/164748?year=2015&surveyNumber=15
- 2016 - https://nces.ed.gov/ipeds/reported-data/164748?year=2016&surveyNumber=15
- 2017 - https://nces.ed.gov/ipeds/reported-data/164748?year=2017&surveyNumber=15
- 2018 - https://nces.ed.gov/ipeds/reported-data/164748?year=2018&surveyNumber=15
- 2019 - https://nces.ed.gov/ipeds/reported-data/164748?year=2019&surveyNumber=15
- 2020 - https://nces.ed.gov/ipeds/reported-data/164748?year=2020&surveyNumber=15
- 2021 - https://nces.ed.gov/ipeds/reported-data/164748?year=2021&surveyNumber=15

IPEDS - Part A - Fall Enrollment - Grand Totals

- 2022 - https://nces.ed.gov/ipeds/reported-data/164748?year=2022&surveyNumber=15
- 2023 - https://nces.ed.gov/ipeds/reported-data/164748?year=2023&surveyNumber=15

California College of the Arts (San Francisco, CA)

IPEDS - Enrollment by race/ethnicity and gender: Fall

- 2001 - https://nces.ed.gov/ipeds/reported-data/110370?year=2001&surveyNumber=2
- 2002 - https://nces.ed.gov/ipeds/reported-data/110370?year=2002&surveyNumber=2
- 2003 - https://nces.ed.gov/ipeds/reported-data/110370?year=2003&surveyNumber=2
- 2004 - https://nces.ed.gov/ipeds/reported-data/110370?year=2004&surveyNumber=2

IPEDS - Part A - Fall Enrollment - Summary by race/ethnicity – Fall

- 2005 - https://nces.ed.gov/ipeds/reported-data/110370?year=2005&surveyNumber=2
- 2006 - https://nces.ed.gov/ipeds/reported-data/110370?year=2006&surveyNumber=2
- 2007 - https://nces.ed.gov/ipeds/reported-data/110370?year=2007&surveyNumber=2
- 2008 - https://nces.ed.gov/ipeds/reported-data/110370?year=2008&surveyNumber=15

IPEDS - Part A - Fall Enrollment Summary

- 2009 - https://nces.ed.gov/ipeds/reported-data/110370?year=2009&surveyNumber=15
- 2010 - https://nces.ed.gov/ipeds/reported-data/110370?year=2010&surveyNumber=15
- 2011 - https://nces.ed.gov/ipeds/reported-data/110370?year=2011&surveyNumber=15
- 2012 - https://nces.ed.gov/ipeds/reported-data/110370?year=2012&surveyNumber=15
- 2013 - https://nces.ed.gov/ipeds/reported-data/110370?year=2013&surveyNumber=15
- 2014 - https://nces.ed.gov/ipeds/reported-data/110370?year=2014&surveyNumber=15
- 2015 - https://nces.ed.gov/ipeds/reported-data/110370?year=2015&surveyNumber=15
- 2016 - https://nces.ed.gov/ipeds/reported-data/110370?year=2016&surveyNumber=15
- 2017 - https://nces.ed.gov/ipeds/reported-data/110370?year=2017&surveyNumber=15
- 2018 - https://nces.ed.gov/ipeds/reported-data/110370?year=2018&surveyNumber=15
- 2019 - https://nces.ed.gov/ipeds/reported-data/110370?year=2019&surveyNumber=15
- 2020 - https://nces.ed.gov/ipeds/reported-data/110370?year=2020&surveyNumber=15
- 2021 - https://nces.ed.gov/ipeds/reported-data/110370?year=2021&surveyNumber=15

IPEDS - Part A - Fall Enrollment – Grand Totals

- 2022 - https://nces.ed.gov/ipeds/reported-data/110370?year=2022&surveyNumber=15
- 2023 - https://nces.ed.gov/ipeds/reported-data/110370?year=2023&surveyNumber=15

California Institute of the Arts (Valencia, CA)

IPEDS - Enrollment by race/ethnicity and gender: Fall

- 2001 - https://nces.ed.gov/ipeds/reported-data/111081?year=2001&surveyNumber=2
- 2002 - https://nces.ed.gov/ipeds/reported-data/111081?year=2002&surveyNumber=2
- 2003 - https://nces.ed.gov/ipeds/reported-data/111081?year=2003&surveyNumber=2
- 2004 - https://nces.ed.gov/ipeds/reported-data/111081?year=2004&surveyNumber=2

IPEDS - Part A - Fall Enrollment - Summary by race/ethnicity – Fall

- 2005 - https://nces.ed.gov/ipeds/reported-data/111081?year=2005&surveyNumber=2
- 2006 - https://nces.ed.gov/ipeds/reported-data/111081?year=2006&surveyNumber=2
- 2007 - https://nces.ed.gov/ipeds/reported-data/111081?year=2007&surveyNumber=2
- 2008 - https://nces.ed.gov/ipeds/reported-data/111081?year=2008&surveyNumber=15

IPEDS - Part A - Fall Enrollment Summary

- 2009 - https://nces.ed.gov/ipeds/reported-data/111081?year=2009&surveyNumber=15
- 2000 - https://nces.ed.gov/ipeds/reported-data/111081?year=2010&surveyNumber=15
- 2011 - https://nces.ed.gov/ipeds/reported-data/111081?year=2011&surveyNumber=15
- 2012 - https://nces.ed.gov/ipeds/reported-data/111081?year=2012&surveyNumber=15
- 2013 - https://nces.ed.gov/ipeds/reported-data/111081?year=2013&surveyNumber=15
- 2014 - https://nces.ed.gov/ipeds/reported-data/111081?year=2014&surveyNumber=15
- 2015 - https://nces.ed.gov/ipeds/reported-data/111081?year=2015&surveyNumber=15
- 2016 - https://nces.ed.gov/ipeds/reported-data/111081?year=2016&surveyNumber=15
- 2017 - https://nces.ed.gov/ipeds/reported-data/111081?year=2017&surveyNumber=15
- 2018 - https://nces.ed.gov/ipeds/reported-data/111081?year=2018&surveyNumber=15
- 2019 - https://nces.ed.gov/ipeds/reported-data/111081?year=2019&surveyNumber=15
- 2020 - https://nces.ed.gov/ipeds/reported-data/111081?year=2020&surveyNumber=15
- 2021 - https://nces.ed.gov/ipeds/reported-data/111081?year=2021&surveyNumber=15

IPEDS - Part A - Fall Enrollment– Grand Totals

- 2022 - https://nces.ed.gov/ipeds/reported-data/111081?year=2022&surveyNumber=15
- 2023 - https://nces.ed.gov/ipeds/reported-data/111081?year=2023&surveyNumber=15

Cleveland Institute of Art (Cleveland, OH)

IPEDS - Enrollment by race/ethnicity and gender: Fall

- 2001 - https://nces.ed.gov/ipeds/reported-data/202046?year=2001&surveyNumber=2
- 2002 - https://nces.ed.gov/ipeds/reported-data/202046?year=2002&surveyNumber=2
- 2003 - https://nces.ed.gov/ipeds/reported-data/202046?year=2003&surveyNumber=2
- 2004 - https://nces.ed.gov/ipeds/reported-data/202046?year=2004&surveyNumber=2

IPEDS - Part A - Fall Enrollment - Summary by race/ethnicity – Fall

- 2005 - https://nces.ed.gov/ipeds/reported-data/202046?year=2005&surveyNumber=2
- 2006 - https://nces.ed.gov/ipeds/reported-data/202046?year=2006&surveyNumber=2
- 2007 - https://nces.ed.gov/ipeds/reported-data/202046?year=2007&surveyNumber=2
- 2008 - https://nces.ed.gov/ipeds/reported-data/202046?year=2008&surveyNumber=15

IPEDS - Part A - Fall Enrollment Summary

- 2010 - https://nces.ed.gov/ipeds/reported-data/202046?year=2009&surveyNumber=15
- 2011 - https://nces.ed.gov/ipeds/reported-data/202046?year=2010&surveyNumber=15
- 2012 - https://nces.ed.gov/ipeds/reported-data/202046?year=2011&surveyNumber=15
- 2013 - https://nces.ed.gov/ipeds/reported-data/202046?year=2012&surveyNumber=15
- 2014 - https://nces.ed.gov/ipeds/reported-data/202046?year=2013&surveyNumber=15
- 2015 - https://nces.ed.gov/ipeds/reported-data/202046?year=2014&surveyNumber=15
- 2016 - https://nces.ed.gov/ipeds/reported-data/202046?year=2015&surveyNumber=15
- 2017 - https://nces.ed.gov/ipeds/reported-data/202046?year=2016&surveyNumber=15
- 2018 - https://nces.ed.gov/ipeds/reported-data/202046?year=2017&surveyNumber=15
- 2019 - https://nces.ed.gov/ipeds/reported-data/202046?year=2018&surveyNumber=15
- 2020 - https://nces.ed.gov/ipeds/reported-data/202046?year=2019&surveyNumber=15
- 2021 - https://nces.ed.gov/ipeds/reported-data/202046?year=2020&surveyNumber=15
- 2022 - https://nces.ed.gov/ipeds/reported-data/202046?year=2021&surveyNumber=15

IPEDS - Part A - Fall Enrollment – Grand Totals

- 2022 - https://nces.ed.gov/ipeds/reported-data/202046?year=2022&surveyNumber=15
- 2023 - https://nces.ed.gov/ipeds/reported-data/202046?year=2023&surveyNumber=15

College for Creative Studies (Detroit, MI)

IPEDS - Enrollment by race/ethnicity and gender: Fall

- 2001 - https://nces.ed.gov/ipeds/reported-data/169442?year=2001&surveyNumber=2
- 2002 - https://nces.ed.gov/ipeds/reported-data/169442?year=2002&surveyNumber=2
- 2003 - https://nces.ed.gov/ipeds/reported-data/169442?year=2003&surveyNumber=2
- 2004 - https://nces.ed.gov/ipeds/reported-data/169442?year=2004&surveyNumber=2

IPEDS - Part A - Fall Enrollment - Summary by race/ethnicity – Fall

- 2005 - https://nces.ed.gov/ipeds/reported-data/169442?year=2005&surveyNumber=2
- 2006 - https://nces.ed.gov/ipeds/reported-data/169442?year=2006&surveyNumber=2
- 2007 - https://nces.ed.gov/ipeds/reported-data/169442?year=2007&surveyNumber=2
- 2008 - https://nces.ed.gov/ipeds/reported-data/169442?year=2008&surveyNumber=15

IPEDS - Part A - Fall Enrollment Summary

- 2009 - https://nces.ed.gov/ipeds/reported-data/169442?year=2009&surveyNumber=15
- 2010 - https://nces.ed.gov/ipeds/reported-data/169442?year=2010&surveyNumber=15
- 2011 - https://nces.ed.gov/ipeds/reported-data/169442?year=2011&surveyNumber=15
- 2012 - https://nces.ed.gov/ipeds/reported-data/169442?year=2012&surveyNumber=15
- 2013 - https://nces.ed.gov/ipeds/reported-data/169442?year=2013&surveyNumber=15
- 2014 - https://nces.ed.gov/ipeds/reported-data/169442?year=2014&surveyNumber=15
- 2015 - https://nces.ed.gov/ipeds/reported-data/169442?year=2015&surveyNumber=15
- 2016 - https://nces.ed.gov/ipeds/reported-data/169442?year=2016&surveyNumber=15
- 2017 - https://nces.ed.gov/ipeds/reported-data/169442?year=2017&surveyNumber=15
- 2018 - https://nces.ed.gov/ipeds/reported-data/169442?year=2018&surveyNumber=15
- 2019 - https://nces.ed.gov/ipeds/reported-data/169442?year=2019&surveyNumber=15
- 2020 - https://nces.ed.gov/ipeds/reported-data/169442?year=2020&surveyNumber=15
- 2021 - https://nces.ed.gov/ipeds/reported-data/169442?year=2021&surveyNumber=15

IPEDS - Part A - Fall Enrollment– Grand Totals

- 2022 - https://nces.ed.gov/ipeds/reported-data/169442?year=2022&surveyNumber=15
- 2023 - https://nces.ed.gov/ipeds/reported-data/169442?year=2023&surveyNumber=15

Columbia College Chicago (Chicago, IL)

IPEDS - Enrollment by race/ethnicity and gender: Fall

- 2001 - https://nces.ed.gov/ipeds/reported-data/144281?year=2001&surveyNumber=2
- 2002 - https://nces.ed.gov/ipeds/reported-data/144281?year=2002&surveyNumber=2
- 2003 - https://nces.ed.gov/ipeds/reported-data/144281?year=2003&surveyNumber=2
- 2004 - https://nces.ed.gov/ipeds/reported-data/144281?year=2004&surveyNumber=2

IPEDS - Part A - Fall Enrollment - Summary by race/ethnicity – Fall

- 2005 - https://nces.ed.gov/ipeds/reported-data/144281?year=2005&surveyNumber=2
- 2006 - https://nces.ed.gov/ipeds/reported-data/144281?year=2006&surveyNumber=2
- 2007 - https://nces.ed.gov/ipeds/reported-data/144281?year=2007&surveyNumber=2
- 2008 - https://nces.ed.gov/ipeds/reported-data/144281?year=2008&surveyNumber=15

IPEDS - Part A - Fall Enrollment Summary

- 2009 - https://nces.ed.gov/ipeds/reported-data/144281?year=2009&surveyNumber=15
- 2010 - https://nces.ed.gov/ipeds/reported-data/144281?year=2010&surveyNumber=15
- 2011 - https://nces.ed.gov/ipeds/reported-data/144281?year=2011&surveyNumber=15
- 2012 - https://nces.ed.gov/ipeds/reported-data/144281?year=2012&surveyNumber=15
- 2013 - https://nces.ed.gov/ipeds/reported-data/144281?year=2013&surveyNumber=15
- 2014 - https://nces.ed.gov/ipeds/reported-data/144281?year=2014&surveyNumber=15
- 2015 - https://nces.ed.gov/ipeds/reported-data/144281?year=2015&surveyNumber=15
- 2016 - https://nces.ed.gov/ipeds/reported-data/144281?year=2016&surveyNumber=15
- 2017 - https://nces.ed.gov/ipeds/reported-data/144281?year=2017&surveyNumber=15
- 2018 - https://nces.ed.gov/ipeds/reported-data/144281?year=2018&surveyNumber=15
- 2019 - https://nces.ed.gov/ipeds/reported-data/144281?year=2019&surveyNumber=15
- 2020 - https://nces.ed.gov/ipeds/reported-data/144281?year=2020&surveyNumber=15
- 2021 - https://nces.ed.gov/ipeds/reported-data/144281?year=2021&surveyNumber=15

IPEDS - Part A - Fall Enrollment– Grand Totals

- 2021 - https://nces.ed.gov/ipeds/reported-data/144281?year=2022&surveyNumber=15
- 2023 - https://nces.ed.gov/ipeds/reported-data/144281?year=2023&surveyNumber=15

Cornish College of the Arts (Seattle, WA)

IPEDS - Enrollment by race/ethnicity and gender: Fall

- 2001 - https://nces.ed.gov/ipeds/reported-data/235024?year=2001&surveyNumber=2
- 2002 - https://nces.ed.gov/ipeds/reported-data/235024?year=2002&surveyNumber=2
- 2003 - https://nces.ed.gov/ipeds/reported-data/235024?year=2003&surveyNumber=2
- 2004 - https://nces.ed.gov/ipeds/reported-data/235024?year=2004&surveyNumber=2

IPEDS - Part A - Fall Enrollment - Summary by race/ethnicity – Fall

- 2005 - https://nces.ed.gov/ipeds/reported-data/235024?year=2005&surveyNumber=2
- 2006 - https://nces.ed.gov/ipeds/reported-data/235024?year=2006&surveyNumber=2
- 2007 - https://nces.ed.gov/ipeds/reported-data/235024?year=2007&surveyNumber=2
- 2008 - https://nces.ed.gov/ipeds/reported-data/235024?year=2008&surveyNumber=15

IPEDS - Part A - Fall Enrollment Summary

- 2009 - https://nces.ed.gov/ipeds/reported-data/235024?year=2009&surveyNumber=15
- 2010 - https://nces.ed.gov/ipeds/reported-data/235024?year=2010&surveyNumber=15
- 2011 - https://nces.ed.gov/ipeds/reported-data/235024?year=2011&surveyNumber=15
- 2012 - https://nces.ed.gov/ipeds/reported-data/235024?year=2012&surveyNumber=15
- 2013- https://nces.ed.gov/ipeds/reported-data/235024?year=2013&surveyNumber=15
- 2014 - https://nces.ed.gov/ipeds/reported-data/235024?year=2014&surveyNumber=15
- 2015 - https://nces.ed.gov/ipeds/reported-data/235024?year=2015&surveyNumber=15
- 2016 - https://nces.ed.gov/ipeds/reported-data/235024?year=2016&surveyNumber=15
- 2017 - https://nces.ed.gov/ipeds/reported-data/235024?year=2017&surveyNumber=15
- 2018 - https://nces.ed.gov/ipeds/reported-data/235024?year=2018&surveyNumber=15
- 2019 - https://nces.ed.gov/ipeds/reported-data/235024?year=2019&surveyNumber=15
- 2020 - https://nces.ed.gov/ipeds/reported-data/235024?year=2020&surveyNumber=15
- 2021 - https://nces.ed.gov/ipeds/reported-data/235024?year=2021&surveyNumber=15

IPEDS - Part A - Fall Enrollment – Grand Totals

- 2010 - https://nces.ed.gov/ipeds/reported-data/235024?year=2022&surveyNumber=15
- 2011 - https://nces.ed.gov/ipeds/reported-data/235024?year=2023&surveyNumber=15

Emerson College (Boston, MA)

IPEDS - Enrollment by race/ethnicity and gender: Fall

- 2001 - https://nces.ed.gov/ipeds/reported-data/165662?year=2001&surveyNumber=2
- 2002 - https://nces.ed.gov/ipeds/reported-data/165662?year=2002&surveyNumber=2
- 2003 - https://nces.ed.gov/ipeds/reported-data/165662?year=2003&surveyNumber=2
- 2004 - https://nces.ed.gov/ipeds/reported-data/165662?year=2004&surveyNumber=2

IPEDS - Part A - Fall Enrollment - Summary by race/ethnicity – Fall

- 2005 - https://nces.ed.gov/ipeds/reported-data/165662?year=2005&surveyNumber=2
- 2006 - https://nces.ed.gov/ipeds/reported-data/165662?year=2006&surveyNumber=2
- 2007 - https://nces.ed.gov/ipeds/reported-data/165662?year=2007&surveyNumber=2
- 2008 - https://nces.ed.gov/ipeds/reported-data/165662?year=2008&surveyNumber=15

IPEDS - Part A - Fall Enrollment Summary

- 2009 - https://nces.ed.gov/ipeds/reported-data/165662?year=2009&surveyNumber=15
- 2010 - https://nces.ed.gov/ipeds/reported-data/165662?year=2010&surveyNumber=15
- 2011 - https://nces.ed.gov/ipeds/reported-data/165662?year=2011&surveyNumber=15
- 2012 - https://nces.ed.gov/ipeds/reported-data/165662?year=2012&surveyNumber=15
- 2013 - https://nces.ed.gov/ipeds/reported-data/165662?year=2013&surveyNumber=15
- 2014 - https://nces.ed.gov/ipeds/reported-data/165662?year=2014&surveyNumber=15
- 2015 - https://nces.ed.gov/ipeds/reported-data/165662?year=2015&surveyNumber=15
- 2016 - https://nces.ed.gov/ipeds/reported-data/165662?year=2016&surveyNumber=15
- 2017 - https://nces.ed.gov/ipeds/reported-data/165662?year=2017&surveyNumber=15
- 2018 - https://nces.ed.gov/ipeds/reported-data/165662?year=2018&surveyNumber=15
- 2019 - https://nces.ed.gov/ipeds/reported-data/165662?year=2019&surveyNumber=15
- 2020 - https://nces.ed.gov/ipeds/reported-data/165662?year=2020&surveyNumber=15
- 2021 - https://nces.ed.gov/ipeds/reported-data/165662?year=2021&surveyNumber=15

IPEDS - Part A - Fall Enrollment - Fall 2022 – Grand Totals

- 2022 - https://nces.ed.gov/ipeds/reported-data/165662?year=2022&surveyNumber=15
- 2023 - https://nces.ed.gov/ipeds/reported-data/165662?year=2023&surveyNumber=15

Maine College of Art & Design (Portland, ME)

IPEDS - Enrollment by race/ethnicity and gender: Fall

- 2001 - https://nces.ed.gov/ipeds/reported-data/161509?year=2001&surveyNumber=2
- 2002 - https://nces.ed.gov/ipeds/reported-data/161509?year=2002&surveyNumber=2
- 2003 - https://nces.ed.gov/ipeds/reported-data/161509?year=2003&surveyNumber=2
- 2004 - https://nces.ed.gov/ipeds/reported-data/161509?year=2004&surveyNumber=2

IPEDS - Part A - Fall Enrollment - Summary by race/ethnicity – Fall

- 2005 - https://nces.ed.gov/ipeds/reported-data/161509?year=2005&surveyNumber=2
- 2006 - https://nces.ed.gov/ipeds/reported-data/161509?year=2006&surveyNumber=2
- 2007 - https://nces.ed.gov/ipeds/reported-data/161509?year=2007&surveyNumber=2
- 2008 - https://nces.ed.gov/ipeds/reported-data/161509?year=2008&surveyNumber=15

IPEDS - Part A - Fall Enrollment Summary

- 2009 - https://nces.ed.gov/ipeds/reported-data/161509?year=2009&surveyNumber=15
- 2010 - https://nces.ed.gov/ipeds/reported-data/161509?year=2010&surveyNumber=15
- 2011 - https://nces.ed.gov/ipeds/reported-data/161509?year=2011&surveyNumber=15
- 2012 - https://nces.ed.gov/ipeds/reported-data/161509?year=2012&surveyNumber=15
- 2013 - https://nces.ed.gov/ipeds/reported-data/161509?year=2013&surveyNumber=15
- 2014 - https://nces.ed.gov/ipeds/reported-data/161509?year=2014&surveyNumber=15
- 2015 - https://nces.ed.gov/ipeds/reported-data/161509?year=2015&surveyNumber=15
- 2016 - https://nces.ed.gov/ipeds/reported-data/161509?year=2016&surveyNumber=15
- 2017 - https://nces.ed.gov/ipeds/reported-data/161509?year=2017&surveyNumber=15
- 2018 - https://nces.ed.gov/ipeds/reported-data/161509?year=2018&surveyNumber=15
- 2019 - https://nces.ed.gov/ipeds/reported-data/161509?year=2019&surveyNumber=15
- 2020 - https://nces.ed.gov/ipeds/reported-data/161509?year=2020&surveyNumber=15
- 2021 - https://nces.ed.gov/ipeds/reported-data/161509?year=2021&surveyNumber=15

IPEDS - Part A - Fall Enrollment - Fall 2022 – Grand Totals

- 2022 - https://nces.ed.gov/ipeds/reported-data/161509?year=2022&surveyNumber=15
- 2023 - https://nces.ed.gov/ipeds/reported-data/161509?year=2023&surveyNumber=15

Manhattan School of Music (New York, NY)

- 2001 - https://nces.ed.gov/ipeds/reported-data/192712?year=2001&surveyNumber=2
- 2002 - NA
- 2003 - https://nces.ed.gov/ipeds/reported-data/192712?year=2003&surveyNumber=2
- 2004 - https://nces.ed.gov/ipeds/reported-data/192712?year=2004&surveyNumber=2

IPEDS - Part A - Fall Enrollment - Summary by race/ethnicity – Fall

- 2005 - https://nces.ed.gov/ipeds/reported-data/192712?year=2005&surveyNumber=2
- 2006 - https://nces.ed.gov/ipeds/reported-data/192712?year=2006&surveyNumber=2
- 2007 - https://nces.ed.gov/ipeds/reported-data/192712?year=2007&surveyNumber=2
- 2008 - https://nces.ed.gov/ipeds/reported-data/192712?year=2008&surveyNumber=15

IPEDS - Part A - Fall Enrollment Summary

- 2009 - https://nces.ed.gov/ipeds/reported-data/192712?year=2009&surveyNumber=15
- 2010 - https://nces.ed.gov/ipeds/reported-data/192712?year=2010&surveyNumber=15
- 2011 - https://nces.ed.gov/ipeds/reported-data/192712?year=2011&surveyNumber=15
- 2012 - https://nces.ed.gov/ipeds/reported-data/192712?year=2012&surveyNumber=15
- 2013 - https://nces.ed.gov/ipeds/reported-data/192712?year=2013&surveyNumber=15
- 2014 - https://nces.ed.gov/ipeds/reported-data/192712?year=2014&surveyNumber=15
- 2015 - https://nces.ed.gov/ipeds/reported-data/192712?year=2015&surveyNumber=15
- 2016 - https://nces.ed.gov/ipeds/reported-data/192712?year=2016&surveyNumber=15
- 2017 - https://nces.ed.gov/ipeds/reported-data/192712?year=2017&surveyNumber=15
- 2018- https://nces.ed.gov/ipeds/reported-data/192712?year=2018&surveyNumber=15
- 2019 - https://nces.ed.gov/ipeds/reported-data/192712?year=2019&surveyNumber=15
- 2020 - https://nces.ed.gov/ipeds/reported-data/192712?year=2020&surveyNumber=15
- 2021 - https://nces.ed.gov/ipeds/reported-data/192712?year=2021&surveyNumber=15

IPEDS - Part A - Fall Enrollment - Fall 2022 – Grand Totals

- 2022 - https://nces.ed.gov/ipeds/reported-data/192712?year=2022&surveyNumber=15
- 2023 - https://nces.ed.gov/ipeds/reported-data/192712?year=2023&surveyNumber=15

Maryland Institute College of Art (Baltimore, MD)

IPEDS - Enrollment by race/ethnicity and gender: Fall

- 2001 - https://nces.ed.gov/ipeds/reported-data/163295?year=2001&surveyNumber=2
- 2002 - https://nces.ed.gov/ipeds/reported-data/163295?year=2002&surveyNumber=2
- 2003 - https://nces.ed.gov/ipeds/reported-data/163295?year=2003&surveyNumber=2
- 2004 - https://nces.ed.gov/ipeds/reported-data/163295?year=2004&surveyNumber=2

IPEDS - Part A - Fall Enrollment - Summary by race/ethnicity – Fall

- 2005 - https://nces.ed.gov/ipeds/reported-data/163295?year=2005&surveyNumber=2
- 2006 - https://nces.ed.gov/ipeds/reported-data/163295?year=2006&surveyNumber=2
- 2007 - https://nces.ed.gov/ipeds/reported-data/163295?year=2007&surveyNumber=2
- 2008 - https://nces.ed.gov/ipeds/reported-data/163295?year=2008&surveyNumber=15

IPEDS - Part A - Fall Enrollment Summary

- 2009 - https://nces.ed.gov/ipeds/reported-data/163295?year=2009&surveyNumber=15
- 2010 - https://nces.ed.gov/ipeds/reported-data/163295?year=2010&surveyNumber=15
- 2011 - https://nces.ed.gov/ipeds/reported-data/163295?year=2011&surveyNumber=15
- 2012 - https://nces.ed.gov/ipeds/reported-data/163295?year=2012&surveyNumber=15
- 2013 - https://nces.ed.gov/ipeds/reported-data/163295?year=2013&surveyNumber=15
- 2014 - https://nces.ed.gov/ipeds/reported-data/163295?year=2014&surveyNumber=15
- 2015 - https://nces.ed.gov/ipeds/reported-data/163295?year=2015&surveyNumber=15
- 2016 - https://nces.ed.gov/ipeds/reported-data/163295?year=2016&surveyNumber=15
- 2017 - https://nces.ed.gov/ipeds/reported-data/163295?year=2017&surveyNumber=15
- 2018 - https://nces.ed.gov/ipeds/reported-data/163295?year=2018&surveyNumber=15
- 2019 - https://nces.ed.gov/ipeds/reported-data/163295?year=2019&surveyNumber=15
- 2020 - https://nces.ed.gov/ipeds/reported-data/163295?year=2020&surveyNumber=15
- 2021 - https://nces.ed.gov/ipeds/reported-data/163295?year=2021&surveyNumber=15

IPEDS - Part A - Fall Enrollment– Grand Totals

- 2022 - https://nces.ed.gov/ipeds/reported-data/163295?year=2022&surveyNumber=15
- 2023 - https://nces.ed.gov/ipeds/reported-data/163295?year=2023&surveyNumber=15

Marymount Manhattan College (New York, NY)

IPEDS - Enrollment by race/ethnicity and gender: Fall

- 2001 - https://nces.ed.gov/ipeds/reported-data/192864?year=2001&surveyNumber=2
- 2002 - https://nces.ed.gov/ipeds/reported-data/192864?year=2002&surveyNumber=2
- 2003 - https://nces.ed.gov/ipeds/reported-data/192864?year=2003&surveyNumber=2
- 2004 - https://nces.ed.gov/ipeds/reported-data/192864?year=2004&surveyNumber=2

IPEDS - Part A - Fall Enrollment - Summary by race/ethnicity

- 2005 - https://nces.ed.gov/ipeds/reported-data/192864?year=2005&surveyNumber=2
- 2006 - https://nces.ed.gov/ipeds/reported-data/192864?year=2006&surveyNumber=2
- 2007 - https://nces.ed.gov/ipeds/reported-data/192864?year=2007&surveyNumber=2
- 2008 - https://nces.ed.gov/ipeds/reported-data/192864?year=2008&surveyNumber=15

IPEDS - Part A - Fall Enrollment Summary

- 2009 - https://nces.ed.gov/ipeds/reported-data/192864?year=2009&surveyNumber=15
- 2010 - https://nces.ed.gov/ipeds/reported-data/192864?year=2010&surveyNumber=15
- 2011 - https://nces.ed.gov/ipeds/reported-data/192864?year=2011&surveyNumber=15
- 2012 - https://nces.ed.gov/ipeds/reported-data/192864?year=2012&surveyNumber=15
- 2013 - https://nces.ed.gov/ipeds/reported-data/192864?year=2013&surveyNumber=15
- 2014 - https://nces.ed.gov/ipeds/reported-data/192864?year=2014&surveyNumber=15
- 2015 - https://nces.ed.gov/ipeds/reported-data/192864?year=2015&surveyNumber=15
- 2016 - https://nces.ed.gov/ipeds/reported-data/192864?year=2016&surveyNumber=15
- 2017 - https://nces.ed.gov/ipeds/reported-data/192864?year=2017&surveyNumber=15
- 2018 - https://nces.ed.gov/ipeds/reported-data/192864?year=2018&surveyNumber=15
- 2019 - https://nces.ed.gov/ipeds/reported-data/192864?year=2019&surveyNumber=15
- 2020 - https://nces.ed.gov/ipeds/reported-data/192864?year=2020&surveyNumber=15
- 2021 - https://nces.ed.gov/ipeds/reported-data/192864?year=2021&surveyNumber=15

IPEDS - Part A - Fall Enrollment– Grand Totals

- 2022 - https://nces.ed.gov/ipeds/reported-data/192864?year=2022&surveyNumber=15
- 2023 - https://nces.ed.gov/ipeds/reported-data/192864?year=2023&surveyNumber=15

Massachusetts College of Art and Design (Boston, MA)

IPEDS - Enrollment by race/ethnicity and gender: Fall

- 2001 - https://nces.ed.gov/ipeds/reported-data/166674?year=2001&surveyNumber=2
- 2002 - https://nces.ed.gov/ipeds/reported-data/166674?year=2002&surveyNumber=2
- 2003 - https://nces.ed.gov/ipeds/reported-data/166674?year=2003&surveyNumber=2
- 2004 - https://nces.ed.gov/ipeds/reported-data/166674?year=2004&surveyNumber=2

IPEDS - Part A - Fall Enrollment - Summary by race/ethnicity – Fall

- 2005 - https://nces.ed.gov/ipeds/reported-data/166674?year=2005&surveyNumber=2
- 2006 - https://nces.ed.gov/ipeds/reported-data/166674?year=2006&surveyNumber=2
- 2007 - https://nces.ed.gov/ipeds/reported-data/166674?year=2007&surveyNumber=2
- 2008 - https://nces.ed.gov/ipeds/reported-data/166674?year=2008&surveyNumber=15

IPEDS - Part A - Fall Enrollment Summary

- 2009 - https://nces.ed.gov/ipeds/reported-data/166674?year=2009&surveyNumber=15
- 2010 - https://nces.ed.gov/ipeds/reported-data/166674?year=2010&surveyNumber=15
- 2011 - https://nces.ed.gov/ipeds/reported-data/166674?year=2011&surveyNumber=15
- 2012 - https://nces.ed.gov/ipeds/reported-data/166674?year=2012&surveyNumber=15
- 2013 - https://nces.ed.gov/ipeds/reported-data/166674?year=2013&surveyNumber=15
- 2014 - https://nces.ed.gov/ipeds/reported-data/166674?year=2014&surveyNumber=15
- 2015 - https://nces.ed.gov/ipeds/reported-data/166674?year=2015&surveyNumber=15
- 2016 - https://nces.ed.gov/ipeds/reported-data/166674?year=2016&surveyNumber=15
- 2017 - https://nces.ed.gov/ipeds/reported-data/166674?year=2017&surveyNumber=15
- 2018 - https://nces.ed.gov/ipeds/reported-data/166674?year=2018&surveyNumber=15
- 2019 - https://nces.ed.gov/ipeds/reported-data/166674?year=2019&surveyNumber=15
- 2020 - https://nces.ed.gov/ipeds/reported-data/166674?year=2020&surveyNumber=15
- 2021 - https://nces.ed.gov/ipeds/reported-data/166674?year=2021&surveyNumber=15

IPEDS - Part A - Fall Enrollment – Grand Totals

- 2022 - https://nces.ed.gov/ipeds/reported-data/166674?year=2022&surveyNumber=15
- 2023 - https://nces.ed.gov/ipeds/reported-data/166674?year=2023&surveyNumber=15

Minneapolis College of Art and Design (Minneapolis, MN)

IPEDS - Enrollment by race/ethnicity and gender: Fall

- 2001 - https://nces.ed.gov/ipeds/reported-data/174127?year=2001&surveyNumber=2
- 2002 - https://nces.ed.gov/ipeds/reported-data/174127?year=2002&surveyNumber=2
- 2003 - https://nces.ed.gov/ipeds/reported-data/174127?year=2003&surveyNumber=2
- 2004 - https://nces.ed.gov/ipeds/reported-data/174127?year=2004&surveyNumber=2

IPEDS - Part A - Fall Enrollment - Summary by race/ethnicity – Fall

- 2005 - https://nces.ed.gov/ipeds/reported-data/174127?year=2005&surveyNumber=2
- 2006 - https://nces.ed.gov/ipeds/reported-data/174127?year=2006&surveyNumber=2
- 2007 - https://nces.ed.gov/ipeds/reported-data/174127?year=2007&surveyNumber=2
- 2008 - https://nces.ed.gov/ipeds/reported-data/174127?year=2008&surveyNumber=15

IPEDS - Part A - Fall Enrollment Summary

- 2009 - https://nces.ed.gov/ipeds/reported-data/174127?year=2009&surveyNumber=15
- 2010 - https://nces.ed.gov/ipeds/reported-data/174127?year=2010&surveyNumber=15
- 2011 - https://nces.ed.gov/ipeds/reported-data/174127?year=2011&surveyNumber=15
- 2012 - https://nces.ed.gov/ipeds/reported-data/174127?year=2012&surveyNumber=15
- 2013 - https://nces.ed.gov/ipeds/reported-data/174127?year=2013&surveyNumber=15
- 2014 - https://nces.ed.gov/ipeds/reported-data/174127?year=2014&surveyNumber=15
- 2015 - https://nces.ed.gov/ipeds/reported-data/174127?year=2015&surveyNumber=15
- 2016 - https://nces.ed.gov/ipeds/reported-data/174127?year=2016&surveyNumber=15
- 2017 - https://nces.ed.gov/ipeds/reported-data/174127?year=2017&surveyNumber=15
- 2018 - https://nces.ed.gov/ipeds/reported-data/174127?year=2018&surveyNumber=15
- 2019 - https://nces.ed.gov/ipeds/reported-data/174127?year=2019&surveyNumber=15
- 2020 - https://nces.ed.gov/ipeds/reported-data/174127?year=2020&surveyNumber=15
- 2021 - https://nces.ed.gov/ipeds/reported-data/174127?year=2021&surveyNumber=15

IPEDS - Part A - Fall Enrollment – Grand Totals

- 2022 - https://nces.ed.gov/ipeds/reported-data/174127?year=2022&surveyNumber=15
- 2023 - https://nces.ed.gov/ipeds/reported-data/174127?year=2023&surveyNumber=15

Montserrat College of Art (Beverly, MA)

IPEDS - Enrollment by race/ethnicity and gender: Fall

- 2001 - NA
- 2002 - https://nces.ed.gov/ipeds/reported-data/166911?year=2002&surveyNumber=2
- 2003 - https://nces.ed.gov/ipeds/reported-data/166911?year=2003&surveyNumber=2
- 2004 - https://nces.ed.gov/ipeds/reported-data/166911?year=2004&surveyNumber=2

IPEDS - Part A - Fall Enrollment - Summary by race/ethnicity – Fall

- 2005 - https://nces.ed.gov/ipeds/reported-data/166911?year=2005&surveyNumber=2
- 2006 - https://nces.ed.gov/ipeds/reported-data/166911?year=2006&surveyNumber=2
- 2007 - https://nces.ed.gov/ipeds/reported-data/166911?year=2007&surveyNumber=2
- 2008 - https://nces.ed.gov/ipeds/reported-data/166911?year=2008&surveyNumber=15

IPEDS - Part A - Fall Enrollment Summary

- 2009 - https://nces.ed.gov/ipeds/reported-data/166911?year=2009&surveyNumber=15
- 2010 - https://nces.ed.gov/ipeds/reported-data/166911?year=2010&surveyNumber=15
- 2011 - https://nces.ed.gov/ipeds/reported-data/166911?year=2011&surveyNumber=15
- 2012 - https://nces.ed.gov/ipeds/reported-data/166911?year=2012&surveyNumber=15
- 2013 - https://nces.ed.gov/ipeds/reported-data/166911?year=2013&surveyNumber=15
- 2014 - https://nces.ed.gov/ipeds/reported-data/166911?year=2014&surveyNumber=15
- 2015 - https://nces.ed.gov/ipeds/reported-data/166911?year=2015&surveyNumber=15
- 2016 - https://nces.ed.gov/ipeds/reported-data/166911?year=2016&surveyNumber=15
- 2017 - https://nces.ed.gov/ipeds/reported-data/166911?year=2017&surveyNumber=15
- 2018 - https://nces.ed.gov/ipeds/reported-data/166911?year=2018&surveyNumber=15
- 2019 - https://nces.ed.gov/ipeds/reported-data/166911?year=2019&surveyNumber=15
- 2020 - https://nces.ed.gov/ipeds/reported-data/166911?year=2020&surveyNumber=15
- 2021 - https://nces.ed.gov/ipeds/reported-data/166911?year=2021&surveyNumber=15

IPEDS - Part A - Fall Enrollment - Fall 2022 – Grand Totals

- 2022 - https://nces.ed.gov/ipeds/reported-data/166911?year=2022&surveyNumber=15
- 2023 - https://nces.ed.gov/ipeds/reported-data/166911?year=2023&surveyNumber=15

Moore College of Art & Design

IPEDS - Enrollment by race/ethnicity and gender

- 2001 - https://nces.ed.gov/ipeds/reported-data/214148?year=2001&surveyNumber=2
- 2002 - https://nces.ed.gov/ipeds/reported-data/214148?year=2002&surveyNumber=2
- 2003 - https://nces.ed.gov/ipeds/reported-data/214148?year=2003&surveyNumber=2
- 2004 - https://nces.ed.gov/ipeds/reported-data/214148?year=2004&surveyNumber=2

IPEDS - Part A - Fall Enrollment - Summary by race/ethnicity

- 2005 - https://nces.ed.gov/ipeds/reported-data/214148?year=2005&surveyNumber=2
- 2006 - https://nces.ed.gov/ipeds/reported-data/214148?year=2006&surveyNumber=2
- 2007 - https://nces.ed.gov/ipeds/reported-data/214148?year=2007&surveyNumber=2
- 2008 - https://nces.ed.gov/ipeds/reported-data/214148?year=2008&surveyNumber=15

IPEDS - Part A - Fall Enrollment - Summary

- 2009 - https://nces.ed.gov/ipeds/reported-data/214148?year=2009&surveyNumber=15
- 2010 - https://nces.ed.gov/ipeds/reported-data/214148?year=2010&surveyNumber=15
- 2011 - https://nces.ed.gov/ipeds/reported-data/214148?year=2011&surveyNumber=15
- 2012 - https://nces.ed.gov/ipeds/reported-data/214148?year=2012&surveyNumber=15
- 2013 - https://nces.ed.gov/ipeds/reported-data/214148?year=2013&surveyNumber=15
- 2014 - https://nces.ed.gov/ipeds/reported-data/214148?year=2014&surveyNumber=15
- 2015 - https://nces.ed.gov/ipeds/reported-data/214148?year=2015&surveyNumber=15
- 2016 - https://nces.ed.gov/ipeds/reported-data/214148?year=2016&surveyNumber=15
- 2017 - https://nces.ed.gov/ipeds/reported-data/214148?year=2017&surveyNumber=15
- 2018 - https://nces.ed.gov/ipeds/reported-data/214148?year=2018&surveyNumber=15
- 2019 - https://nces.ed.gov/ipeds/reported-data/214148?year=2019&surveyNumber=15
- 2020 - https://nces.ed.gov/ipeds/reported-data/214148?year=2020&surveyNumber=15
- 2021 - https://nces.ed.gov/ipeds/reported-data/214148?year=2021&surveyNumber=15

IPEDS - Part A - Fall Enrollment - Fall 2022 – Grand Totals

- 2022 - https://nces.ed.gov/ipeds/reported-data/214148?year=2022&surveyNumber=15
- 2023 - https://nces.ed.gov/ipeds/reported-data/214148?year=2023&surveyNumber=15

Otis College of Art and Design (Los Angeles, CA)

IPEDS - Enrollment by race/ethnicity and gender: Fall

- 2001 - https://nces.ed.gov/ipeds/reported-data/120403?year=2001&surveyNumber=2
- 2002 - https://nces.ed.gov/ipeds/reported-data/120403?year=2002&surveyNumber=2
- 2003 - https://nces.ed.gov/ipeds/reported-data/120403?year=2003&surveyNumber=2
- 2004 - https://nces.ed.gov/ipeds/reported-data/120403?year=2004&surveyNumber=2

IPEDS - Part A - Fall Enrollment - Summary by race/ethnicity – Fall

- 2005 - https://nces.ed.gov/ipeds/reported-data/120403?year=2005&surveyNumber=2
- 2006 - https://nces.ed.gov/ipeds/reported-data/120403?year=2006&surveyNumber=2
- 2007 - https://nces.ed.gov/ipeds/reported-data/120403?year=2007&surveyNumber=2
- 2008 - https://nces.ed.gov/ipeds/reported-data/120403?year=2008&surveyNumber=15

IPEDS - Part A - Fall Enrollment Summary

- 2009 - https://nces.ed.gov/ipeds/reported-data/120403?year=2009&surveyNumber=15
- 2010 - https://nces.ed.gov/ipeds/reported-data/120403?year=2010&surveyNumber=15
- 2011 - https://nces.ed.gov/ipeds/reported-data/120403?year=2011&surveyNumber=15
- 2012 - https://nces.ed.gov/ipeds/reported-data/120403?year=2012&surveyNumber=15
- 2013 - https://nces.ed.gov/ipeds/reported-data/120403?year=2013&surveyNumber=15
- 2014 - https://nces.ed.gov/ipeds/reported-data/120403?year=2014&surveyNumber=15
- 2015 - https://nces.ed.gov/ipeds/reported-data/120403?year=2015&surveyNumber=15
- 2016 - https://nces.ed.gov/ipeds/reported-data/120403?year=2016&surveyNumber=15
- 2017 - https://nces.ed.gov/ipeds/reported-data/120403?year=2017&surveyNumber=15
- 2018 - https://nces.ed.gov/ipeds/reported-data/120403?year=2018&surveyNumber=15
- 2019 - https://nces.ed.gov/ipeds/reported-data/120403?year=2019&surveyNumber=15
- 2020 - https://nces.ed.gov/ipeds/reported-data/120403?year=2020&surveyNumber=15
- 2021 - https://nces.ed.gov/ipeds/reported-data/120403?year=2021&surveyNumber=15

IPEDS - Part A - Fall Enrollment – Grand Totals

- 2022 - https://nces.ed.gov/ipeds/reported-data/120403?year=2022&surveyNumber=15
- 2023 - https://nces.ed.gov/ipeds/reported-data/120403?year=2023&surveyNumber=15

Pennsylvania Academy of the Fine Arts

IPEDS - Enrollment by race/ethnicity and gender

- 2001 - https://nces.ed.gov/ipeds/reported-data/214971?year=2001&surveyNumber=2
- 2002 - https://nces.ed.gov/ipeds/reported-data/214971?year=2002&surveyNumber=2
- 2003 - https://nces.ed.gov/ipeds/reported-data/214971?year=2003&surveyNumber=2
- 2004 - https://nces.ed.gov/ipeds/reported-data/214971?year=2004&surveyNumber=2

IPEDS - Part A - Fall Enrollment - Summary by race/ethnicity

- 2005 - https://nces.ed.gov/ipeds/reported-data/214971?year=2005&surveyNumber=2
- 2006 - https://nces.ed.gov/ipeds/reported-data/214971?year=2006&surveyNumber=2
- 2007 - https://nces.ed.gov/ipeds/reported-data/214971?year=2007&surveyNumber=2
- 2008 - https://nces.ed.gov/ipeds/reported-data/214971?year=2008&surveyNumber=15

IPEDS - Part A - Fall Enrollment - Summary

- 2009 - https://nces.ed.gov/ipeds/reported-data/214971?year=2009&surveyNumber=15
- 2010 - https://nces.ed.gov/ipeds/reported-data/214971?year=2010&surveyNumber=15
- 2011 - https://nces.ed.gov/ipeds/reported-data/214971?year=2011&surveyNumber=15
- 2012 - https://nces.ed.gov/ipeds/reported-data/214971?year=2012&surveyNumber=15
- 2013 - https://nces.ed.gov/ipeds/reported-data/214971?year=2013&surveyNumber=15
- 2014 - https://nces.ed.gov/ipeds/reported-data/214971?year=2014&surveyNumber=15
- 2015 - https://nces.ed.gov/ipeds/reported-data/214971?year=2015&surveyNumber=15
- 2016 - https://nces.ed.gov/ipeds/reported-data/214971?year=2016&surveyNumber=15
- 2017 - https://nces.ed.gov/ipeds/reported-data/214971?year=2017&surveyNumber=15
- 2018 - https://nces.ed.gov/ipeds/reported-data/214971?year=2018&surveyNumber=15
- 2019 - https://nces.ed.gov/ipeds/reported-data/214971?year=2019&surveyNumber=15
- 2020 - https://nces.ed.gov/ipeds/reported-data/214971?year=2020&surveyNumber=15
- 2021 - https://nces.ed.gov/ipeds/reported-data/214971?year=2021&surveyNumber=15

IPEDS - Part A - Fall Enrollment - Fall 2022 – Grand Totals

- 2022 - https://nces.ed.gov/ipeds/reported-data/214971?year=2022&surveyNumber=15
- 2023 - https://nces.ed.gov/ipeds/reported-data/214971?year=2023&surveyNumber=15

Pennsylvania College of Art and Design (Lancaster, PA)

IPEDS - Enrollment by race/ethnicity and gender: Fall

- 2001 - https://nces.ed.gov/ipeds/reported-data/215053?year=2001&surveyNumber=2
- 2002 - https://nces.ed.gov/ipeds/reported-data/215053?year=2002&surveyNumber=2
- 2003 - https://nces.ed.gov/ipeds/reported-data/215053?year=2003&surveyNumber=2
- 2004 - https://nces.ed.gov/ipeds/reported-data/215053?year=2004&surveyNumber=2

IPEDS - Part A - Fall Enrollment - Summary by race/ethnicity – Fall

- 2005 - https://nces.ed.gov/ipeds/reported-data/215053?year=2005&surveyNumber=2
- 2006 - https://nces.ed.gov/ipeds/reported-data/215053?year=2006&surveyNumber=2
- 2007 - https://nces.ed.gov/ipeds/reported-data/215053?year=2007&surveyNumber=2
- 2008 - https://nces.ed.gov/ipeds/reported-data/215053?year=2008&surveyNumber=15

IPEDS - Part A - Fall Enrollment Summary

- 2009 - https://nces.ed.gov/ipeds/reported-data/215053?year=2009&surveyNumber=15
- 2010 - https://nces.ed.gov/ipeds/reported-data/215053?year=2010&surveyNumber=15
- 2011 - https://nces.ed.gov/ipeds/reported-data/215053?year=2011&surveyNumber=15
- 2012 - https://nces.ed.gov/ipeds/reported-data/215053?year=2012&surveyNumber=15
- 2013 - https://nces.ed.gov/ipeds/reported-data/215053?year=2013&surveyNumber=15
- 2014 - https://nces.ed.gov/ipeds/reported-data/215053?year=2014&surveyNumber=15
- 2015 - https://nces.ed.gov/ipeds/reported-data/215053?year=2015&surveyNumber=15
- 2016 - https://nces.ed.gov/ipeds/reported-data/215053?year=2016&surveyNumber=15
- 2017 - https://nces.ed.gov/ipeds/reported-data/215053?year=2017&surveyNumber=15
- 2018 - https://nces.ed.gov/ipeds/reported-data/215053?year=2018&surveyNumber=15
- 2019 - https://nces.ed.gov/ipeds/reported-data/215053?year=2019&surveyNumber=15
- 2020 - https://nces.ed.gov/ipeds/reported-data/215053?year=2020&surveyNumber=15
- 2021 - https://nces.ed.gov/ipeds/reported-data/215053?year=2021&surveyNumber=15

IPEDS - Part A - Fall Enrollment – Grand Totals

- 2022 - https://nces.ed.gov/ipeds/reported-data/215053?year=2022&surveyNumber=15
- 2023 - https://nces.ed.gov/ipeds/reported-data/215053?year=2023&surveyNumber=15

Point Park University (Pittsburgh, PA)

IPEDS - Enrollment by race/ethnicity and gender: Fall

- 2001 - https://nces.ed.gov/ipeds/reported-data/215442?year=2001&surveyNumber=2
- 2002 - https://nces.ed.gov/ipeds/reported-data/215442?year=2002&surveyNumber=2
- 2003 - https://nces.ed.gov/ipeds/reported-data/215442?year=2003&surveyNumber=2
- 2004 - https://nces.ed.gov/ipeds/reported-data/215442?year=2004&surveyNumber=2

IPEDS - Part A - Fall Enrollment - Summary by race/ethnicity – Fall

- 2005 - https://nces.ed.gov/ipeds/reported-data/215442?year=2005&surveyNumber=2
- 2006 - https://nces.ed.gov/ipeds/reported-data/215442?year=2006&surveyNumber=2
- 2007 - https://nces.ed.gov/ipeds/reported-data/215442?year=2007&surveyNumber=2
- 2008 - https://nces.ed.gov/ipeds/reported-data/215442?year=2008&surveyNumber=15

IPEDS - Part A - Fall Enrollment Summary

- 2009 - https://nces.ed.gov/ipeds/reported-data/215442?year=2009&surveyNumber=15
- 2010 - https://nces.ed.gov/ipeds/reported-data/215442?year=2010&surveyNumber=15
- 2011 - https://nces.ed.gov/ipeds/reported-data/215442?year=2011&surveyNumber=15
- 2012 - https://nces.ed.gov/ipeds/reported-data/215442?year=2012&surveyNumber=15
- 2013 - https://nces.ed.gov/ipeds/reported-data/215442?year=2013&surveyNumber=15
- 2014 - https://nces.ed.gov/ipeds/reported-data/215442?year=2014&surveyNumber=15
- 2015 - https://nces.ed.gov/ipeds/reported-data/215442?year=2015&surveyNumber=15
- 2016 - https://nces.ed.gov/ipeds/reported-data/215442?year=2016&surveyNumber=15
- 2017 - https://nces.ed.gov/ipeds/reported-data/215442?year=2017&surveyNumber=15
- 2018 - https://nces.ed.gov/ipeds/reported-data/215442?year=2018&surveyNumber=15
- 2019 - https://nces.ed.gov/ipeds/reported-data/215442?year=2019&surveyNumber=15
- 2020 - https://nces.ed.gov/ipeds/reported-data/215442?year=2020&surveyNumber=15
- 2021 - https://nces.ed.gov/ipeds/reported-data/215442?year=2021&surveyNumber=15

IPEDS - Part A - Fall Enrollment – Grand Totals

- 2022 - https://nces.ed.gov/ipeds/reported-data/215442?year=2022&surveyNumber=15
- 2023 - https://nces.ed.gov/ipeds/reported-data/215442?year=2023&surveyNumber=15

Pratt Institute-Main (Brooklyn, NY)

IPEDS - Enrollment by race/ethnicity and gender: Fall

- 2001 - https://nces.ed.gov/ipeds/reported-data/194578?year=2001&surveyNumber=2
- 2002 - https://nces.ed.gov/ipeds/reported-data/194578?year=2002&surveyNumber=2
- 2003 - https://nces.ed.gov/ipeds/reported-data/194578?year=2003&surveyNumber=2
- 2004 - https://nces.ed.gov/ipeds/reported-data/194578?year=2004&surveyNumber=2

IPEDS - Part A - Fall Enrollment - Summary by race/ethnicity – Fall

- 2005 - https://nces.ed.gov/ipeds/reported-data/194578?year=2005&surveyNumber=2
- 2006 - https://nces.ed.gov/ipeds/reported-data/194578?year=2006&surveyNumber=2
- 2007 - NA
- 2008 - https://nces.ed.gov/ipeds/reported-data/194578?year=2008&surveyNumber=15

IPEDS - Part A - Fall Enrollment Summary

- 2009 - https://nces.ed.gov/ipeds/reported-data/194578?year=2009&surveyNumber=15
- 2010 - https://nces.ed.gov/ipeds/reported-data/194578?year=2010&surveyNumber=15
- 2011 - https://nces.ed.gov/ipeds/reported-data/194578?year=2011&surveyNumber=15
- 2012 - https://nces.ed.gov/ipeds/reported-data/194578?year=2012&surveyNumber=15
- 2013 - https://nces.ed.gov/ipeds/reported-data/194578?year=2013&surveyNumber=15
- 2014 - https://nces.ed.gov/ipeds/reported-data/194578?year=2014&surveyNumber=15
- 2015 - https://nces.ed.gov/ipeds/reported-data/194578?year=2015&surveyNumber=15
- 2016 - https://nces.ed.gov/ipeds/reported-data/194578?year=2016&surveyNumber=15
- 2017 - https://nces.ed.gov/ipeds/reported-data/194578?year=2017&surveyNumber=15
- 2018 - https://nces.ed.gov/ipeds/reported-data/194578?year=2018&surveyNumber=15
- 2019 - https://nces.ed.gov/ipeds/reported-data/194578?year=2019&surveyNumber=15
- 2020 - https://nces.ed.gov/ipeds/reported-data/194578?year=2020&surveyNumber=15
- 2021 - https://nces.ed.gov/ipeds/reported-data/194578?year=2021&surveyNumber=15

IPEDS - Part A - Fall Enrollment – Grand Totals

- 2022 - https://nces.ed.gov/ipeds/reported-data/194578?year=2022&surveyNumber=15
- 2023 - https://nces.ed.gov/ipeds/reported-data/194578?year=2023&surveyNumber=15

Rhode Island School of Design (Providence, RI)

IPEDS - Enrollment by race/ethnicity and gender: Fall

- 2001 - https://nces.ed.gov/ipeds/reported-data/217493?year=2001&surveyNumber=2
- 2002 - https://nces.ed.gov/ipeds/reported-data/217493?year=2002&surveyNumber=2
- 2003 - https://nces.ed.gov/ipeds/reported-data/217493?year=2003&surveyNumber=2
- 2004 - https://nces.ed.gov/ipeds/reported-data/217493?year=2004&surveyNumber=2

IPEDS - Part A - Fall Enrollment - Summary by race/ethnicity – Fall

- 2004 - https://nces.ed.gov/ipeds/reported-data/217493?year=2005&surveyNumber=2
- 2005 - https://nces.ed.gov/ipeds/reported-data/217493?year=2006&surveyNumber=2
- 2007 - https://nces.ed.gov/ipeds/reported-data/217493?year=2007&surveyNumber=2
- 2008 - https://nces.ed.gov/ipeds/reported-data/217493?year=2008&surveyNumber=15

IPEDS - Part A - Fall Enrollment Summary

- 2009 - https://nces.ed.gov/ipeds/reported-data/217493?year=2009&surveyNumber=15
- 2010 - https://nces.ed.gov/ipeds/reported-data/217493?year=2010&surveyNumber=15
- 2011 - https://nces.ed.gov/ipeds/reported-data/217493?year=2011&surveyNumber=15
- 2012 - https://nces.ed.gov/ipeds/reported-data/217493?year=2012&surveyNumber=15
- 2013 - https://nces.ed.gov/ipeds/reported-data/217493?year=2013&surveyNumber=15
- 2014 - https://nces.ed.gov/ipeds/reported-data/217493?year=2014&surveyNumber=15
- 2015 - https://nces.ed.gov/ipeds/reported-data/217493?year=2015&surveyNumber=15
- 2016 - https://nces.ed.gov/ipeds/reported-data/217493?year=2016&surveyNumber=15
- 2017 - https://nces.ed.gov/ipeds/reported-data/217493?year=2017&surveyNumber=15
- 2018 - https://nces.ed.gov/ipeds/reported-data/217493?year=2018&surveyNumber=15
- 2019 - https://nces.ed.gov/ipeds/reported-data/217493?year=2019&surveyNumber=15
- 2020 - https://nces.ed.gov/ipeds/reported-data/217493?year=2020&surveyNumber=15
- 2021 - https://nces.ed.gov/ipeds/reported-data/217493?year=2021&surveyNumber=15

IPEDS - Part A - Fall Enrollment – Grand Totals

- 2022 - https://nces.ed.gov/ipeds/reported-data/217493?year=2022&surveyNumber=15
- 2023 - https://nces.ed.gov/ipeds/reported-data/217493?year=2023&surveyNumber=15

Ringling College of Art and Design (Sarasota, FL)

IPEDS - Enrollment by race/ethnicity and gender: Fall

- 2001 - https://nces.ed.gov/ipeds/reported-data/136774?year=2001&surveyNumber=2
- 2002 - https://nces.ed.gov/ipeds/reported-data/136774?year=2002&surveyNumber=2
- 2003 - https://nces.ed.gov/ipeds/reported-data/136774?year=2003&surveyNumber=2
- 2004 - https://nces.ed.gov/ipeds/reported-data/136774?year=2004&surveyNumber=2

IPEDS - Part A - Fall Enrollment - Summary by race/ethnicity – Fall

- 2005 - https://nces.ed.gov/ipeds/reported-data/136774?year=2005&surveyNumber=2
- 2006 - https://nces.ed.gov/ipeds/reported-data/136774?year=2006&surveyNumber=2
- 2007 - https://nces.ed.gov/ipeds/reported-data/136774?year=2007&surveyNumber=2
- 2008 - https://nces.ed.gov/ipeds/reported-data/136774?year=2008&surveyNumber=15

IPEDS - Part A - Fall Enrollment Summary

- 2009 - https://nces.ed.gov/ipeds/reported-data/136774?year=2009&surveyNumber=15
- 2010 - https://nces.ed.gov/ipeds/reported-data/136774?year=2010&surveyNumber=15
- 2011 - https://nces.ed.gov/ipeds/reported-data/136774?year=2011&surveyNumber=15
- 2012 - https://nces.ed.gov/ipeds/reported-data/136774?year=2012&surveyNumber=15
- 2013 - https://nces.ed.gov/ipeds/reported-data/136774?year=2013&surveyNumber=15
- 2014 - https://nces.ed.gov/ipeds/reported-data/136774?year=2014&surveyNumber=15
- 2015 - https://nces.ed.gov/ipeds/reported-data/136774?year=2015&surveyNumber=15
- 2016 - https://nces.ed.gov/ipeds/reported-data/136774?year=2016&surveyNumber=15
- 2017 - https://nces.ed.gov/ipeds/reported-data/136774?year=2017&surveyNumber=15
- 2018 - https://nces.ed.gov/ipeds/reported-data/136774?year=2018&surveyNumber=15
- 2019 - https://nces.ed.gov/ipeds/reported-data/136774?year=2019&surveyNumber=15
- 2020 - https://nces.ed.gov/ipeds/reported-data/136774?year=2020&surveyNumber=15
- 2021 - https://nces.ed.gov/ipeds/reported-data/136774?year=2021&surveyNumber=15

IPEDS - Part A - Fall Enrollment – Grand Totals

- 2022 - https://nces.ed.gov/ipeds/reported-data/136774?year=2022&surveyNumber=15
- 2023 - https://nces.ed.gov/ipeds/reported-data/136774?year=2023&surveyNumber=15

Savannah College of Art and Design (Savannah, GA)

IPEDS - Enrollment by race/ethnicity and gender: Fall

- 2001 - https://nces.ed.gov/ipeds/reported-data/140951?year=2001&surveyNumber=2
- 2002 - https://nces.ed.gov/ipeds/reported-data/140951?year=2002&surveyNumber=2
- 2003 - https://nces.ed.gov/ipeds/reported-data/140951?year=2003&surveyNumber=2
- 2004 - https://nces.ed.gov/ipeds/reported-data/140951?year=2004&surveyNumber=2

IPEDS - Part A - Fall Enrollment - Summary by race/ethnicity – Fall

- 2005 - https://nces.ed.gov/ipeds/reported-data/140951?year=2005&surveyNumber=2
- 2006 - https://nces.ed.gov/ipeds/reported-data/140951?year=2006&surveyNumber=2
- 2007 - https://nces.ed.gov/ipeds/reported-data/140951?year=2007&surveyNumber=2
- 2008 - https://nces.ed.gov/ipeds/reported-data/140951?year=2008&surveyNumber=15

IPEDS - Part A - Fall Enrollment Summary

- 2009 - https://nces.ed.gov/ipeds/reported-data/140951?year=2009&surveyNumber=15
- 2010 - https://nces.ed.gov/ipeds/reported-data/140951?year=2010&surveyNumber=15
- 2011 - https://nces.ed.gov/ipeds/reported-data/140951?year=2011&surveyNumber=15
- 2012 - https://nces.ed.gov/ipeds/reported-data/140951?year=2012&surveyNumber=15
- 2013 - https://nces.ed.gov/ipeds/reported-data/140951?year=2013&surveyNumber=15
- 2014 - https://nces.ed.gov/ipeds/reported-data/140951?year=2014&surveyNumber=15
- 2015 - https://nces.ed.gov/ipeds/reported-data/140951?year=2015&surveyNumber=15
- 2016 - https://nces.ed.gov/ipeds/reported-data/140951?year=2016&surveyNumber=15
- 2017 - https://nces.ed.gov/ipeds/reported-data/140951?year=2017&surveyNumber=15
- 2018 - https://nces.ed.gov/ipeds/reported-data/140951?year=2018&surveyNumber=15
- 2019 - https://nces.ed.gov/ipeds/reported-data/140951?year=2019&surveyNumber=15
- 2020 - https://nces.ed.gov/ipeds/reported-data/140951?year=2020&surveyNumber=15
- 2021 - https://nces.ed.gov/ipeds/reported-data/140951?year=2021&surveyNumber=15

IPEDS - Part A - Fall Enrollment – Grand Totals

- 2022 - https://nces.ed.gov/ipeds/reported-data/140951?year=2022&surveyNumber=15
- 2023 - https://nces.ed.gov/ipeds/reported-data/140951?year=2023&surveyNumber=15

School of the Art Institute of Chicago (Chicago, IL)

IPEDS - Enrollment by race/ethnicity and gender: Fall

- 2001 - https://nces.ed.gov/ipeds/reported-data/143048?year=2001&surveyNumber=2
- 2002 - https://nces.ed.gov/ipeds/reported-data/143048?year=2002&surveyNumber=2
- 2003 - https://nces.ed.gov/ipeds/reported-data/143048?year=2003&surveyNumber=2
- 2004 - https://nces.ed.gov/ipeds/reported-data/143048?year=2004&surveyNumber=2

IPEDS - Part A - Fall Enrollment - Summary by race/ethnicity – Fall

- 2005 - https://nces.ed.gov/ipeds/reported-data/143048?year=2005&surveyNumber=2
- 2006 - https://nces.ed.gov/ipeds/reported-data/143048?year=2006&surveyNumber=2
- 2007 - https://nces.ed.gov/ipeds/reported-data/143048?year=2007&surveyNumber=2
- 2008 - https://nces.ed.gov/ipeds/reported-data/143048?year=2008&surveyNumber=15

IPEDS - Part A - Fall Enrollment Summary

- 2009 - https://nces.ed.gov/ipeds/reported-data/143048?year=2009&surveyNumber=15
- 2010 - https://nces.ed.gov/ipeds/reported-data/143048?year=2010&surveyNumber=15
- 2011 - https://nces.ed.gov/ipeds/reported-data/143048?year=2011&surveyNumber=15
- 2012 - https://nces.ed.gov/ipeds/reported-data/143048?year=2012&surveyNumber=15
- 2013 - https://nces.ed.gov/ipeds/reported-data/143048?year=2013&surveyNumber=15
- 2014 - https://nces.ed.gov/ipeds/reported-data/143048?year=2014&surveyNumber=15
- 2015 - https://nces.ed.gov/ipeds/reported-data/143048?year=2015&surveyNumber=15
- 2016 - https://nces.ed.gov/ipeds/reported-data/143048?year=2016&surveyNumber=15
- 2017 - https://nces.ed.gov/ipeds/reported-data/143048?year=2017&surveyNumber=15
- 2018 - https://nces.ed.gov/ipeds/reported-data/143048?year=2018&surveyNumber=15
- 2019 - https://nces.ed.gov/ipeds/reported-data/143048?year=2019&surveyNumber=15
- 2020 - https://nces.ed.gov/ipeds/reported-data/143048?year=2020&surveyNumber=15
- 2021 - https://nces.ed.gov/ipeds/reported-data/143048?year=2021&surveyNumber=15

IPEDS - Part A - Fall Enrollment – Grand Totals

- 2022 - https://nces.ed.gov/ipeds/reported-data/143048?year=2022&surveyNumber=15
- 2023 - https://nces.ed.gov/ipeds/reported-data/143048?year=2023&surveyNumber=15

School of Visual Arts (New York, NY)

IPEDS - Enrollment by race/ethnicity and gender: Fall

- 2001 - https://nces.ed.gov/ipeds/reported-data/197151?year=2001&surveyNumber=1
- 2002 - https://nces.ed.gov/ipeds/reported-data/197151?year=2002&surveyNumber=1
- 2003 - https://nces.ed.gov/ipeds/reported-data/197151?year=2003&surveyNumber=2
- 2004 - https://nces.ed.gov/ipeds/reported-data/197151?year=2004&surveyNumber=2

IPEDS - Part A - Fall Enrollment - Summary by race/ethnicity – Fall

- 2005 - https://nces.ed.gov/ipeds/reported-data/197151?year=2005&surveyNumber=2
- 2006 - https://nces.ed.gov/ipeds/reported-data/197151?year=2006&surveyNumber=2
- 2007 - https://nces.ed.gov/ipeds/reported-data/197151?year=2007&surveyNumber=2
- 2008 - https://nces.ed.gov/ipeds/reported-data/197151?year=2008&surveyNumber=15

IPEDS - Part A - Fall Enrollment Summary

- 2009 - https://nces.ed.gov/ipeds/reported-data/197151?year=2009&surveyNumber=15
- 2010 - https://nces.ed.gov/ipeds/reported-data/197151?year=2010&surveyNumber=15
- 2011 - https://nces.ed.gov/ipeds/reported-data/197151?year=2011&surveyNumber=15
- 2012 - https://nces.ed.gov/ipeds/reported-data/197151?year=2012&surveyNumber=15
- 2013 - https://nces.ed.gov/ipeds/reported-data/197151?year=2013&surveyNumber=15
- 2014 - https://nces.ed.gov/ipeds/reported-data/197151?year=2014&surveyNumber=15
- 2015 - https://nces.ed.gov/ipeds/reported-data/197151?year=2015&surveyNumber=15
- 2016 - https://nces.ed.gov/ipeds/reported-data/197151?year=2016&surveyNumber=15
- 2017 - https://nces.ed.gov/ipeds/reported-data/197151?year=2017&surveyNumber=15
- 2018 - https://nces.ed.gov/ipeds/reported-data/197151?year=2018&surveyNumber=15
- 2019 - https://nces.ed.gov/ipeds/reported-data/197151?year=2019&surveyNumber=15
- 2020 - https://nces.ed.gov/ipeds/reported-data/197151?year=2020&surveyNumber=15
- 2021 - https://nces.ed.gov/ipeds/reported-data/197151?year=2021&surveyNumber=15

IPEDS - Part A - Fall Enrollment – Grand Totals

- 2022 - https://nces.ed.gov/ipeds/reported-data/197151?year=2022&surveyNumber=15
- 2023 - https://nces.ed.gov/ipeds/reported-data/197151?year=2023&surveyNumber=15

The New School (New York, NY)

IPEDS - Enrollment by race/ethnicity and gender: Fall

- 2001 - https://nces.ed.gov/ipeds/reported-data/193654?year=2001&surveyNumber=1
- 2002 - https://nces.ed.gov/ipeds/reported-data/193654?year=2002&surveyNumber=2
- 2003 - https://nces.ed.gov/ipeds/reported-data/193654?year=2004&surveyNumber=2
- 2004 - https://nces.ed.gov/ipeds/reported-data/193654?year=2005&surveyNumber=2

IPEDS - Part A - Fall Enrollment - Summary by race/ethnicity – Fall

- 2005 - https://nces.ed.gov/ipeds/reported-data/193654?year=2005&surveyNumber=2
- 2006 - https://nces.ed.gov/ipeds/reported-data/193654?year=2006&surveyNumber=2
- 2007 - https://nces.ed.gov/ipeds/reported-data/193654?year=2007&surveyNumber=2
- 2008 - https://nces.ed.gov/ipeds/reported-data/193654?year=2008&surveyNumber=15

IPEDS - Part A - Fall Enrollment Summary

- 2009 - https://nces.ed.gov/ipeds/reported-data/193654?year=2009&surveyNumber=15
- 2010 - https://nces.ed.gov/ipeds/reported-data/193654?year=2010&surveyNumber=15
- 2011 - https://nces.ed.gov/ipeds/reported-data/193654?year=2011&surveyNumber=15
- 2012 - https://nces.ed.gov/ipeds/reported-data/193654?year=2012&surveyNumber=15
- 2013 - https://nces.ed.gov/ipeds/reported-data/193654?year=2013&surveyNumber=15
- 2014 - https://nces.ed.gov/ipeds/reported-data/193654?year=2014&surveyNumber=15
- 2015 - https://nces.ed.gov/ipeds/reported-data/193654?year=2015&surveyNumber=15
- 2016 - https://nces.ed.gov/ipeds/reported-data/193654?year=2016&surveyNumber=15
- 2017 - https://nces.ed.gov/ipeds/reported-data/193654?year=2017&surveyNumber=15
- 2018 - https://nces.ed.gov/ipeds/reported-data/193654?year=2018&surveyNumber=15
- 2019 - https://nces.ed.gov/ipeds/reported-data/193654?year=2019&surveyNumber=15
- 2020 - https://nces.ed.gov/ipeds/reported-data/193654?year=2020&surveyNumber=15
- 2021 - https://nces.ed.gov/ipeds/reported-data/193654?year=2021&surveyNumber=15

IPEDS - Part A - Fall Enrollment – Grand Totals

- 2022 - https://nces.ed.gov/ipeds/reported-data/193654?year=2022&surveyNumber=15
- 2023 - https://nces.ed.gov/ipeds/reported-data/193654?year=2023&surveyNumber=15

University of North Carolina School of the Arts (Winston Salem, NC)

IPEDS - Enrollment by race/ethnicity and gender: Fall

- 2001 - https://nces.ed.gov/ipeds/reported-data/199184?year=2001&surveyNumber=2
- 2002 - https://nces.ed.gov/ipeds/reported-data/199184?year=2002&surveyNumber=2
- 2003 - https://nces.ed.gov/ipeds/reported-data/199184?year=2003&surveyNumber=2
- 2004 - https://nces.ed.gov/ipeds/reported-data/199184?year=2004&surveyNumber=2

IPEDS - Part A - Fall Enrollment - Summary by race/ethnicity – Fall

- 2005 - https://nces.ed.gov/ipeds/reported-data/199184?year=2005&surveyNumber=2
- 2006 - https://nces.ed.gov/ipeds/reported-data/199184?year=2006&surveyNumber=2
- 2007 - https://nces.ed.gov/ipeds/reported-data/199184?year=2007&surveyNumber=2
- 2008 - https://nces.ed.gov/ipeds/reported-data/199184?year=2008&surveyNumber=15

IPEDS - Part A - Fall Enrollment Summary

- 2009 - https://nces.ed.gov/ipeds/reported-data/199184?year=2009&surveyNumber=15
- 2010 - https://nces.ed.gov/ipeds/reported-data/199184?year=2010&surveyNumber=15
- 2011 - https://nces.ed.gov/ipeds/reported-data/199184?year=2011&surveyNumber=15
- 2012 - https://nces.ed.gov/ipeds/reported-data/199184?year=2012&surveyNumber=15
- 2013 - https://nces.ed.gov/ipeds/reported-data/199184?year=2013&surveyNumber=15
- 2014 - https://nces.ed.gov/ipeds/reported-data/199184?year=2014&surveyNumber=15
- 2015 - https://nces.ed.gov/ipeds/reported-data/199184?year=2015&surveyNumber=15
- 2016 - https://nces.ed.gov/ipeds/reported-data/199184?year=2016&surveyNumber=15
- 2017 - https://nces.ed.gov/ipeds/reported-data/199184?year=2017&surveyNumber=15
- 2018 - https://nces.ed.gov/ipeds/reported-data/199184?year=2018&surveyNumber=15
- 2019 - https://nces.ed.gov/ipeds/reported-data/199184?year=2019&surveyNumber=15
- 2020 - https://nces.ed.gov/ipeds/reported-data/199184?year=2020&surveyNumber=15
- 2021 - https://nces.ed.gov/ipeds/reported-data/199184?year=2021&surveyNumber=15

IPEDS - Part A - Fall Enrollment – Grand Totals

- 2022 - https://nces.ed.gov/ipeds/reported-data/199184?year=2022&surveyNumber=15
- 2023 - https://nces.ed.gov/ipeds/reported-data/199184?year=2023&surveyNumber=15

University of the Arts

IPEDS - Enrollment by race/ethnicity and gender

- 2001 - https://nces.ed.gov/ipeds/reported-data/215105?year=2001&surveyNumber=2
- 2002 - https://nces.ed.gov/ipeds/reported-data/215105?year=2002&surveyNumber=2
- 2003 - https://nces.ed.gov/ipeds/reported-data/215105?year=2003&surveyNumber=2
- 2004 - https://nces.ed.gov/ipeds/reported-data/215105?year=2004&surveyNumber=2

IPEDS – Part A - Fall Enrollment - Summary by race/ethnicity

- 2005 - https://nces.ed.gov/ipeds/reported-data/215105?year=2005&surveyNumber=2
- 2006 - https://nces.ed.gov/ipeds/reported-data/215105?year=2006&surveyNumber=2
- 2007 - https://nces.ed.gov/ipeds/reported-data/215105?year=2007&surveyNumber=2
- 2008 - https://nces.ed.gov/ipeds/reported-data/215105?year=2008&surveyNumber=15

IPEDS – Part A - Fall Enrollment – Summary

- 2009 - https://nces.ed.gov/ipeds/reported-data/215105?year=2009&surveyNumber=15
- 2010 - https://nces.ed.gov/ipeds/reported-data/215105?year=2010&surveyNumber=15
- 2011 - https://nces.ed.gov/ipeds/reported-data/215105?year=2011&surveyNumber=15
- 2011 - https://nces.ed.gov/ipeds/reported-data/215105?year=2012&surveyNumber=15
- 2012 - https://nces.ed.gov/ipeds/reported-data/215105?year=2013&surveyNumber=15
- 2013 - https://nces.ed.gov/ipeds/reported-data/215105?year=2014&surveyNumber=15
- 2014 - https://nces.ed.gov/ipeds/reported-data/215105?year=2015&surveyNumber=15
- 2015 - https://nces.ed.gov/ipeds/reported-data/215105?year=2016&surveyNumber=15
- 2016 - https://nces.ed.gov/ipeds/reported-data/215105?year=2017&surveyNumber=15
- 2017 - https://nces.ed.gov/ipeds/reported-data/215105?year=2018&surveyNumber=15
- 2018 - https://nces.ed.gov/ipeds/reported-data/215105?year=2019&surveyNumber=15
- 2019 - https://nces.ed.gov/ipeds/reported-data/215105?year=2020&surveyNumber=15
- 2020 - https://nces.ed.gov/ipeds/reported-data/215105?year=2021&surveyNumber=15

IPEDS – Part A - Fall Enrollment – Summary – Grand Totals

- 2021 - https://nces.ed.gov/ipeds/reported-data/215105?year=2022&surveyNumber=15
- 2022 - https://nces.ed.gov/ipeds/reported-data/215105?year=2023&surveyNumber=15

Fair Use Notice

Select quotations from the United Academics of Philadelphia blog are included under the fair-use provisions of U.S. Copyright Law (17 U.S.C. § 107) for purposes of criticism, commentary, and academic analysis. All quoted materials are limited in scope, accurately cited, and used to illustrate key points concerning institutional governance, transparency, and labor relations in higher education.

www.ingramcontent.com/pod-product-compliance
Lightning Source LLC
Chambersburg PA
CBHW051339120626
46547CB00016B/2606